Frantz Fanon's *Black Skin, White Masks*

MANCHESTER
1824

Manchester University Press

(TEXTS · IN · CULTURE

SERIES EDITORS
Jeff Wallace and John Whale

FOUNDING EDITORS
Stephen Copley and Jeff Wallace

ADVISORY EDITORS
Lynda Nead, Birbeck College, London
Gillian Beer, Girton College, Cambridge
Roy Porter, Wellcome Institute for the History of Medicine
Anne Janowitz, University of Warwick

This series offers specially commissioned, cross-disciplinary essays on texts of seminal importance to Western culture. Each text has had an impact on the way we think, write and live beyond the confines of its original discipline, and it is only through an understanding of its multiple meanings that we can fully appreciate its importance.

ALREADY PUBLISHED

Charles Darwin's *The Origin of Species*
David Amigoni, Jeff Wallace (eds)

Adam Smith's *The Wealth of Nations*
Stephen Copley, Kathryn Sutherland (eds)

Niccolò Machiavelli's *The Prince*
Martin Coyle (ed.)

Simone de Beauvoir's *The Second Sex*
Ruth Evans (ed.)

Sigmund Freud's *Interpretation of Dreams*
Laura Marcus (ed.)

Francis Bacon's *New Atlantis*
Bronwen Price (ed.)

The Great Exhibition of 1851
Louise Purbrick (ed.)

Edmund Burke's *Reflections on the Revolution in France*
John Whale (ed.)

TEXTS·IN·CULTURE

Frantz Fanon's
BLACK SKIN, WHITE MASKS

New interdisciplinary essays

MAX SILVERMAN

editor

Manchester University Press
Manchester and New York

distributed exclusively in the USA by Palgrave

Published by Manchester University Press
Oxford Road, Manchester M13 9NR, UK
and Room 400, 175 Fifth Avenue, New York, NY 10010, USA
www.manchesteruniversitypress.co.uk

Distributed exclusively in the USA by
Palgrave, 175 Fifth Avenue, New York, NY 10010, USA

Distributed exclusively in Canada by
UBC Press, University of British Columbia, 2029 West Mall, Vancouver, BC, Canada V6T 1Z2

British Library Cataloguing-in-Publication Data
A catalogue record is available from the British Library

Library of Congress Cataloging-in-Publication Data applied for

ISBN 0 7190 6448 1 *hardback*
EAN 978 0 7190 6448 7

First published 2005

14 13 12 11 10 09 08 07 06 05   10 9 8 7 6 5 4 3 2 1

Typeset in Apollo
by Koinonia, Manchester
Printed in Great Britain
by Bell & Bain, Glasgow

Contents

Series introduction

Texts are produced in particular cultures and in particular historical circumstances. In turn, they shape and are shaped by those cultures as they are read and re-read in changing circumstances by different groups with different commitments, engagements and interests. Such readings are themselves then re-absorbed into the ideological frameworks within which the cultures develop. The seminal works drawn on by cultures thus have multiple existences within them, exerting their influence in distinct and perhaps contradictory ways. As these texts have been 'claimed' by particular academic disciplines, however, their larger cultural significance has often been obscured.

Recent work in cultural history and textual theory has stimulated critical awareness of the complex relations between texts and cultures, highlighting the limits of current academic formations and opening the possibility of new approaches to interdisciplinarity. At the same time, however, the difficulties of interdisciplinary work have become increasingly apparent at all levels of research and teaching. On the one hand the abandonment of disciplinary specialisms may lead to amorphousness rather than challenging interdisciplinarity; on the other, interdisciplinary approaches may in the end simply create new specialisms or sub-specialisms, with their own well-guarded boundaries. In these circumstances, yesterday's ground-breaking interdisciplinary study may become today's autonomous (and so potentially circumscribed) discipline, as has happened, it might be argued, in the case of some forms of History of Ideas.

The volumes in this series highlight the advantages of interdisciplinary work while at the same time encouraging a critical reflexiveness about its limits and possibilities; they seek to stimulate consideration both of the distinctiveness and integrity of individual disciplines, and of the transgressive potential of interdisciplinarity. Each volume offers a collection of new essays on a text of seminal intellectual and cultural importance, displaying the insights to be gained from the juxtaposition of disciplinary perspectives and from the negotiation of disciplinary boundaries. The volumes represent a challenge to the conception of authorship which locates the significance of the text in the individual act of creation; but we assume that no issues (including those of interdisciplinarity and authorship) are foreclosed, and that individual volumes drawing contributions from a broad range of disciplinary standpoints, will raise questions about the texts they examine more by the perceived disparities of approach that they encompass than by any interpretative consensus that they demonstrate.

All essays are specially commissioned for the series and are designed to be approachable to non-specialist as well as specialist readers: substantial editorial introductions provide a framework for the debates conducted in each volume, and highlight the issues involved.

We would, finally, like to dedicate the series to the memory of our colleague Stephen Copley, whose insight and energy started it all.

Jeff Wallace, University of Glamorgan
John Whale, University of Leeds
General editors

Preface

All references to *Peau noire, masques blancs* will be to the following edition: F. Fanon (1952) *Peau noire, masques blancs*, Paris: Seuil/Points. This will be abbreviated throughout the collection as *Peau noire*. The translation, by Charles Lam Markmann, is *Black Skin, White Masks*. This was first published by Grove Press (New York) in 1967 but the edition used here will be London: Pluto Press, 1986. The page references for both editions are the same. This will be abbreviated throughout the collection as *Black Skin*. Some of the contributors have modified the Markmann translation, indicated by tr. mod. in the text, or have used their own translations (also indicated in the text). All quotations from *Peau noire* consist of the French original followed by the English translation. Translations of short quotations will follow the original in the body of the text while translations of longer quotations will be in footnotes.

I wish to thank all the contributors to this collection. I would also like to thank Manchester University Press for their patience in waiting for the manuscript. My special thanks go to my family, who are my source of inspiration.

Chronology

1635 Caribs on Martinique ousted by invading European conquistadors. Martinique claimed for France by Pierre Belain d'Esnambuc

1802 Having been part of the French Empire of the *ancien régime*, then lost temporarily to Britain for several years in the eighteenth century, Martinique reverts to French rule and remains a French possession to the present day

1830 France invades Algeria

1848 France abolishes slavery. Algeria officially integrated into France

1925 Frantz Fanon born in Fort-de-France, Martinique

1936 Léopold Senghor first uses term 'Negritude'

1938 Aimé Césaire, *Cahier d'un retour au pays natal*

1943 Fanon joins the Free French forces

1946 Following Second World War, when Martinique was under Vichy control, the island's status changes from colony to overseas department of France (département d'outre-mer); Jean-Paul Sartre, *Réflexions sur la question juive*

1947 Fanon studies medicine, and then specialises in psychiatry, Lyons

1947 René Maran, *Un homme pareil aux autres*

1948 Léopold Senghor (ed.), *Anthologie de la nouvelle poésie nègre et malgache de langue française* (with introduction by Jean-Paul Sartre entitled *Orphée noir*); Mayotte Capécia, *Je suis martiniquaise*

1950 Aimé Césaire, *Discours sur le colonialisme*; Germaine Guex, *La Névrose d'abandon*; Octave Mannoni, *Psychologie de la colonisation*

1952 *Peau noire, masques blancs*

1953 Fanon appointed head of the psychiatry department at the Blida-Joinville hospital in Algeria

1954 Beginning of Algerian war of independence. Fanon supports and works for the Front de Libération Nationale (FLN)

1957 Having resigned his post with the French government the previous year because of the effects on his patients of torture and oppression, Fanon goes into exile in Tunis. He continues to practise as a psychiatrist while working for the FLN and writing for its newspaper, *El Moudjahid*

1957 Albert Memmi, *Portrait du colonisé*

1959 *L'An V de la révolution algérienne* (English translation, *Studies in a Dying Colonialism*, 1965)

1960 Provisional Algerian government appoints Fanon ambassador to Ghana

1961 *Les Damnés de la terre* (English translation, *The Wretched of the Earth*, 1965)

1961 Death of Fanon from leukemia in Maryland, USA

1962 Independence for Algeria

1964 Posthumous publication of collected essays, *Pour la Révolution africaine* (English translation, *Toward the African Revolution*, 1967)

1960s Fanon's ideas influential in Black Panther movement in America and, more generally, in Third World struggles against the West

1967 Translation into English of *Black Skin, White Masks* by Charles Lam Markmann

1971 New edition in French of *Peau noire, masques blancs*

1981 Edouard Glissant, *Le Discours antillais*

1986 Major conference on Fanon in Brazzaville, the Congo; reprint of English translation of *Black Skin, White Masks*, with an introduction by Homi K. Bhabha

1993 J. Bernabé, P. Chamoiseau and R. Confiant, *Eloge de la créolité*

1995 Isaac Julien's film *Black Skin, White Mask* shown on BBC

1997 Patrick Chamoiseau, *Ecrire en pays dominé*

1990s to present Fanon's work and ideas (especially *Black Skin, White Masks*) central to the development of cultural and postcolonial studies in the anglophone academy. Numerous critical works and biographies in English appear on Fanon including Gordon, *Fanon and the Crisis of European Man* (1995); Gordon, White and Sharpley-Whiting (eds), *Fanon: A Critical Reader* (1996);

Sekyi-Otu, *Fanon's Dialectic of Experience* (1996); Sharpley-Whiting, *Frantz Fanon: Conflicts and Feminism* (1998); Alessandrini (ed.), *Frantz Fanon: Critical Perspectives* (1999); Gibson (ed.), *Rethinking Fanon: The Continuing Dialogue* (1999); Cherki, *Frantz Fanon, Portrait* (2000); Macey, *Frantz Fanon: A Life* (2000); Gibson, *Fanon: The Postcolonial Imagination* (2003)

2001 New editions in French of *L'An V de la révolution algérienne* and *Pour la Révolution africaine*

2002 New edition in French of *Les Damnés de la terre*

Introduction

MAX SILVERMAN

All he'd ever wanted, from earliest childhood on, was to be free: not black, not even white – just on his own and free. (Philip Roth, *The Human Stain*)

Nos frères de couleur ...
Je crois en toi, Homme ...
(Our coloured brothers ... Mankind, I believe in you) (Frantz Fanon, *Peau noire, masques blancs*)

Frantz Fanon's *Peau noire, masques blancs* (*Black Skin, White Masks*) was published by the Paris-based publishing house Editions du Seuil in 1952 when Fanon was twenty-seven. At the time of writing, Fanon, born in the French overseas department of Martinique, was studying medicine in Lyons. *Peau noire* was his first work, apart from an essay published the previous year in the journal *Esprit* under the title 'L'Expérience vécue du noir' ('The lived experience of the black man') which, with only one minor change, would become Chapter 5 of *Peau noire* (Fanon 1951).[1] After its publication, *Peau noire* had a life of relative obscurity. However, since the 1980s, the text has become known, at least in the anglophone world, as one of the most important anti-colonial and anti-racist works in the post-war period. Ironically, given its specifically francophone context, the text has not received the same treatment in France or the francophone world and remains a relatively minor work (cf. Gibson 1999a: 10).

In his recent biography of Fanon, David Macey (2000), one of the contributors to this collection, comments on (and takes issue with) this rather strange posthumous trajectory of man and work. He notes the way in which, since his death in December 1961, Fanon has first been adopted as the Third World champion of 'the wretched of the earth', then celebrated as one of the inspirations to the Black Power movement in America in the 1960s and, more recently, established as an icon of theorists of cultural and postcolonial studies in the anglophone academy and absorbed into their more textual preoccupations with identity and sexual and racial politics.[2] Macey also criticises the way in which the American translation of *Peau noire* in 1967 dislocates Fanon from a francophone context and, through mistranslation, transforms him into the archetypal Negro from the American deep south. Many readers of *Peau noire* in English, whose only acquaintance with the text is via this version, have little or no access to the multi-layered francophone context within which Fanon's ideas evolved. To counter these simplified (and often inaccurate) representations of Fanon, Macey's biography retrieves the complexity of the man and his work, especially the geographical, historical and socio-political aspects of his francophone heritage.

I would broadly endorse this characterisation of the afterlife of man and text. However, while agreeing that the anglophone postcolonial appropriation of Fanon and *Peau noire* has often erased important contexts within which the text should usefully be situated (especially the francophone context), I also believe that the power of the text resides in its ability to travel across the frontiers of place, history and politics and speak in different voices to different readers. The tension between the specific and the universal is a theme running through many of the essays in this collection. For *Peau noire* is about anti-Black racism in the colonial context and also race and racism in general; it is about Martinique and the French metropole and yet resonates far beyond those places; and it is about the immediate post-war period – in which the economic, political and ideological power of the West to colonise the minds and bodies of others was being challenged by new discourses and struggles of liberation by the victims of that power – and yet still profoundly relevant today when forms of oppression and power have evolved but by no means disappeared.

Peau noire is justifiably a classic text because of its breadth and scope. It is far from a simple denunciation of colonialism and racism and Fanon's voice is not that of the oppressed Negro of the American deep south prior to civil rights (as the translation might have us believe). *Peau noire* is, instead, both an intellectual critique and an existential project, an exposé of the ideological apparatus of colonialism and a passionate cry from deep within a body alienated by that system and in search of liberation from it. Fanon's canvas is large. He engages not only with the French metropolitan system which, through official and scholarly texts and popular culture, overtly produces negative images of the Black, but also with the wider spread of western liberal thought which more covertly colludes in the perpetuation of a Manichaean binary opposition between the West and its others. Discourses of liberation such as psychoanalysis, the Hegelian dialectic and phenomenology are adopted as useful tools for prising open the nature and extent of white oppression but are also exposed as false universalisms when confronted by the specificities of 'the lived experience of the black man'. Aware of the conscious and unconscious effects of the western gaze, Fanon's text is a profound exploration of the power of that gaze to alienate mind *and* body.

Fanon also engages with the Negritude writers, Léopold Senghor, Aimé Césaire and others, and their challenge to white oppression of Blacks. Here, too, Fanon's position oscillates between intellectual critique and emotional empathy. The ambiguities in the text that arise from this slippage of languages are further reinforced when we view Fanon's reflections on black and white writings on race in the context of his own unconscious fears and desires. For example, Fanon's treatment of the articulation of racial and sexual relations in the colonial context – his stinging critique of the female protagonist in Mayotte Capécia's auto-biographical novel *Je suis martiniquaise* in Chapter 2 compared to his sympathetic understanding of the male protagonist Jean Veneuse in René Maran's semi-autobiographical novel *Un homme pareil aux autres* in Chapter 3 – could be seen as symptomatic of his own ambivalent affective life. When we consider *Peau noire* across these different levels, we begin to get a sense of the complexity, power and fascination of the text but also its

inevitable contradictions. In the same way that Fanon describes
the black body as an overdetermined phobic object in a white
world, so *Peau noire* itself might be seen as an overdetermined
text, proposing divergent meanings which arise inevitably from
the multi-layered intellectual and existential enterprise undertaken.

In Chapter 1 David Macey develops the theme of the francophone contextualisation of *Peau noire* mentioned above by
concentrating on the specifically Martinican references in the
text which have either been effaced or distorted in subsequent
representations of Fanon. By teasing out these references, Macey
relocates Fanon within a very specific space and time and blocks
the over-hasty tendency to universalise his ideas. So, for example,
the 'comparison' culture of Martinique, whereby social distinctions are constructed around different shadings of colour, will be
in stark contrast to the cruder dichotomy between black and
white which Fanon will encounter in metropolitan France. Not
only will this difference in reading colour reveal to Fanon the
unstable nature of racial classifications and their status as
situated social constructions rather than natural characteristics,
but it will also establish a tension between Martinican and
metropolitan culture and history which is at the heart of Fanon's
'lived experience'. 'White' for Fanon is already overlaid by the
Martinican experience of the 'béké' (the white master of colonial
rule). It is his racialising and inferiorising look which will be
recalled (if unconsciously) when, in a train, Fanon is cast as the
demonic Negro in the eyes of the white boy with his mother. This
moment in France is therefore overlaid with (and overdetermined
by) another history: the trauma of slavery and colonisation at the
hands of the white master. The universalising of that experience
of racialised otherness can lose sight of the historical specificity
so important to its meaning.

Macey's approach also manages to tease out the profound
tension at the heart of the text between the desire for a new
beginning and the weight of the past. By retrieving the specific
cultural and historical significance attached to particular linguistic
items in the text, Macey reveals the unconscious traces of a
history which Fanon consciously wants to expunge. It is precisely
the question of expunging the past which is central to the

argument of Françoise Vergès in Chapter 2. She argues that Fanon's desire for a violent rupture with the past and a new beginning rules out the possibility of a Creole conception of Caribbean history and culture associated today with the writers Edouard Glissant, Jean Bernabé, Patrick Chamoiseau and Raphaël Confiant. The celebration of a mixed and impure culture central to 'créolité', with its complex notion of time as 'mixed long and short temporalities', is antithetical to Fanon's insistence on a break with cultural traditions which have contributed only to the alienation of the colonised. His concept of time is that of 'rupture time', a new dawn following anti-colonial revolution, the present turned only towards the future, never back to the past.[3]

Although Vergès is wary of Fanon's negative view of culture (especially his critical attitude towards his own Martinican heritage) and has, herself, more affinities with the 'créolité' of Edouard Glissant, she is nevertheless conscious of what has been lost in this switch from violent rejection of tradition to the cultivation of a hybrid past. Today's emphasis on culture and memory ('le devoir de mémoire') has the effect of transforming the politics of anger, revolution and emancipation into a blander and more apolitical concern with reparation and justice. 'Créolité's culturalist concern with diversity, hybridity, multilingualism and impurity implicitly rejects Fanon's vision of a new beginning within the framework of a new nation. Yet, according to Vergès, elements of Fanon's critique (slavery, colonialism, alienation, diglossia) are still intensely relevant to an understanding of Creole societies. Moreover, we would be wise not to dismiss out of hand older methods of resistance to new forms of oppression and exclusion. Fanon's concept of 'where to begin?' ruled out creolisation, but creolisation should not necessarily rule out Fanon.

In Chapter 3 Jim House situates *Peau noire* in the context of racism in metropolitan France. Fanon makes a number of references to this tradition but is also unaware of some previous militant black writing on white racism and assimilationism in France and the colonies. For example, there is no mention of the journal *Légitime défense*, whose only issue in 1932 was a 'brutal denunciation of social conditions in Martinique' (Macey 2000: 131), and no awareness of the similarity between his own famous 'train scene' in *Peau noire* and one of the scenes in the 1937 novel *Mirages de Paris* by the Senegalese writer Ousmane Socé. House cites numerous other instances of political and cultural denunciations of popular racism and black stereotyping in the interwar period in France which constitute an important context for the elaboration of Fanon's own theories, even if Fanon himself makes little or no reference to many of these in *Peau noire*.

Yet, for House, *Peau noire* is particularly significant in terms of what it adds to preceding analysis and writing. By contrasting his own lived experience with the social and ideological structures of colonial racism, Fanon was adept at highlighting the gap between the universalist rhetoric of French republicanism and the reality for Blacks from non-metropolitan France. Moreover, he was one of the first writers and activists to see the similarities between his own situation and that of victims of other forms of racism. Fanon's comparative approach was not without its contradictions, as it slides between the cases of Martinicans, Antilleans and Blacks in general and both draws together and distinguishes between anti-Black racism and anti-Semitism. Yet it added a different dimension to understanding racism. Racism had hitherto been conceptualised in France more or less exclusively within the tradition of universal human rights based on the model of anti-Semitism. By drawing together different forms of racism, Fanon highlighted the 'inter-relatedness' of the metropolitan centre and colonial periphery and allowed for a more complex understanding of levels of racial exclusion.

The next three chapters explore different aspects of Fanon's engagement with Sartre in *Peau noire*. In Chapter 4 Bryan Cheyette focuses specifically on the relationship between anti-Semitism and anti-Black racism. He argues that Fanon's discussion of Sartre's *Réflexions sur la question juive* (*Anti-Semite and Jew*, 1946) establishes a fascinating dialogue in *Peau noire* between the discourses on Jews and Blacks. At times these converge around a universalising notion of oppression, the Black and the Jew racialised equally within the European imaginary. At others they diverge as Fanon pursues the specificities of each rather than their commonalities. Interestingly, when Fanon highlights the distinctions between the Jew and the Black, especially by defining them in terms of mind and body respectively, he occasionally reinforces a dichotomy which is the very stuff of stereotype so vehemently decried elsewhere in the text.

Cheyette suggests that, despite the tension between the opposing pulls of universalism and particularism (which will at times place the Jew in the camp of the white European master, at times in the camp of the victim of the master's objectifying and racialising gaze), Fanon will ultimately tend towards particularism so as to avoid being caught up in the pitfalls of a liberal universalising of humanity and to emphasise the distinctiveness of the Black's lived experience. In a sense, then, the uncertainties and contradictions in *Peau noire* concerning Blacks and Jews which arise from Fanon's attempt both to employ and resist Sartre's model of racism are resolved in the effort to challenge, at all costs, a Eurocentric universalising of difference.

In Chapter 5 Robert Bernasconi discusses Fanon's engagement with another of Sartre's texts, 'Orphée noir', which he wrote as introduction to Léopold Senghor's *Anthologie de la nouvelle poésie nègre et malgache de langue française*. Fanon's response to this text shows how the white philosopher not only destroys black enthusiasm – by viewing Negritude as simply a stage in the Hegelian dialectic, a passing phase, a 'becoming' rather than a state, a bit actor in the drama of a 'white history' – but, perhaps more importantly, destroys the existential force of black experience, lived through the body, by intellectualising it in this fashion. Sartre cannot 'know' (i.e. understand) the situation of the Black because, as a White, he has not 'known' (experienced) the black body's lived existence in a 'white-washed' world. Bernasconi argues, then, like Cheyette, that the levels of overlap and difference between white and black experience ultimately come down on the side of difference. Fanon's view that 'l'Européen sait et ne sait pas' implies that there is a fundamental gap in knowledge between black and white which no amount of sympathetic understanding (as demonstrated, for example, by Sartre) will bridge.

For Bernasconi, Fanon's corrective to Sartre's (white) perception of blackness is also a lesson in differential readings of Fanon's text: the understanding will be different by Whites and Blacks because their experience as already situated racialised beings is itself different. The text is therefore not exclusively about black identity but also has important things to say about white identity. Fanon's insistence on the very specificity of the black experience should act as a warning to white commentators whose hasty readings risk imposing misleading meanings on his text.

In my chapter (Chapter 6) I also discuss Fanon's engagement with Sartre and the tension between universalism and particularism. However, my purpose is to suggest that the slippages and contradictions between these positions in *Peau noire* are never resolved but are symptomatic, instead, of the restless nature of a text both trapped within and at odds with the binary structure itself. I place Fanon's text alongside two other post-war texts – Robert Antelme's *L'Espèce humaine* (1947) and Claude Lévi-Strauss's *Race et histoire* (1952) – which also deal, in different ways, with the struggle to redefine the human in the wake of the disastrous effects of systems of racialised violence in the West. I propose that, although none of these works amounts to a fully developed post-humanist vision of 'Man' in the aftermath of the war and at a time of the crisis of western imperialism and ideology, nevertheless they all demonstrate the engagement with otherness beyond the Enlightenment straitjacket of assimilation and exclusion which would henceforth characterise the post-humanist critique of the West in the post-war period.

The final two chapters of the collection are studies of the psychic, existential and political dimensions of racial ideology in *Peau noire*. In Chapter 7 Vicky Lebeau traces Fanon's treatment of unconscious processes informing Negrophobia. Through her analysis of the famous scene in which a young white boy cries out 'Maman, regarde le nègre, j'ai peur' ('Mummy, look at the Negro! I'm frightened') (*Peau noire*: 90; tr. mod.: 112), she demonstrates that it is not simply a generalised anxiety and fear which, mediated unconsciously through the cultural and institutional apparatus of the colonial order, is transferred onto the objectified black man; it is, more specifically, the *sexualised* nature of that fear which lends the negrophobic fantasy its awesome power in western society. It marks the child's transition into both the sexual and symbolic life of culture. For Fanon, Negrophobia is the source of his own alienation – as he experiences the White's unconscious sexualised fears, anxieties and desires projected onto his own body – and the socially constructed racial myth at the heart of colonialism. By drawing an analogy with the murder in 1993 of the black teenager Stephen Lawrence and the subsequent Macpherson Report which criticised police handling of the case, Lebeau suggests that the western imago of 'the Negro' analysed by Fanon is still present in the unconscious life of western culture and responsible for racist violence.

Lebeau's essay specifically highlights Fanon's treatment of this fantasy as both the child's sexualised anxiety of difference and a cultural institutionalisation of racial hatred and violence. However, Lebeau is also critical of Fanon's use of female sexuality to explain the white child's anxiety. Fanon's vision of a feminine sexualised fantasy – in which a masochistic white woman cries out to be raped by a black man – is a problematic understanding of the articulation between anxiety, desire and racial violence. Fanon's use of a multi-layered conceptual framework for unpacking the overdetermined nature of the phobic object can lead to confusing conflations. Nevertheless, by dramatising the scene of phobia through the white boy's encounter with the black man, Fanon opens up the articulation between anxiety and racialised object in a way which is still highly resonant today.

In the final chapter, David Marriott's point of departure, drawing on Harold Rosenberg's criticism of *Hamlet*, is the incommensurable gap between being and seeming (or acting), described by Hamlet himself as 'that within which passeth show'. In Shakespeare's play it is summoned up by the ghost of the dead father. Marriott argues that this is precisely the conflict played out not only in Fanon's work but also in the work of René Maran, whose semi-autobiographical novel *Un homme pareil aux autres* is discussed at length by Fanon in Chapter 3 of *Peau noire*: the sense of black life as haunted, doubled, out of joint, as it hovers between the disguises of the white imago and the anxieties of lived experience.

Marriott explores the ways in which this 'spectral logic of racism' is dramatised in Maran and Fanon, especially in terms of its appropriation and manipulation of the black man's desire. In the desire for a white woman resides the whole panoply of emotions and neuroses of the black colonised man, including

hatred, self-hatred and masochism, revenge, the need to be loved
and to possess self and others, the search for black manhood. In a
fascinating analysis of the scene in which Fanon describes a black
man crying out the name of Schoelcher (who was instrumental in
the abolition of slavery in 1848) while making love to a blonde
white woman, Marriott uncovers the strange mixture of unconscious desires and neuroses which haunt the black man in a white
world. In an equally fascinating account of Maran, and of Fanon's
treatment of Maran's hero in *Un homme pareil aux autres*, Jean
Veneuse, Marriott portrays the anguished nature of the alienated
black man, whose life and fictions are driven by an obsessive and
endlessly repeated sense of loss and absence in their hopeless
quest for white recognition. At the heart of this quest is,
ultimately, a mourning for the lost object par excellence, the
mother who has abandoned the black son to the demands of
white law and culture. Finally, Marriott will locate the figure of
Orpheus as key to Fanon's own quest. In his black incarnation
(following Sartre's depiction in 'Orphée noir' but here transformed), this is an Orpheus who must decline an eventual unity
with his white Eurydice but open himself to the tension and
difference of his 'en moi' which is 'neither white nor black but
beyond the Manichaean'.

The essays in this collection situate *Peau noire* within a variety of
discourses, spaces and histories and thereby open up the multi-
faceted and often contradictory nature of the text. No 'authentic'
Fanon emerges from these essays but a thinker who is both of his
time and place and yet speaks to us all across time and place in
different ways.

Notes

1 The only change is the removal of three sentences in the paragraph
  beginning 'La honte. La honte et le mépris de moi-même …' ('Shame.
  Shame and self-contempt …') (*Peau noire*: 94; *Black Skin*: 116; Fanon 1951:
  662).

2 For a discussion of the different 'stages' of Fanon studies since Fanon's
  death, see Gordon, Sharpley-Whiting and White 1996. For a justification
  of the American cultural studies approach to Fanon studies, and a critique
  of the perspective offered in Gordon *et al.* 1996, see Alessandrini 1999. For

a critique of the Anglo-American cultural studies approach which, like Macey's review of Fanon studies, attacks the misrepresentations of a constructed 'Fanon', see Gibson 1999b.

3 Cf. the title of his book *L'An V de la révolution algérienne*, which is clearly premised on the new calendar following the French Revolution of 1789.

References

Alessandrini, A. C. (1999) 'Introduction: Fanon studies, cultural studies, cultural politics' in A. C. Alessandrini (ed.), *Frantz Fanon: Critical Perspectives*, London and New York: Routledge, 1–17

Fanon, F. (1951) 'L'Expérience vécue du noir', *Esprit*, no. 179, May, 657–79

Gibson, N. C. (1999a) 'Introduction' in N. C. Gibson (ed.), *Rethinking Fanon: The Continuing Dialogue*, New York: Humanity Books, 9–46

—— (1999b) 'Fanon and the pitfalls of cultural studies' in A. C. Alessandrini (ed.), *Frantz Fanon: Critical Perspectives*, London and New York: Routledge, 99–125

Gordon, L. R., Sharpley-Whiting, T. D. and White, R. T. (1996) 'Introduction: five stages of Fanon studies' in L. R. Gordon, T. D. Sharpley-Whiting and R. T. White (eds), *Fanon: A Critical Reader*, Oxford: Blackwell, 1–8

Macey, D. (2000) *Frantz Fanon: A Life*, London: Granta

1

Adieu foulard. Adieu madras

DAVID MACEY

> Nos observations et nos conclusions ne valent que pour les Antilles. (Our observations and our conclusions apply only to the West Indies.) (*Peau noire*: 11)[1]

In the first chapter of *Peau noire* Fanon imagines (or recalls) a young man on the point of leaving Martinique for metropolitan France. Perhaps he is recalling his own departure from the island in 1946. The young man is about to embark on the steamer that will, after ten to twelve days at sea, deposit him in Le Havre. From there, he will take the train to Paris. The young man 'lit sa puissance, sa mutation' ('reads his power, his mutation') in the eyes of those who have come to see him off. He dreams of the 'cercle magique' of 'Paris, Marseille, La Sorbonne, Pigalle'. He dreams of the white women he will sleep with. And he whistles or hums to himself '"Adieu madras, adieu foulard..."' (*Peau noire*: 18).

Although Fanon places the phrase in inverted commas, he provides no gloss for his allusion. The quotation is in fact slightly inaccurate and should read 'Adieu foulard, adieu madras', but the reference is transparent to any reader acquainted with Martinique. It is a reference to the title and refrain of a popular Creole song in which a young Martinican woman says a tearful farewell to the white lover or 'doudou' who has abandoned her: 'Adieu foulard, adieu madras / Adieu graine d'or, adieu collier chou / Doudou a moi, lui parti / Hélas, hélas, c'est pou toujou' ('Farewell foulard, farewell madras / Farewell graine d'or, farewell collier chou / My loverman gone / Alas alas / gone for ever') (cited in Lemoine 1982: 46). The 'foulard' is a scarf twisted into a headdress; the 'madras' a checked cotton dress. The 'graine d'or' and the 'collier chou' are highly prized (and highly expensive) pieces of gold jewellery. The story behind the song is obviously not uncommon in the literatures of Empire; to restrict discussion to the French sphere of influence, what has been called the paradigm of 'landing–loving–leaving' also appears, for instance, in fictions about Indochina (Cooper 2001: 167). It is the story of the unfortunate heroine of Abdoulay Sadji's novel, *Nini: mulâtresse du Sénégal* (1988), which was published in 1951, just in time to be discussed in *Peau noire*. It is, of course, also the tale of Mayotte Capécia (1948), whom Fanon criticises so brutally: she wanted her white officer to marry her even though she knew that white men did not marry black women. And she was right. She was abandoned and left to bring up his child.[2]

Although the paradigm of 'landing–loving–leaving' is universal, there is something highly specific about Fanon's allusion to the song. The story is not always told with this accent. Thanks to an inversion of gender, a melancholy lament sung by a young woman becomes a young man's ironic farewell to his native home. The song itself is part of a network of signifiers that all signify 'Martinique'. Women dressed in 'foulards' and 'madras' are key signifiers in the exoticism that surrounds so many images of Martinique in both literature and promotional material addressed to potential tourists. Fanon's allusion to the song is also a farewell to the literature of 'doudouism', a form of exoticism that celebrates the beauty of both the 'île des fleurs' and its female population in such a way that 'beautiful young black woman' becomes a metonym for 'Martinique'.[3] If the young man boarding the ship is the emblematic black man, it would seem that his 'expérience vécue' ('lived experience') is emblematic of Martinique. He is not 'just' a black man, just as the lived experience of colonialism and racism is at once specific and universal. As Edouard Glissant remarks, 'La Martinique n'est pas une île de la Polynésie' ('Martinique is not an island in Polynesia') (Glissant 1981: 11).

The Martinican specificity of *Peau noire* has been obscured by a number of factors and agencies. There is of course a degree of indeterminacy about the text itself; Fanon's insistence that he

is speaking of Martinique or the West Indies is somewhat
discordant with more generalised statements about a universal
experience,[4] just as it is never quite certain whether *Les Damnés
de la terre* is 'about' Algeria or the more universal Third World –
'en face de l'Europe comme une masse colossale' ('facing Europe
like a colossal mass') (Fanon 1961: 241) – it did so much to bring
into being. After his death, Fanon was transformed into an apostle
of Black Power by American activists, and by the publicists of
Grove Press who, in 1964, described Constance Farrington's
translation of *Les Damnés de la terre* as a handbook for 'a negro
revolution that is sweeping the white world'. Activists such as
Eldridge Cleaver and Stokely Carmichael relocated Fanon from
Martinique and Algeria to the rooftops of the ghettos of Watts
and Detroit. The relocation was also a mutilating distortion. No
reader of the concluding pages of *Peau noire* will be convinced by
claims that Fanon was a believer in black nationalism: 'Le nègre
n'est pas. Pas plus que le Blanc' ('The Negro does not exist. No
more so than the White') (*Peau noire*: 187). Those pages are a very
Sartrean ode to freedom in which consciousness wrenches itself
free from all determinations – historical, psychological and racial
– and leaps into total freedom.

More disturbingly, but also more intriguingly, strands
within postcolonial theory appear to have completely delocalised
and detemporalised a Fanon who now exists outside time and
space. In a very influential article, Homi K. Bhabha remarks, for
instance, that Fanon's first book 'rarely historicises the colonial
experience' (Bhabha 1994: 42).[5] A more detailed reading suggests
that *Peau noire* does not deal with anything so general as 'the
colonial experience' – always assuming that such an abstraction,
as opposed to different experiences of different colonialisms,
ever existed – but with the colonial experience of Martinique in
Fanon's youth, though it could be argued that it 'geographi-
calises' that experience rather than historicising it. If, however, it
is read together with the 1955 essay 'Antillais et Africains', it
becomes apparent that the book's referent is at least to some
extent Martinique in the period 1940–43, when the island was
blockaded by the US navy and ruled by the authoritarian Admiral
Georges Robert – a sort of Pétain in white tropical uniform who
supported the Vichy regime in the metropolis and established its

Caribbean equivalent (see Chauvet 1985 and the historical documents collected in Leotin 1993). The island was now submerged by a shore-bound population of French sailors who behaved 'en racistes authentiques' ('as authentic racists'); its population began to doubt if they really were the French citizens they had always believed themselves to be ('Antillais et Africains' in Fanon 1969: 27).

The 'Robert' episode is a theme to which Martinique's novelists return again and again (see, for instance, Confiant 1988 ; Delpech 1991; Delsham 1994). Indeed, *Tan Robè* is so much part of the collective Martinican memory that even people far too young to have lived through it will spontaneously use it as a synonym for 'hard times'. The reintroduction of the historical, even historicist, dimension also suggests that Fanon's hostility towards Mayotte Capécia is not purely gender-based. *Je suis martiniquaise* is set during 'Robert time' ('an tan Robè' in Creole). Capécia's heroine-spokeswoman shares her lover's pro-Vichy views and describes the volunteers who joined the Free French forces that overthrew Robert in 1943 as 'nègres de la plus basse catégorie' ('niggers of the lowest category') (Capécia 1948: 172). Fanon was one of their number.

It is surprisingly difficult to insert Martinique into the classic paradigm of colonialism, as its history and constitutional status have always been highly ambiguous. Like Guadeloupe, Guyane and Réunion, Martinique was one of the 'old colonies' which were remnants of the pre-revolutionary empire that was largely surrendered to Britain under the terms of the peace treaty signed in 1763 (on Réunion, see Vergès 1999). When slavery was abolished in 1848, universal suffrage was introduced and the peoples of the old colonies became full French citizens, at least in theory. Although it had an appointed colonial governor, Martinique also had a powerful elected regional council and returned députés to the Assemblée nationale in Paris. In 1946, the old colonies became overseas departments (départements d'outre-mer) and their constitutional status is identical to that of any metropolitan département. 'Départementalisation' was not something that was foisted upon the population of Martinique; they voted in favour of it. The official French view is that 'départementalisation' was an alternative form of decolonisation (see, for instance,

Deville and Georges 1996); dissidents such as the novelist Patrick Chamoiseau take the view that it was the beginning of 'une modernisation anesthyésiante' ('an anaesthetising modernisation') and a very successful colonisation (Chamoiseau 1997a: 70). Being an integral part of France, Martinique is now part of the European Community. Those with good eyesight can locate it on the schematic maps printed on Euro notes.

Martinique has never been home to a true independence movement, still less an armed liberation struggle. Even today, Alfred Marie-Jeanne, député and leader of the tiny independence party, concedes that independence is not a viable goal in the immediate, and argues the case for greater autonomy: 'Je ne réclame pas l'impossible, je réclame tout le champ du possible'.[6] Historically, independence has had a greater appeal for the indigenous white population than for the black population; planter revolts were always a threat during the colonial period. One of the reasons why so many young men supported the Free French in 1943–4 is that they regarded metropolitan France as a force that could defend them against the white plantocracy.

Although Fanon's analysis of racial intersubjectivity relies heavily upon a Sartrean-Hegelian problematic, it is true to say that he does not view history as a process or as the teleological unfolding of some dialectic. His vision is of history as *tabula rasa*, punctuated by absolute beginnings and, presumably, endings that are equally absolute.[7] The very title of *L'An V de la révolution algérienne* (Fanon 1959) obviously implies that 1954 was year one, or the absolute beginning of a new era. And this in turn implies that the opening words of *Peau noire* are a reproach to a Martinique, where there can be no new beginning. This is a place where, to Fanon's obvious chagrin, 'l'explosion n'aura pas lieu aujourd'hui. Il est trop tôt … ou trop tard' ('the explosion will not take place today. It's too early … or too late') (*Peau noire*: 5). Even when serious riots did break out in 1959, and when blood did flow in the streets of Fort-de-France, the longed-for explosion did not occur.[8] In public, Fanon claimed that Martinique was seeing the birth of a national spirit; in private he told a friend that the flash of anger was no more than a wet dream that would come to nothing (see 'Le sang coule aux Antilles sous domination française' in Fanon 1969 and Juminer 1962). The explosion came in Algeria in late October 1954, and Fanon's eschatological vision was consonant with the mythology of the FLN, which was eager to present and represent itself as having been created *ex nihilo* by the will and violence of its members, and as a movement that had no prehistory.

Fanon does not, for instance, trace the long and bloody history of the slave revolts that broke out so regularly between 1635, when Martinique was first colonised, and 1848, when slavery was finally abolished. And yet Martinique's history, or a mytho-poetic version thereof, is still present throughout. The image of revolt in *Peau noire* (pp. 160–1) is borrowed from Aimé Césaire's account of a doomed slave rebellion in the Caribbean;[9] that it reappears unchanged in *Les Damnés de la terre* (pp. 64–6), where the icon of revolt might have been expected to be provided by an Algerian 'moudjahid' with gun in hand rather than a rebel slave armed with a 'coutelas', or machete, further indicates that – perhaps despite himself – Fanon does remain one of Martinique's native sons. If, to paraphrase Barthes (1984: 49), history is 'ce qui s'enseigne' ('that which is taught'),[10] the absence of any overt historical perspective in *Peau noire* can be explained by pedagogic practice: the history of Martinique is not taught in the schools of Martinique, where students learn of a sequence of kings, emperors and presidents of republics, but not the history of the 'marrons' or runaway slaves. It has been left to a later generation of novelists, or word-scratchers ('marqueurs de paroles'), as Chamoiseau calls them,[11] to reconstruct an alternative history drawing on the historical record, Creolisms and a folklore which Fanon, being the son of a good upwardly mobile family, had been taught to despise on the grounds that 'le folklore martiniquais est pauvre' ('Martinique's folklore is poor') (*Peau noire*: 124).

Most of the indications that *Peau noire* is an account of the lived experience of being Martinican are fairly minor lexical items, but they are deeply embedded in the fabric of the text (and disappear in the published translation, which succeeds in transforming the Martinican Fanon into the archetypal Black of the Deep South). At times Fanon reverts, that is, to a vocabulary that could be used only by someone from Martinique (or perhaps Guadeloupe). A mother scolds her children for daring to speak

Creole rather than 'proper' French and calls them 'tibandes'
(*Peau noire*: 15), the irony being that she has to use Creole to scold
them for using it: 'tibandes' ('petites bandes') were the 'little
gangs' of children who worked in the cane fields, clearing up the
pieces of cane missed by the women ('amarreuses') who tied them
into neat bundles. Few metropolitan readers would recognise the
expression, just as few metropolitan readers would realise that
'souventefois' (*Peau noire*: 73) is neither a misprint nor a condensation of 'souvent' and 'maintes fois', but a standard Creolism
meaning 'often'. Fanon insists on the need to achieve 'une
compréhension totale' ('a complete understanding') and remarks
'ce n'est pas la peine de venir, avec des airs de "crabe-c'est-ma-
faute" proclamer qu'il s'agit de sauver l'âme' ('It's not worth
coming along, looking like a crabe-c'est-ma-faute, and proclaim-
ing that it's a matter of saving souls') (*Peau noire*: 9). The
expression is traditional,[12] and the beast in question is one of
Martinique's many crustaceans. In the male, one claw is much
larger than the other. As it waves that claw, which is an offensive
weapon as well as a limb used to grasp food, it appears to be
beating its chest and saying 'mea culpa'. It belongs to the genus
Ucas, and is known in English as a fiddler crab. The many species
of the genus are very widely distributed, but it is only in the
French West Indies that the animal is known as a 'crabe-c'est-ma-
faute' (literally 'an I'm-sorry-crab').

Fanon rails against the 'comparaison' culture of Martinique,
and asks his Martinican readers to 'déterminer la plus
"comparaison" des rues de Fort-de-France. La rue Schoelcher, la
rue Victor-Hugo, certainement pas la rue François-Arago' ('determine the most "comparison" street in Fort-de-France. The rue
Schoelcher, la rue Victor Hugo … certainly not the rue François
Arago') (*Peau noire*: 171). The rue Schoelcher and the rue Victor-
Hugo were – and are – middle-class streets, one running parallel
to and the other perpendicular to the rue de la République,
where Fanon's family lived in (relative) middle-class comfort.
Slightly to the west, the rue François Arago was significantly
poorer and 'blacker'. The population of the rue Schoelcher and
the rue Victor Hugo are 'nègres comparaison' in that they
'compare' themselves with their neighbours in order to
determine where they stand in a hierarchy of pigmentation,

lighter skin being equated with higher social status. They are preoccupied with their self-valorisation at the expense of others and with their ego-ideals, or in other words with the racial-economic model to which they attempt to conform. As the proverb has it, '(t)out nègre riche, c'est mulâtre, tout mulâtre pauvre, c'est nègre' ('any rich negro is a mulatto, any poor mulatto is a negro') (cited in Giraud 1979: 174). Fanon himself is by no means immune to the 'comparison' syndrome. He describes how, as a boy, he went with friends to look at a visiting philosophy teacher from Guadeloupe who was so 'excessivement noir' ('excessively black') as to be 'bleu' ('blue') in local parlance (*Peau noire*: 132n).

Although Fanon works within a Hegelian-existentialist tradition, and maps Black–White on to a self–other, master–slave dichotomy, he is in fact forced to admit, albeit almost in passing, that the schema is not really applicable to Martinique, observing that '(i)l y avait aussi aux Antilles ce petit hiatus qui existe entre la békaille, la mulâtraille et la négraille' ('there was in the French West Indies also that small hiatus that exists between "la békaille, la mulâtraille" and "la négraille"') (*Peau noire*: 89). As in Jamaica and elsewhere in the Caribbean, the racial system is three-tiered, being divided into the White, the Brown and the Black, and whiteness is more a matter of appearance than genealogy. The Jamaican philosopher Charles W. Mills (2002: 156) remarks that, whereas he is a 'black man' when teaching in the United States, he is a 'red man' when he goes home to Jamaica. If he went to Martinique, Mills would presumably be a 'chabin': a light-skinned 'black man' with blue eyes and red-brown hair. *Mutatis mutandis*, it is when Fanon or any other 'black' Martinican goes to France that he 'becomes' black. Indeed, the complexities of Martinique's ethnic groups are even greater than this: Fanon makes no mention of the Indian 'coolies', who are descended from the indentured workers imported to work the cane fields when slavery was abolished, or the 'Syrians' who still have a monopoly on the garment trade (they are in fact of Lebanese descent). Significantly, the crucial encounter with the white other (*Peau noire*: 88–93) occurs not in Martinique but in metropolitan France. As a child at home in Martinique, remarks Fanon, 'Je suis un nègre – mais naturellement je ne le

sais pas, parce que je le suis' ('I am a negro, but naturally I don't
know that because that is what I am') (*Peau noire*: 155).

The 'Creolist' movement that developed around Raphaël
Confiant and Patrick Chamoiseau in the 1980s and 1990s is in part
an attempt to come to terms with this complex 'racial' heritage:
'Ni Européens, ni Africains, ni Asiatiques, nous nous proclamons
Créoles' ('Neither Europeans, nor Africans, nor Asians, we
proclaim ourselves Creoles') (Bernabé, Chamoiseau and Confiant
1993: 13). The modern Creolists regard Fanon as one of their
immediate forebears, and set themselves this goal: 'A la suite de
Frantz Fanon, explorer notre réel dans une perspective
cathartique' ('Exploring our real from a cathartic perspective,
following the example of Frantz Fanon') (Bernabé, Chamoiseau
and Confiant 1993: 22). In the 1950s, 'Creolism' was simply not an
option. Fanon speaks admiringly of 'l'arrivée de Césaire' ('the
arrival of Césaire') in 1939 and declares (with some exaggeration[13])
that he is the first man in Martinique to assume his Negritude
and to say, in his great *Cahier d'un retour au pays natal*, that 'il est
beau et bon d'être nègre' ('it is fine and good to be a negro',
'Antillais et Africains' in Fanon 1969: 26).[14] The appropriation of
a stigma and its transformation into a badge of honour ('Black is
beautiful') has become a paradigmatic response to perceived
oppression, but this was not an easy proclamation to make in pre-
war times and, despite its post-war success in France, the *Cahier*
was not popular in Martinique. And it would still be a long time
before even the hero of a novel could state with pride: 'Un
mulâtre, voilà ce que je suis, oui!' ('A mulatto, that's what I am,
yes!') (Confiant 2000: 380).

The phrasing of the description of Martinique's three-tiered
racial structure (which is calqued on 'canaille', meaning 'rabble'
or 'riff-raff') is Fanon's, but it again refers to a specific reality and
a very specific colonial experience on the part of the black man.
The 'béké' – the word tends to be used in the singular and its
etymology is obscure – is not just a white man, and nor is he just
a white settler. There were white settlers in France's African
colonies and 'pieds noirs' were born in Algeria, but there were
no 'békés' outside the Caribbean. A béké is a descendant of the
first plantation owners who populated Martinique with slaves. A
béké is as much a native of Martinique as any mulatto or Black,

but is also extremely proud of 'being white'. He is fluent in Creole, a *lingua franca* that originally developed as a means of communication between master and slave on the sugar plantations ('habitations'). That the béké is not metropolitan French is significant, and allows the population of Martinique to unite in despising any 'in-coming' 'Béké-France' – a term that is never used with friendly intent.

Unlike the former French colonies in West Africa or Algeria, Martinique has no pre-colonial past to which it can turn or which it can reclaim. Hence, of course, the appeal of a more or less imaginary Africa in some forms of Negritude. The aboriginal population of Arawaks was wiped out by the Caribs, and the Caribs themselves were, from 1635 onwards, the object of what can only be described as a colonial genocide. Almost no trace of them remains, apart from a few artefacts in dusty museums and some enigmatic carved stones deep in the forests.[15] Martinique's history began with colonisation and slavery, with an encounter with an absolute white other. This is how Edouard Glissant's mytho-poetic fictional history of the island commences: with the arrival of the *Rose-Marie* and her cargo of slaves, watched by 'le maître au regard bleu' ('the blue gaze of the master'), by 'l'homme aux yeux bleus' ('the man with blue eyes') (Glissant 1990: 21 and 24). In Aimé Césaire's Caribbean reworking of *The Tempest*, it is the gaze of Prospero that imposes on Caliban his self-image as 'un sous-développé … un sous-capable … voilà comment tu m'as obligé à me voir' ('an under-developed, under-capable man … That's how you've made me see myself') (Césaire 1969: 88). Although it is not made explicit, the same imagery permeates *Peau noire*, which can thus be read as part of an intertext grounded in Martinique's experience of the trauma of colonisation.

Fanon first refers to the trope of 'blue eyes' in his discussion of Mayotte Capécia. Dismissively paraphrasing the theme of her novel as 'Je l'aimais parce qu'il avait les yeux bleus, les cheveux blonds et le teint pâle', he adds 'et nous qui sommes Antillais, nous ne le savons que trop: le nègre craint les yeux bleus, répète-t-on là-bas' (p. 34).[16] The allusion is to the proverbial saying 'les yeux béké ont brûlé les yeux nègres' ('the eyes of the béké burned to eyes of the negro'). This is how Confiant's Creole lexicon defines the 'béké': 'Le bleu de ses yeux brûlait le regard du nègre au temps-l'esclavage. Débarqué de Normandie, Poitou ou Bretagne, il extermina par le fer et le feu les indigènes caraïbes' (Confiant 1993: 253).[17] The history of Martinique begins with the trauma of colonisation and slavery, and it begins under the burning gaze of the man with blue eyes. And it is that trauma that is repeated and reactivated during Fanon's encounter with a child in a train. The child turns to its mother: 'Tiens, un nègre … Maman, regarde le nègre, j'ai peur' ('Look, a negro … Mum, look at the negro. I'm frightened') (*Peau noire*: 90). Fanon's account of his reaction is couched in phenomenological terms derived from Sartre's account of the gaze and 'être pour autrui' ('being for others') and especially from Merleau-Ponty's description of the 'bodily schema' in *Phénoménologie de la perception*. But whilst this is a universal encounter with the other, it is also racialised, and it is racialised in very specific terms: 'Toute cette blancheur me calcine' ('All this whiteness is burning me up') (*Peau noire*: 92). A chance encounter with a child who has learned to recognize 'a black man' reactivates the original trauma of the encounter with the blue eyes of the white man with blond hair, with the eyes that burn.

Fanon is describing a moment of trauma, schematically defined in psychiatric terms as a confrontation with some external event that is an actual or perceived threat to the life of personal integrity (here, the corporeal schema), and as an emotive response to that event: 'le schéma corporel, attaqué en plusieurs points, s'écroula, cédant la place à un schéma épidermique racial' (p. 90). He experiences nausea and dizziness, and then states: 'J'étais tout à la fois responsable de mon corps, responsable de ma race, de mes ancêtres. Je promenai sur moi un regard objectif, découvris ma noirceur, mes caractères ethniques, – et me défoncèrent le tympan l'anthropophagie, l'arriération mentale, le fétichisme, les tares raciales, les négriers, et surtout, et surtout: "Y a bon banania"' (p. 90).[18] This is a description of a common feature of trauma: the sudden shift from amnesia, or an inability to remember, to hypermensia, or an inability to forget. External events or stimuli – the gaze of a child, the sight of a poster advertising Banania – a grinning colonial soldier spooning proprietary cocoa into his mouth – trigger the inescapable memory of the burning gaze of the first béké.

In his discussion of 'The Negro and psychopathology' (Chapter 6), Fanon contends that all neuroses can be traced back to 'des *Erlebnis* déterminées' ('determinate lived experiences') (*Peau noire*: 117) that are repressed into the unconscious, and supports his contention with a long quotation from Freud. This is in fact his only direct quotation from Freud, but a closer reading demonstrates that it actually refutes Fanon's claims. Although Fanon gives no reference, the quotations are from the lectures on psychoanalysis delivered by Freud at Clark University in 1909. Freud is retrospectively describing his early work with Breuer, in which 'seduction theory' provides an explanation for the occurrence of neurosis. In Freudian terminology, 'seduction' is a rather prudish euphemism for what is now commonly described as the sexual abuse of children: neurosis stems from the childhood trauma of abuse or even rape (see respectively, 'The aetiology of hysteria' (1896), vol. 2 and 'Five lectures on psychoanalysis', vol. 11 in Freud 1954–74). In his lectures, Freud describes how he came to abandon that theory and to conclude that neurosis stems not from actual abuse at the hands of an adult but from the incestuous and Oedipal fantasies and desires of the child.

What orthodox psychoanalysis would see as Fanon's misreading of Freud is in fact consistent with certain other surprising statements, and, most strikingly, with the denial that the Oedipus complex exists in Martinique:

> On oublie trop souvent que la névrose n'est pas constitutive de la réalité humaine. Qu'on le veuille ou non, le complexe d'Oedipe n'est pas près de voir le jour chez les nègres ... il nous serait relativement facile de montrer qu'aux Antilles françaises, 97% des familles sont incapables de donner naissance à une névrose oedipienne. (*Peau noire*: 123–4)[19]

No psychoanalyst – and it cannot be pointed out too often that Fanon was a psychiatrist and not a psychoanalyst – would endorse this claim, and many psychoanalysts would object that the Oedipus is not a neurosis but a complex that generates neurosis. Even more astonishing, from a psychoanalytic point of view, is the claim that the absence of the Oedipus complex explains why there is no 'présence manifeste de pédérastie en Martinique' ('manifest presence of pederasty in Martinique'),

even though there are 'des hommes habillés en dames' ('some
men dressed as ladies') (*Peau noire*: 146, note 44).[20] With what
sounds like something of an effort on his part, Fanon adds that he
is 'persuadé qu'ils ont une vie sexuelle normale' ('convinced that
they have a normal sexual life') (*Peau noire*: 146, note 44).

   Such statements fly in the face of both psychoanalytic
wisdom and observable reality, but they may have a logic of
their own. They explain, for instance, the appeal of Germaine's
Guex's *Le Syndrôme d'abandon* (1973), first published in 1951
under the title *La Névrose d'abandon*. Guex was a Swiss psychoanalyst and her major work describes a clinical picture dominated
by fears and anxieties about abandonment and insecurity. The
'abandonment neurosis' is described as being pre-Oedipal. An
'abandonic' patient, that is, has never entered the classic Oedipal
phase, which represents too great a threat to his or her security.
The neurosis is therefore attributable to a fundamental
disturbance of the ego. Guex's book is not especially well known
and her speculations about the abandonment neurosis have not
gained wide currency within the psychoanalytic community.
Fanon invokes it in his discussion of René Maran's novel *Un
homme pareil aux autres* (1947) and describes its hero Jean
Veneuse, a Martinican raised in Bordeaux who worked as a
colonial administrator in sub-Saharan Africa, thus: '(U)n jour …
j'ai esquissé une relation objectale et j'ai été *abandonné*. Je n'ai
jamais pardonné à ma mère. Ayant été abandonné, je ferai
souffrir l'autre, et l'abandonner sera l'expression directe de mon
besoin de revanche' (*Peau noire*: 60–1).[21] Guex's theory provides
Fanon with a nosography consistent with the claim that the
Oedipus complex is non-existent in Martinique. Ironically, it is
also consistent with one of the most pernicious of colonial myths,
namely the idea that Martinique is one of France's 'daughters'
and that she fears that she will be abandoned by 'la mère-patrie'
(see Burton 1994 and Vergès 1999).

   It should be noted that most of the patients Fanon saw in his
professional capacity as a psychiatrist probably were suffering
from the effects of trauma. As a newly qualified doctor working
in Lyons, he met North African immigrants traumatised by their
experience and describes his typical patient as a man 'menacé
dans son affectivité, menacé dans son activité sociale, menacé

dans son appartenance à la cité, le Nord-Africain réunie toutes les conditions qui font un homme malade. Qu'y a-t-il de plus pathétique que cet homme aux muscles robustes qui nous dit de sa voix véritablement cassée: "Docteur, je vais mourir"' ('Le syndrome nord-africain' in Fanon 1969: 18, first published in *Esprit*, February 1952).[22] As Fanon's mentor François Tosquelles put it, 'Inutile de faire de la psychothérapie à un mort, c'est trop tard. Inutile aussi d'interpréter son oralité à quelqu'un qui a faim, ou son complexe de castration à l'homme qui a une jambe de bois' (cited in Arveiller 1995: 667).[23] And as Fanon puts it in *Peau noire* when he objects to Mannoni's claim that when a Malgache dreams of a 'tirailleur sénégalais' (a colonial infantry-man) with a rifle he is dreaming of a penis or of phallic symbols, we must not 'perdre de vue le réel' ('lose sight of the real') (*Peau noire*: 67).

It is obvious from the case notes included in the fourth chapter of *Les Damnés de la terre* that the patients Fanon saw in Algeria – and they included both the victims and the perpe-trators of torture – were suffering from the very real condition of post-traumatic stress disorder. Fanon's view of therapy is that its goal is to 'conscienciser' ('bring to consciousness') the uncon-scious, to free the patient from his unconscious desire and to orient him towards social change (*Peau noire*: 80, 81). If, that is, the aetiology of mental illness lies in the social domain – and not in sexuality – no talking cure can take away the need for social change. In that sense, the anecdote about the peasant who returns to Martinique after spending a few months in Paris takes on an almost emblematic status. The returnee catches sight of a piece of ploughing equipment and asks his father what it is. 'Pour toute réponse, son père le lui lâche sur les pieds, et l'amnésie disparaît' ('His father's only response is to drop it on his feet. The amnesia disappears'). Fanon comments: 'Singulière thérapeutique' ('A singular form of therapy') (*Peau noire*: 18). It is indeed 'singular': the therapeutic effect is not brought about by a talking cure, but by a sudden and no doubt painful encounter with the real (understood in prosaic terms, and not in the Lacanian sense).

Fanon's ultimate response to the encounter with the white gaze of the child, and to its mother's embarrassed attempts to defuse the situation, is aggression: '"Regarde, il est beau, ce nègre ... ", "Le beau nègre vous emmerde, madame!"' ('"Look how handsome this negro is ...", "The handsome negro says piss off, Madame!"') (*Peau noire*: 92). A similar view is proposed on the grand scale in *Les Damnés de la terre*: violence overcomes the depersonalisation and alienation induced by colonial violence, and has a cleansing cathartic effect on individual and society alike. There is little or no clinical evidence to back up this thesis; Fanon's own case notes make it quite clear that violence has a pathogenic effect on both its victims and its perpetrators. Its political validity is, of course, a different matter and it is the case that a 'French Algeria' born of violence did die a violent death. In Martinique, it is still too early, or too late, for the explosion to take place.

The claim that Martinique knows nothing of either the Oedipus complex or homosexuality is, to say the least, hard to sustain or substantiate at the level of fact, but it may make sense at the level of fantasy. According to Fanon, '(u)n enfant noir normal, ayant grandi au sein d'une famille normale, s'anormalisera au moindre contact avec le monde blanc' ('A normal black child, who has grown up in a normal family, will become abnormal at the slightest contact with the white world') (*Peau noire*: 117). It is immediately after he has put forward this claim that he refers to Freud's 'seduction theory' and to trauma. It would seem, then, that what Fanon understands by 'normality' is the state that existed before the first encounter with the burning eyes of the first white master. It is a sort of utopia or prelapsarian state that can have existed before the beginning. Utopian appeals to Africa are not uncommon in the literature of Negritude, and this prelapsarian Martinique appears to fulfil a similar function.

In 1998, France celebrated an unexpected victory over Brazil in the football World Cup and, in much more muted fashion, the one hundred and fiftieth anniversary of the abolition of slavery. That 1848 was also the year in which an annexed Algeria became part of a greater metropolitan France was passed over in embarrassed silence. The daily newspapers *Le Monde* and *Libération* dispatched special correspondents to the French West Indies to investigate the lingering effects of slavery.[24] Their reports could have been taken from the pages of *Peau noire*. A light-skinned boy of twenty told *Libération*'s Béatrice Bantman that he was convinced that girls went out with him only because they could not find a 'real' white boyfriend. A lycéenne called 'Catherine' told *Le Monde*'s correspondent that 'on a l'impression qu'éclaircir la race est le seul moyen d'accéder à la liberté et à la reconnaissance sociale' ('You get the impression that lightening the race is the only way to achieve freedom and social recognition'). Whether or not these young people had read Fanon is not on record; that they would have known what he was talking about, and would have recognised their problems in a text written over forty years earlier, is quite obvious. *Peau noire* remains tragically relevant to contemporary Martinique. Perhaps a copy should be presented to every tourist who boards an aircraft for Fort-de-France. It might help to dispel the lingering effects of 'doudouisme' and of the erotic exoticism of photographs of young women in 'foulards' and 'madras'.

Notes

1 All translations are my own.

2 See also Capécia's *La Négresse blanche* (1950). The most complete account of Capécia's life and career is Christiane Makward's *Mayotte Capécia, ou l'aliénation selon Fanon* (1999). Unfortunately, Makward's claim that Fanon's case against Capécia is determined by her gender is undermined by her contention that his criticisms are simply based upon 'le manichéisme racial qui sous-tend sa vision de jeune mulâtre en colère' ('the racial Manichaeism that subtends the vision of "an angry young mulatto"') (p. 21). Whilst there is no denying that Fanon is a very masculinist author, such claims do little to advance the debate. I have argued elsewhere (Macey 2000) that Fanon's criticisms of Capécia are not purely gender-based and centre on the evident bad faith signalled by the 'I know but ...' trope.

3 For a brief account, see Chapter 10 of Régis Antoine's *La Littérature franco-antillaise: Haïti, Guadeloupe et Martinique* (1992). Bitter critiques of 'doudoisme' are frequent in the literature of Caribbean Negritude. 'Doudouism' can, however, overlap with some forms of Negritude, as is evident from the 'dedication' to Gilbert Gratiant's 'La Petite Demoiselle' in Senghor (ed.) 1948.

4 'Nous élargissons le secteur de notre description, et par-delà l'Antillais nous visons tout homme colonisé' ('We will extend the sector of our description beyond the West Indian, and will apply it to all colonised men') (*Peau noire*: 14).

5 Cf. the same author's preface to the 1986 Pluto reprint of Charles Lam Markmann's translation of *Black Skin, White Masks*.

6 'I am not asking for the impossible, I am asking for the whole field of the possible', cited Jean-Louis Saux, 'Les DOM attendent un rebond économique des réformes politiques', *Le Monde*, 30 Jan. 2003.

7 Cf. 'Cette sorte de table rase qui définit au départ toute décolonisation [...] La décolonisation est véritablement création d'hommes nouveaux' ('this sort of tabula rasa that defines all decolonisation from the outset [...] Decolonisation really is the creation of new men') (Fanon 1961: 29–30).

8 The riots were provoked by a minor traffic accident involving a white incomer and a black docker, and left three dead. For semi-fictional accounts, see Placoly 1973 and Confiant 1994.

9 Césaire 1970. The opening line (p. 73) reads: 'Bien sûr qu'il va mourir le Rebelle' ('Of course the Rebel is going to die').

10 Barthes originally said 'La littérature est ce qui s'enseigne' ('Literature is that which is taught').

11 See in particular his *Texaco*. The novel traces the history of Texaco, a slum on the outskirts of Fort-de-France that grew and spread like some urban mangrove swamp. The history of Martinique is traced through the history of the homes built by its inhabitants: from huts built from logs to shacks built from blocks of ferro-concrete. For a sympathetic but by no means uncritical account, see Derek Walcott's 'Letter to Chamoiseau' in his *What the Twilight Says* (1998).

12 See the 'Creole lexicon' appended to Raphaël Confiant's *Ravines du devant-jour* (1993: 256): 'Quelle faute a-t-il commise pour se battre sans arrêt la couple de la grosse pince démesurée, presque aussi grosse que son corps? Seul le diable des mangroves le sait' ('What sin has he committed to make him constantly beat his chest with his big oversized claw, which is almost as big as his body? Only the devil of the mangroves knows').

13 Many of Césaire's – and Fanon's – themes can already be found in the one issue of the journal *Légitime défense* published in Paris in 1932. Reprinted in facsimile and with an introduction by René Méni (Paris: Editions Jean-Michel Place, 1979).

14 The most useful edition of the *Cahier* is the bilingual French–English *Notebook of a Return to My Native Land*, trans. Mireille Rosello with Annie Pritchard (Newcastle upon Tyne: Bloodaxe Books, 1995).

15 For a powerfully lyrical account of a runaway slave's encounter with one such stone, see Patrick Chamoiseau's *L'Esclave vieil homme et le molosse* (1997b).

16 'I loved him because he had blond hair, blue eyes and pale skin ... And those of us who are West Indian know it only too well; back there, they repeat "the negro fears blue eyes".'

17 'The blue of his eyes burned the gaze of the negro during slave-time. When he disembarked from Normandy, Poitou or Britanny, he exterminated the native Caribs with fire and the sword.'

18 'Attacked in several places, the corporeal schema collapsed, giving way to
     a racial epidermal schema ... All at once I was responsible for my body,
     responsible for my race, my ancestors. I took an objective look at myself,
     discovered my blackness, my ethnic characteristics – and my ears were
     deafened with cannibalism, mental retardation, fetishism, racial flaws,
     slave traders and, above all, above all "Y a bon banania".'

19 'It is too often forgotten that neurosis is not constitutive of human reality.
     Like it or not, the Oedipus complex is not likely to emerge amongst
     negroes ... It would be relatively easy for me to show that in the French
     West Indies, 97% of families are incapable of giving birth to an Oedipal
     neurosis.'

20 The most astonishing feature of this notorious claim is that it appears to be
     either a misquotation from or a reminiscence of Octave Mannoni's account
     of colonisation in Madagascar: 'On ne rencontre guère d'homosexualité ...
     chez les Malgaches typiques ... le cas curieux des hommes-femmes ...
     s'habillant en femme, et agissant comme des femmes, mais pour vivre avec
     les femmes ... et, assure-t-on, avec une sexualité normale' ('One encounters
     almost no homosexuality ... amongst typical Malgaches ... the curious case
     of men-women ... they dress as women and act as women, but they do so
     in order to live amongst women and, we are assured, enjoy a normal
     sexuality') (Mannoni, 1984. Fanon refers to the first edition, published in
     1951 as *Psychologie de la colonisation*). For the moment, I can offer no
     explanation for this similarity.

21 'One day ... I began to establish an object-relationship, and I was
     abandoned. I have never forgiven my mother. Having been abandoned, I
     will make the other suffer, and abandoning him will be the direct
     expression of my need for revenge.'

22 'Threatened in affectivity, threatened in his social activity, threatened in
     his membership of the polis, the North African brings together all the
     conditions that make a man ill. What could be more pathetic than this man
     with robust muscles who says to us in his truly broken voice: "Doctor, I
     am going to die."'

23 'No point in psychotherapy for a dead man, it's too late. No point either in
     interpreting the orality of someone who is hungry, or the castration
     complex of a man with a wooden leg.'

24 See Annick Cojean, 'L' "Héritage" de l'esclavage aux Antilles', *Le Monde*
     24 Apr. 1998; Béatrice Bantman, 'Martinique, terre des castes', *Libération*
     25–6 Apr. 1998.

References

Antoine, R. (1992) *La Littérature franco-antillaise: Haïti, Guadeloupe et
     Martinique*, Paris: Karthala
Arveiller, J. (1995) 'Mon Maître Tosquelles', *Evolution psychiatrique*, vol. 60,
     no. 3

Barthes, R. (1984) 'Réflexions sur un manuel' in *Le Bruissement de la langue: essais critiques IV*, Paris: Seuil (Collection Points)

Bernabé, J., Chamoiseau, P. and Confiant, R. (1993) *Eloge de la créolité*, Paris: Gallimard

Bhabha, H. K. (1994) 'Interrogating identity: Frantz Fanon and the post-colonial prerogative' in *The Location of Culture*, London: Routledge

Burton, R. D. E. (1994) *La Famille coloniale: la Martinique et la mère-patrie 1789–1993*, Paris: L'Harmattan

Capécia, M. (1948) *Je suis martiniquaise*, Paris: Editions Corréa

—— (1950) *La Négresse blanche*, Paris: Editions Corréa

—— (1969) *Une Tempête*, Paris: Seuil

Césaire, A. (1970) 'Et les chiens se taisaient' (1946) in *Les Armes miraculeuses*, Paris: Gallimard/Poésie

Chamoiseau, P. (1992) *Texaco*, Paris: Gallimard (English trans. Rose-Myriam Réjouis and Val Vonkurov, London: Granta, 1997)

—— (1997a) *Ecrire en pays dominé*, Paris: Gallimard

—— (1997b) *L'Esclave vieil homme et le molosse*, Paris: Gallimard

Chauvet, C. (1985) 'La Martinique au temps de l'Amiral Robert (1939–1943)' in *Historial antillais*, vol. 5, Fort-de France: Société Dajani

Cooper, N. (2001) *France in Indochina: Colonial Encounters*, Oxford and New York: Berg

Confiant, R. (1988) *Le Nègre et l'amiral*, Paris: Grasset

—— (1993) *Ravines du devant-jour*, Paris: Folio

—— (1994) *L'Allée des soupirs*, Paris: Grasset

—— (2000) *Régisseur du rhum*, Paris: Pocket

Delpech, A. (1991) *La Dissidence*, Paris: L'Harmattan

Delsham, T. (1994) *An Tan Robè*, Schoelcher, Martinique: Editions MGG

Deville, R. and Georges, N. (1996) *Les Départements d'outre-mer: l'autre décolonisation*, Paris: Découvertes/Gallimard

Fanon, F. (1959) *L'An V de la révolution algérienne*, Paris: Maspero

—— (1961) *Les Damnés de la terre*, Paris: Maspero

—— (1969) *Pour la révolution africaine*, Paris: Petite Collection Maspero

Freud, S. (1954–74) *The Standard Edition of the Psychological Works of Sigmund Freud* (24 vols), London: Hogarth Press and the Institute of Psychoanalysis

Giraud, M. (1979) *Races et classes à la Martinique*, Paris: Editions Anthropos

Glissant, E. (1981) *Le Discours antillais*, Paris: Seuil

—— (1990) *Le Quatrième Siècle*, Paris: Gallimard/L'Imaginaire (first pub. 1964)

Guex, G. (1973) *Le Syndrôme d'abandon*, Paris: PUF

Juminer, B. (1962) 'Homage à Frantz Fanon', *Présence africaine*, 40, 138–9

Lemoine, M. (1982) *Le Mal antillais: leurs ancêtres les gaulois*, Paris: L'Harmattan

Leotin, M.-H. (1993) *La Martinique pendant la seconde guerre mondiale*, Fort-de-France, Archives départmentales, Centre Régional de Documentation Pédagogique des Antilles et de la Guyane

Macey, D. (2000) *Frantz Fanon: A Life*, London: Granta

Makward, C. P. (1999) *Mayotte Capécia, ou l'aliénation selon Fanon*, Paris: Karthala

Mannoni, O. (1984) *Prospéro et Caliban: psychologie de la colonisation*, Paris: Editions Universitaires

Maran, R. (1947) *Un homme pareil aux autres*, Paris: Editions Arc-en-ciel
Mills, C. W. (2002) 'Red shift: politically embodied/embodied politics' in George Yancy (ed.), *The Philosophical I: Personal Reflections on Life in Philosophy*, Lanham, MD: Rowman & Littlefield
Placoly, V. (1973) *L'Eau-de-morte guildive*, Paris: Denoël
Sadji, A. (1988) *Nini: mulâtresse du Sénégal*, Paris and Dakar: Présence Africaine
Senghor, L. S. (ed.) (1948) *Anthologie de la nouvelle poésie nègre et malgache*, Paris: Presses Universitaires de France
Vergès, F. (1999) *Monsters and Revolutionaries: Colonial Family Romance and Métissage*, Durham, NC: Duke University Press
Walcott, D. (1998) *What the Twilight Says*, London: Faber and Faber

2

Where to begin? 'Le commencement' in *Peau noire, masques blancs* and in creolisation

FRANÇOISE VERGÉS

> Nous ne tendons à rien de moins qu'à libérer l'homme de couleur de lui-même. Nous irons très lentement, car il y a deux camps: le blanc et le noir (I propose nothing short of the liberation of the man of color from himself. We shall go very slowly, for there are two camps: the white and the black) (*Peau noire*: 6; *Black Skin*: 10)

'Where to begin?' is a political question. The 'where' refers to a space and a time invested by individuals who accept the need to debate common issues. It is about marking out the ground upon which women and men will agree to start discussing what social and political organisation they want to build. The question 'where to begin?' introduces a community which imagines being united by something greater than affinities, by the desire to act collectively. It is a question about temporality and spatialisation. It often involves a founding scene, whether fictional or real. Such a scene may happen at any time or in any place: during the day, in a public institution, the gathering of revolutionary brothers swearing allegiance to the republic, with the exclusion of sisters and slaves; a clandestine gathering of slaves at night, conspiring for their freedom, murmuring words of courage; the massacre of innocents on a day in 1945 at Setif, Algeria; a mutiny in India; a strike in Bolivia.

'Where to begin?' Where indeed? The moment, the time, the

space of the 'where to begin' already indicate a choice, for whether fictional or real, the primary *mise-en-scène* sets up a series of characters, positive and negative, and a goal to fight for – liberty, fraternity, the nation, independence. In other words, this moment establishes the time and space of a politics. Will the time include the reinterpreted past and the imagined future, or will it choose to begin now, grounded in a present which rejects any reference to the past and projects itself into an imagined future, or will it wish to be imagined as an ongoing present, in which neither the past nor the future have a role?

In this essay I want to suggest that Fanon's conception of the 'where to begin' forecloses a Creole conception of the past and by doing so suggests a conception of the collective that condemns the Creole communities to the perpetual hell of alienation. I believe that a discussion of Fanon's theoretical position today can no longer ignore its vexed relation to creolisation. However, I do not wish to reject entirely his notion of radical temporality. His understanding of 'le commencement' (the beginning, the starting point) as rupture, as the inauguration of a new spatial and temporal organisation, acknowledges the necessity of an epistemo-logical revolution, the need for a radical change of horizon. In Fanon, there is a refusal to lessen the harshness and the violence of colonial and racial relations. This is particularly useful today when the politics of brutality and force seek to prevail again. Though the world is no longer divided between 'us and them' as Fanon believed (colonised and colonisers), the current practices of symbolic and economic violence speak of the recurrent attacks against 'les conditions d'existence idéales d'un monde humain' ('the ideal conditions of existence for a human world') (*Peau noire*: 188; *Black Skin*: 231). The new predatory politics in which human life is again trafficked on a great scale, in which human beings no longer 'count' even as matter to exploit (workers and soldiers can be leased, moved around), mean that we need to reconsider the notion of brutality in the world of politics. Moral condemnation is not sufficient; new theoretical tools are needed. Fanon's analysis of violence and his understanding of its effects on human beings – notably during the brutish war in Algeria – are useful here. They hark back to Aimé Césaire's *Discours sur le colonialisme* (*Discourse on Colonialism*) and his indictment of 'la machine à écraser, à broyer, à abrutir les peuples' ('the machine for crushing, for grinding, for degrading peoples') (Césaire 1989: 58; Césaire 2000: 77). There is thus a need for rupture, for a new imagination. And yet, when Fanon imagined 'where to begin', he could not include in his world-view a temporality with which he was familiar: the temporality of the Creole world. Had he included that temporality, Fanon would have opened up another space. To develop that point, I will turn to the territories of French Creole societies – Martinique, Guadeloupe, Réunion – which were born out of slavery, colonisation and forced migrations and became, in 1946, French overseas departments.

The world, according to Fanon, is a battlefield. Love is fragile, desire cannot be trusted, language is deceptive, the entire world offers no respite. However, there is hope, although only in violent emancipation because violence is necessary to shake the burden of colonialism and racism. Where to begin that movement? Is there a space? How will the man of colour know that the time has come to move, that it is time to begin the struggle for liberation? Will there be a sign, something like a flash, the tearing of the mask that blinds the man of colour? Or must he wait for a collective organisation which would show him the way? In actual fact, this is not what Fanon has in mind. His conception of 'where to begin?' is an awakening which takes the form of a psychological *tabula rasa*. The event takes place in the man of colour's unconscious and his liberation occurs on two levels: on the one hand, emancipation from himself and from the white world; and, on the other hand, a swift and trenchant rupture with the old world, for there is no emancipation without a violent break. There is no time for hesitation, contemplation or meditation.

Fanon answered the question 'where to begin?' with 'now and from myself'. The individual needs to forget the past and start from entirely new grounds. The past is a hindrance; it imposes psychological shackles that imprison the individual. There is no time for reminiscences of what went wrong a long time ago. The individual must cut the links that connect him with the past. This is the only road to salvation. The new grounds find their sources in an idea of man that transcends racial barriers. The Fanonian agora – space, assembly and words – is constituted by men freed of the past. 'Le problème envisagé ici se situe dans la temporalité. Seront désaliénés Nègres et Blancs qui auront refusé de se laisser enfermer dans la Tour substantialisée du Passé,' Fanon argued. And again: 'Les Vietnamiens qui meurent devant le peloton d'exécution n'espèrent pas que leur sacrifice permettra la réapparition d'un passé. C'est au nom du présent et de l'avenir qu'ils acceptent de mourir' (*Peau noire*: 183, 184).[1] 'Je ne me fais l'homme d'aucun passé', he wrote ('I will not make myself the man of any past') (*Peau noire*: 183; *Black Skin*: 226), insisting upon his refusal to ground the 'where to begin?' on either a retrieval or a reinterpretation of the past. He is a man with no past because his past is one of humiliation, brutality and rape. What can be done about that? What would be the political value of retrieving that past? 'Chanter le passé aux dépens de mon présent et de mon avenir' ('to exalt the past at the expense of my present and of my future') is a dead end (*Peau noire*: 183; *Black Skin*: 226). The exaltation of the past forecloses the possibility of living in the present and for the future. Fanon would not approve of the current interest in memory. He saw memory as belonging to culture and it was not culture that led people to revolt: 'Ce n'est pas parce que l'Indochinois a découvert une culture propre qu'il s'est révolté. C'est parce que "tout simplement" il lui devenait, à plus d'un titre, impossible de respirer' (*Peau noire*: 183).[2]

Any conception of history implies a conceptualisation of time. Cultural experience is also an experience of time. There exist a colonial conception of time, an anti-colonial conception of time and a Creole conception of time. The colonial conception of time is linear: the colonised are in prehistory, in *pre-time*, and can expect to reach 'civilisation' and history (time) if they accept subjection by and guidance from western colonisers. It was usually understood that the majority of the colonised would never reach that time, except for a minority of 'évolués'. Anti-colonial time is understood as revolutionary time, a time of rupture with the colonial power. Rupture would lead to recovery of the land, the past and the self. Colonial time is thus temporary, a time of interruption that the struggle for liberation will displace. It is up to the revolutionary – his/her determination and refusal to 'wait' – to shorten the time of interruption. Fanonian revolutionary time is not about patience but about speed, rapidity, boldness and steadfastness.

Fanon showed impatience with the West, with the Antilleans and with the men and women of colour who did not understand that it was imperative to fight back against racism resolutely, without a hint of hesitation. *Peau noire* is full of pleas for swift action, though Fanon thought that it was too late for the Antilleans. They had lost the opportunity to free themselves. Martinicans were too 'avides de sécurité' ('greedy for security') (*Peau noire*: 172; *Black Skin*: 212). Nothing collective could be expected from them because each of them was 'un atome isolé, aride, trenchant' ('an isolated, sterile, salient atom') (*Peau noire*: 172; *Black Skin*: 212). According to Fanon, Martinican society was inhabited by petty individuals. They are envious and jealous, constantly comparing what each other has and constantly expressing their desire to dominate the other. 'Toute action de l'Antillais passe par l'Autre. Non parce que l'Autre demeure le but final de son action dans la perspective de la communion humaine que décrit Adler, mais plus simplement parce que c'est l'Autre qui l'affirme dans son besoin de valorisation' (*Peau noire*: 172).[3] Alterity in Creole societies does not offer the grounds for a new community because alterity is denied and rejected outside the self as something upon which the ego finds a space for a comparison which reinforces its narcissism. Thus, Creole societies are not societies which invent a new politics of emancipation. Their culture has been destroyed, the past looms too large and they have lost the notion of time required by revolution, that is, the desire to act quickly and without hesitation. Creole societies have not fought for their freedom; they are the slaves of their past. 'Le nègre français est condamné à se mordre et à mordre' ('The French Negro is doomed to bite himself and just to bite') (*Peau noire*: 179; *Black Skin*: 221). There are no real battles, no real war, no defeats and no victory. The only politics is one of resentment.

Fanon's harsh judgement of Martinicans – subsequently understood as a judgement on Creole societies which emerged from slavery in French colonies – has been paradoxically adopted by the very people whom Fanon indicted for their alienation. People from Martinique, Guadeloupe or Réunion Island have no hesitation among themselves in expressing a deep contempt for their own. Yet they differ from Fanon because their comments belong to a doxa rather than to an analysis of the roots of such contempt. None of the theories on Creole societies – whether developed by Edouard Glissant, or by Jean Bernabé, Patrick Chamoiseau and Raphaël Confiant – takes any of Fanon's observations as its starting-point. Fanon is politely dismissed. Yet his legacy deserves better treatment. Inheritance is what we receive. We have no choice in the matter. As Jacques Derrida has argued, it is rather inheritance which chooses us ('c'est lui qui nous élit violemment', Derrida and Roudinesco 2001: 16). We obey two injunctions: to preserve and reaffirm the past and to reinterpret and criticise the past so that history – as what is unforeseeable and unpredictable – may occur (Derrida and Roudinesco 2001: 17). Fanon's texts constitute a theoretical corpus which we *must* receive and reinterpret for there is a responsibility involved in the dynamics of inheritance: we are forced to receive and forced to choose, and this process involves excluding and rejecting some aspects of the inheritance.

I look at that inheritance from the point of view of a Creole. I base my argument upon my experience of a particular Creole society, that of Réunion Island (in the Indian Ocean). I draw from my work on slavery and abolitionism in French colonies and my continuous interest in the processes and practices of creolisation. I understand creolisation differently from the thinkers of Creoleness. Creolisation results from the tension between two phenomena that are produced by the *same* structures. These two phenomena are, on the one hand, the presence of strong contrasts and differences and, on the other, the creation of a unity (the Creole symbolic world). They first emerged in the world of the plantation. From different worlds, thrown together by the yoke of history on a land, slaves created a language and a culture, that of the Creole world. Yet unity was constantly reworked and reconfigured by the arrivals of new groups – slaves, indentured workers, colonists. They brought new practices, adapted existing ones and participated in the creation of new ones. Diversity and unity are in tension in creolisation. One cannot exist without the other for one is the condition of the other. My notion of creolisation is close to that of Edouard Glissant, that is, a practice with unforeseeable results, whereas for the thinkers of Creoleness it is an 'interior attitude' (Bernabé, Chamoiseau and Confiant 1993: 75). Creolisation thus refers to practices and processes that are never finished, always threatened by new contrasts and differences. Though Fanon only marginally addressed the Creole world, his analysis of its making (slavery, colonisation) and experience (alienation, bilingualism, diglossia) is still relevant.

Rupture time

The temporality of emancipation leaves no space for contemplation or meditation. It is *speed time, rupture time*, but also a time of the present entirely turned to the future, a present burdened with the future. The future is a promise whose condition for existing is contained in the temporality of rupture. The success of the rupture depends on establishing a relation between present and future. The past has no role in this conceptualisation of time. It is an obstacle for reaching the future of emancipation. 'Je suis mon propre fondement' ('I am my own foundation'), Fanon claimed (*Peau noire*: 187; *Black Skin*: 231). To build a present pregnant with the future, the past has to be erased. Memory cannot play a role because it leads to anxiety. 'La douleur morale devant la densité du Passé?' will fix me in the past. 'Mais je n'ai pas le droit de me laisser ancrer. Je n'ai pas le droit d'admettre la moindre parcelle d'être dans mon existence. Je n'ai pas le droit de me laisser engluer par les déterminations du passé' (*Peau noire*: 186).[4] The past is an anchor that immobilises my movement. Here there is no duty of memory ('devoir de mémoire'), which is so often invoked today among victims of crimes (slavery, genocide, colonialism, mass massacre, ethnic cleansing). According to Fanon, the politics of reparation is rooted in the making of the present and future, not in the celebration of the past. In his theatre of redemption, the scenes of subjection have no place. The temporality of emancipation is a temporality of heroism.

In the West, linearity remains the dominant understanding of time. To summarise briefly, since Augustine, whose *Confessions* explicated the western notion of time, the present integrates three levels of temporality: the past as memory or story; the present itself; and the future, which is immanent in the present. These three aspects of the present open up a space for the

construction of human time. In its Christian version, linearity
leads to an end, the time of eternity. In its secularised version,
time is still homogeneous and structured according to past and
future; but there is no eternity. The relation between past, present
and future has remained a vexed question in western philosophy. The role of the past is fundamental. Henri Bergson, who
renewed the philosophical discourse on time, gave the past an
important role. In *Time and Free Will*, he argued that the present
is interwoven with the past and the future. Their interdepen-
dence means that the present is constantly created in unforeseeable
ways. For Bergson, time is heterogeneous and always in motion.
The experience of the past, the present and the future emerges
from a perspective of inner time. Here time is a qualitative
experience; it is flux, *duration*. There is a productive relation
between past and present and the present must be understood as
'becoming'.

For Fanon, the productive relation is *between present and
future*. It is duration as actualisation. If, for Bergson, that
actualisation is involuntary and the subject is created through
perceptions and actions that send constantly new stimuli to
memory and consciousness, for Fanon, actualisation is voluntary,
the conscious creation of time and subjectivity. The emancipa-
tory gesture is to stop time as it has been defined – that is, a time
in which the past informs the present. One must voluntarily
operate a rupture in temporal linearity. In his *Theses on the
Philosophy of History*, Walter Benjamin argued that revolutions
are lived as suspended time, as interruption of chronology.
Fanon's notion of time is interrupted time, the time of 'now'. It is
a notion influenced by Marx's idea of history as praxis, concrete
activity as the essence and origin of man. Through the revolutionary praxis of national emancipation, the man of colour will
become a historical being, an identity which had been denied by
colonialism. The Fanonian present is a time of 'becoming now'.
The time of emancipation never ends. After the state of emergency
that was colonialism must succeed the time of emergency that is
revolution: a 'time of history' in which the fundamental event is
always in the making and whose goal is not in the future but
always already in the present (Agamben 1989: 127).

Fanon's conception of time as rupture, as a present unburdened by the past, is heuristically useful for the postcolonial world. It cannot constitute a politics – the world of power and resistance – but it can constitute a strategy of resistance. In recent years, we have witnessed what seems to be an inexorable movement towards demanding apology, restitution and compensation for the past, towards a politics of reparation and recovery, accompanied by a narrative that insists on wounds and damages. These demands for restitution, reparation and apology have opened up the space for the voices of victims, the history of the vanquished. The past is the scene of those who have vanished, whose stories are still to be heard. The politics of reparation has led to a profound reassessment of the ways in which history is written, blame is distributed and payment for the crime is assessed. The demand for restitution has produced a cosmo-politics: the circulation of notions, practices and narratives (see the innovative work of Ariel Colonomos 2001).

This is a revolutionary move: history is no longer written exclusively by the heroes but also by the weak, the dispossessed. It has forced states, international institutions, banks and museums to confront their passive or active complicity with spoliation and plunder. Yet I wish to point to the other side of this politics which invokes the past to freeze the present, to burden it under the weight of past wrongs. Fanon claimed that the past should not be a burden. He wanted to liberate us from the ruins, the spectres and the phantoms of the past, for they barred the road to the future and hindered the present.

Elsewhere I have challenged Fanon's belief that it is possible to erase the past, to start anew, to operate a *tabula rasa* (see for example Verges 1996a, 1996b and 1999). This view is based not only on the illusion of self-creation but also on the belief that there exists a core self. Fanon's programme adopted the vision of ideologies of decolonisation and cultural disalienation: the belief that popular culture constituted an autonomous space with its own symbolic coherence. Fanon could not consider the practices of creolisation because they were not *revolutionary* practices. Yet Fanon's affirmation contains an important insight about the politics of recovery: it is an *apolitical politics*, a narcissistic use of the past to compensate for a troubling present whose responsibility cannot be mine. Fanon foresaw, in the politics of recovery, a politics of 'projection': projecting outside the (national, cultural) body the deep ambiguities, the passions, the sentiments of hatred and animosity that nonetheless animate the (post)colonial unconscious and consciousness. As such, it is an ideology that seeks to protect individuals from loss and mourning and to transform politics into a field in which conflicts are regulated by justice rather than through a confrontation with the plurality of positions. There are moments when time must be imagined as rupture. Fanon started from that fact: colonisation was a violent act. In a world created by violence, whose cultural and social organisation was shaped by the economy and symbolic form of predatory practices, *human being as matter*, the colonised must answer with a violence which is a gesture of self-defence rather than one of mimicry.

Creole time

Creole societies have in recent years been celebrated for their resistance, their ability to endure and to create under the violent and stressful environments of slavery and colonisation. In *In Praise of Creoleness* (1993), the Martinican authors Jean Bernabé, Patrick Chamoiseau and Raphaël Confiant do not once invoke Frantz Fanon. He is absent from their pantheon. He was too connected with an ideology which the authors reject, one of redemptive violence, idealisation of Africa and the maroon, and nationalism. Their world is one of openness, of 'the nontotalitarian consciousness of a preserved diversity' (Bernabé, Chamoiseau and Confiant 1993: 89). Creativity is rooted in Creole language, though it must open itself to Creoleness. Bernabé, Chamoiseau and Confiant dream of a 'multi-partisan, multi-unionist and pluralist regime' which would federate the Caribbean Archipelago. They are suspicious of the ideologies that prevailed in the "Third World", those of nationalism and providential man (Bernabé *et al.* 1993: 116–17). Their vision could not be further from that of Fanon. Their 'where to begin?' is curiously apolitical and ahistorical. The figures of the past are absent in their *materiality*; they are evoked simply as literary figures. Creole society seems to come into being out of a series of literary discourses (folklore, Negritude, Caribbean-ness) and culminate in 'Créolité', Creoleness.

For the thinkers of Creoleness, social time is linear. Yet their work acknowledges the cultural time of creolisation. Creole time consists of the processes and practices of creolisation, between the 'longue durée' and short bursts of rupture. By restoring the complex role of mixed long and short temporalities in the making of Creole societies, Bernabé, Chamoiseau and Confiant question Fanon's conception of time and demonstrate that creolisation offers the grounds for resistance to the hegemony of purity and monolingualism.

In *In Praise of Creoleness* the development of Creole identity is described as a series of steps, each one authentic in its time but which must be overcome by a new one. Each step builds on the preceding one and announces the next. The first period was mimetic expression, both in French and Creole language (Bernabé *et al.* 1993: 76). The authors then claim that there is a move to 'Césaire's Négritude that opened us to the path for the actuality of a Caribbeanness' (Bernabé *et al.* 1993: 80). This preceded Edouard Glissant's Caribbeanness which, in turn, preceded Creoleness. For Bernabé, Chamoiseau and Confiant temporality is associated with space: each historical moment is dependent on an imagined space, from the (alienated) West/Creole world to fantasmatic Africa to the authentic soil of the Caribbean celebrated by Césaire. Each time/space produced a (male) character: the first was the oral poet who rediscovered the proverbs and wisdom of the people. Césaire, who wished to be the 'mouth of those calamities that have no mouth' ('ma bouche sera la bouche des malheurs qui n'ont point de bouche') introduced the heroic character, the Maroon, the Rebel. If each time/space was authentic, each constituted a trap (except for Creoleness). The heroism of the Rebel permeated the time/space of Negritude. In this narrative, Fanon is a lone figure, heroic to be sure, but belonging to a distant era (see Chamoiseau 1997: 59). Subsequently, Glissant questioned the demiurge impulse in Caribbean discourse and attempted to assert the polyphony of the creolised collective presence. Yet, for the writers of Creoleness, Caribbeanness still lacked an 'interior vision' which Creoleness would provide (Bernabé *et al.* 1993: 87). Creoleness is '"the world diffracted but recomposed", a maelstrom of signifieds in a single signifier: a Totality' (Bernabé *et al.* 1993: 88).

The temporality of Creoleness is linear time. Creoleness is contained within a geographical space – the Caribbean – that prefigures the world. History as action plays a marginal role. Bernabé, Chamoiseau and Confiant write '(o)ur chronicle is behind the dates, behind the known facts: *we are Words behind writing*' (Bernabé et al. 1993: 99; emphasis in text). They assume a transparent world whose signs they can decipher. They replace old fantasies with new ones. They repeat the gesture they criticise: to create a new fantasmatic and redemptive figure, a Messiah. However, what these authors bring to the theory of creolisation is their desire to ground it in space (even if their notion of space remains geographical). This is the space of culture rather than the space of nationalism and its time is that of relation and difference.

Creolisation requires a rupture with and a forgetting of the origins. More importantly, it requires the conscious will to reject a 'right to return'. Origins have been lost for ever and the cauldron of slavery and colonisation is the matrix of creolisation. A violent rupture inaugurates the space of creolisation. It is a rupture which has not been chosen but has been forced upon the future Creole. The machine of creolisation (which made Africans, Malagasy, Hindus, slaves and indentured workers into Creoles) operates through different temporalities: the time of capture, being sold, crossing the sea (the Middle Passage), arrival, adjustment on the plantation, and meeting older slaves who have learned the ropes of resistance. Creole time, the time of creolisation, is both rupture and unification. It is not linear time because, to survive as such, creolisation requires a time of being challenged and rendered fragile by new arrivals that weaken older forms. Newly arrived slaves had to imitate, to mimic the behaviour of formerly arrived slaves in order to survive and to fit in. However, this was a reciprocal process, for the established slaves also imitated the rituals and attitudes brought by the newer slaves. Creole time mocks a European time of ineluctable progress: it has integrated the notion of slowness in human social and political enterprise. It is not a time for revolutionary politics – quick seizure of power – but a time for surviving and creating a space.

Between time as rupture and linear time there is Creole time, a time based on repetition, mimicry and invention. It is a time which mixes the speed of mimicry and the slowness of repetition. It is the time of the maroon, that nomadic figure. Fanon left Martinique for France, France for Algeria, and finally Algeria for Tunisia when he decided that the colonial war would hinder his practice as a psychiatrist. His life suggests a nomadic identity. Time was rupture; life was wandering. He was a cosmopolitan nomad, but one who never reclaimed his Creoleness. Creole time eluded Fanon. He dreamed that the time of rupture and freedom from all forms of alienation could be contained in one's life. His desire to free himself from the burden put upon him by history (having to be responsible for the past of slavery) and from the burden of racism (being labelled a 'black' man when he wanted to be simply a 'man') led him to desire freedom from all kinds of connections. Creole time – which concerns the ephemeral nature of one's life (a singular contribution to the process of creolisation but simply one contribution among so many others) – allows space *in the time of one's life* for conceiving emancipation not only as rupture but also as an ongoing practice.

Notes

1 'The problem (emancipation) considered here (was) one of time. Those Negroes and white men will be disalienated who refuse to let themselves be sealed away in the materialised Tower of the Past.' 'The Vietnamese who die before the firing squads are not hoping that their sacrifice will bring about the reappearance of a past. It is for the sake of the present and of the future that they are willing to die' (*Black Skin*: 226, 227).

2 'It is not because the Indo-Chinese has discovered a culture of his own that he is in revolt. It is because "quite simply" it was, in more than one way, becoming impossible for him to breathe' (*Black Skin*: 226).

3 'Everything that an Antillean does is done for The Other. Not because The Other is the ultimate objective of his action in the sense of communication between people that Adler describes, but, more primitively, because it is The Other who corroborates him in his search for self-validation' (*Black Skin*: 212–13).

4 'Moral anguish in the face of the massiveness of the Past? ... But I do not have the right to allow myself to bog down. I do not have the right to allow the slightest fragment to remain in my existence. I do not have the right to allow myself to be mired in what the past has determined' (*Black Skin*: 230).

References

Agamben, G. (1989) *Enfance et histoire: dépérissement de l'expérience et origine de l'histoire*, Paris: PUF

Bernabé, J., Chamoiseau, P. and Confiant, R. (1993) *Eloge de la créolité/In Praise of Creoleness*, Paris: Gallimard (bilingual edn, trans. M. B. Taleb-Khyar)

Césaire, A. (1989) *Discours sur le colonialisme*, Paris: Présence Africaine (*Discourse on Colonialism*, trans. J. Pinkham, New York: Monthly Review Press, 2000)

Chamoiseau, P. (1997) *Ecrire en pays dominé*, Paris: Gallimard

Colonomos, A. (2001) 'L'exigence croissante de justice sans frontières: le cas de la demande de restitution des biens juifs spoliés', *Les Etudes du CERI*, 78, July, 1–37

Derrida, J. and Roudinesco, E. (2001) *De quoi demain …*, Paris: Fayard/Galilée

Verges, F. (1996a) 'Chains of madness, chains of colonialism: Fanon and freedom' in A. Read (ed.), *The Fact of Blackness – Frantz Fanon and Visual Representation*, London: ICA, 46–75

—— (1996b) 'To cure and to free: the Fanonian project of "decolonized psychiatry"' in L. R. Gordon, R. T. White and T. D. Sharpley-Whiting (eds), *Fanon: A Critical Reader*, Oxford: Blackwell, 85–99

—— (1999) '"I am not the slave of slavery": the politics of reparation in (French) postslavery communites' in A. Alessandrini (ed.), *Frantz Fanon: Critical Perspectives*, London and New York: Routledge, 258–75

3

Colonial racisms in the 'métropole': reading *Peau noire, masques blancs* in context

JIM HOUSE

This chapter aims to provide a historical reading of the many examples of racism in 'metropolitan' France that Fanon cites and comments upon. It also analyses the significance of *Peau noire* for our understanding of the various cultures of colonial racism, evaluating the text in relation to the different currents within the opposition to racism circulating in France from the 1930s to the early 1960s. Fanon's preoccupation with racism on the level of attitudes and practices in particular had a number of precedents in the writing of black people in France during the inter-war years. These examples will be called upon to assess just where, how and to what extent *Peau noire* breaks with previous analyses of white racism and racism as lived experience. Fanon certainly writes as a Martinican man, but he does so from France (Macey 1999). *Peau noire* can therefore be usefully understood as an essential contribution to a debate that had begun after the First World War and was to continue until decolonisation regarding the way in which living in 'metropolitan' France affected the perspectives from which black people viewed the dynamics of the racialised French colonial order. I will argue that Fanon's novelty lies in the way in which he questioned the republican tradition and its mythologisation of a 'non-racist' France from an experiential position and highlighted the need for a political agency that went beyond a limiting reformism. Fanon also developed an analysis from this perspective that is not purely inspired by Marxism, while giving due weight to the socio-economic factors structuring and reinforcing racial alienation. I will also argue that Fanon was one of the earliest thinkers to establish fruitful comparison between anti-Black, anti-Jewish and anti-North African racisms, a framework that was to continue throughout the 1950s and beyond.

Peau noire is characterised by a number of tensions that result from Fanon's wish to study his own individual experiences as a black person (along with those of other black people whose experiences he quotes) while also examining the wider systemic racialised order within which such experiences have to be situated and understood. Thus the text navigates an at times uneasy course: alongside succinct analyses of the divisive, differentiated forms of racism that (for example) pit Antilleans against the Senegalese – where these mutually reinforcing forms of racism are also in some respects analytically distinct – Fanon makes more generalising denunciations of white racism. As Fanon put it, in an attempt to bring together these two equally necessary approaches, 'il y une ambiguïté dans la situation universelle du nègre, qui se résout toutefois dans son existence concrète' ('in the universal situation of the Negro there is an ambiguity, which is, however, resolved in his concrete existence') (*Peau noire*: 140; *Black Skin*: 173).[1] Furthermore, while Fanon states that 'il est utopique de rechercher en quoi un comportement inhumain se différencie d'un autre comportement inhumain' ('it is utopian to try to ascertain in what ways one kind of inhuman behaviour differs from another kind of inhuman behaviour') (*Peau noire*: 69; *Black Skin*: 98), his comparative approach to various forms of racism often belies this statement. It is precisely the way in which Fanon's analytical approach integrates and interrogates the experiential that makes *Peau noire* so insightful for our understanding of the political, social and cultural context of post-war colonial France.

Fanon's trajectory

It is necessary to retrace the impact of Fanon's own political and social trajectory prior to and during his writing (1950–1) of *Peau noire* (Macey 2000: 127) to understand how and why he comes to focus on certain themes. By the time Fanon came to study in Lyons he had already had the opportunity to observe and experience many different cultures of racism within the French colonial order. In this important respect, it is Fanon's experiences prior to *Peau noire* that distinguish his essay from much (but not all) of the inter-war writing – whether fictional or otherwise – by black intellectuals from the colonies in France, since his experiences in France would merely confirm and strengthen (as opposed to trigger off, in the inter-war case) an already deeply held suspicion, disappointment and hence anger towards a post-war French society that was structurally racist. Fanon's 'journey of experience' (Sekyi-Otu 1996: 29) had already taught him to reject the prior assumptions about a non-racist France inculcated by colonial ideology. The crucial 'train scene' was emblematic of the low point of Fanon's experiences of white racist attitudes (see below and *Peau noire*: 90–2; *Black Skin*: 111–14), yet the personal alienation this serves to highlight – and the collective alienation Fanon observes elsewhere – had been subjects on which Fanon had been reflecting for some years. The calls in *Peau noire* for a collective de-alienation of the colonised (of whatever origin) should be understood within that perspective.

First, Fanon had experienced the occupation of Martinique by French officers and sailors during the Vichy period. This had brought another example of racism to Martinique, one that then co-existed with the longer-standing, sedimented racist culture of the 'békés' (white Creoles) as well as that of the 'metropolitan' French functionaries. While the Vichy regime no doubt highlighted the responsibilities that the 'mother-country' (France) played in the inequities that Martinicans experienced on an everyday level, there was of course the reassuring perspective that 'real' (i.e. republican) France was not racist – an extremely well-established rhetorical theme shared by the mainstream right and left. In 'imitating' Germany, with decrees institutionalising and codifying racist discrimination, the Vichy regime seemed to stand for all that 'Free France' was not.[2] At this time, there was widespread belief throughout French colonies that the European settler populations were 'universally' more racist than their counterparts in the 'métropole'. Whilst this assumption may have had some foundation, this idea tended to assume that white French colonial officials or settlers arrived in the colonies free of any colonialist baggage and that the 'métropole' had little to do with colonialism (Sayad 1999: 147–8; Stoler and Cooper 1997). *Peau noire*'s examples will contradict any such impression.

Secondly, Fanon had witnessed the racial stratification in the (Free French) army that reproduced the colonial order more generally, with its sliding hierarchy of groups: white 'metropolitan' French, white colonial settler French, Antilleans and other non-white French citizens, Arab-Berber North Africans and black Africans. The military administration reserved differential treatment for each category both on and off the battlefield (cf. Macey 2000: 91–100 *passim*). Such practices were not new (Dornel 1995; Stovall 1993). Fanon had seen glimpses of colonial Morocco and Algeria, and observed the way in which the 'Senegalese' troops (in fact, sub-Saharan Africans whether from Senegal or not) were considered the 'lowest of the low' by the French army and indeed by many North Africans themselves (cf. *Peau noire*: 20, 21, 83–6; *Black Skin*: 28, 103–7). When in Morocco Fanon failed to wear the correct military uniform to distinguish him from the African soldiers, he was mistaken for a 'Senegalese' soldier (Cherki 2000: 23). Fanon was the unwitting and unwilling participant in the French army's racial order.

Thirdly, once Fanon was in metropolitan France as a soldier, he was made acutely aware of the differentiated racism of the French population. White French women welcomed African American soldiers rather than black French soldiers from the Caribbean or Africa (cf. Manville 1992: 69). It is easy to see how, by the time he returned to France in 1946 to study in Paris and then Lyons, Fanon was already more than disillusioned by the promises of a new society being forged in the Liberation period (Macey 2000: 110). Fanon therefore comes to dissect 'metropolitan' French society with a particularly sharp scalpel, looking at racism and its manifestations in a great variety of degrees and forms, amongst social classes, generations and professions. Fanon probably has a unique experience in his overview of the different colonial contexts, from Fort-de-France to Lyons, from Paris to Meknès.

Finally, the city of Lyons was the site for the spatial

reproduction of colonial power relations, as North Africans
(almost exclusively Algerians) arrived there in increasing numbers
following legislation in 1947 instituting 'free' circulation between
Algeria and France (cf. MacMaster 1997). It was in this area that
Fanon had his first real human contact with Algerians beyond
the relative superficiality of his wartime experiences (Macey
2000: 120–1). The racialisation of space was well underway:
increasingly relegated to the outer urban margins (as opposed to
the inner-city districts where Fanon had direct contact with
them), Algerians were subjected to popular protest and petitions
on the rare occasions when public authorities took steps to
provide them with adequate housing. On a national level, succes-
sive anti-Algerian press campaigns in the 1947–50 period had
reintroduced the inter-war stereotype of Algerian males as
dangerous criminals. Once again in Lyons, as in Morocco and
Algeria, Fanon was not just an observer – albeit a 'participant
observer' – of colonial racism, whatever forms it took. He was the
object of it himself; he was 'objectified' by it. In 1952 Fanon told
his mentor in psychiatry, François Tosquelles, that when walking
in Lyons with his (white) fiancée, he was arrested and spent
hours at the police station, accused of being involved in white
slavery (Tosquelles 2001: 169).

   Yet the 'metropolitan' French did not 'read' skin colour in
the way that Fanon had been used to in Martinique, since they
had not been sensitised to the interaction between skin colour
and class position that predominated in Martinique and which
made that society a 'société "comparaison"' ('a society of
"comparison"'), that is, one where individuals continually compare
one another's skin colour (*Peau noire*: 172; *Black Skin*: 213; cf.
Bonniol 1992; Guérin 1956; Leiris 1955/1987). The process of
epidermalisation in the 'metropolitan' context tended to lose
some of its 'subtlety' (in the sense that it was less differentiating).
Non-whites were often seen as an indistinct group – itself a
common component of racialisation (cf. Guillaumin 1972; Taguieff
1987), thus distorting skin colour as a signifier. By contrast, in
the Martinican and Senegalese contexts Fanon describes extensively in *Peau noire*, the smallest degree of change in skin colour
could affect the racial economy, as Fanon's choice of literary
examples (Capécia, Maran, Sadji) is intended to show. Intra-Black

diversity is largely lost within this 'metropolitan' racialising gaze. As Fanon says, for a Martinican in Europe 'quand on parlera de nègres il saura qu'il s'agit de lui aussi bien que du Sénégalais' ('when he hears Negroes mentioned he will realise that the word includes himself as well as the Senegalese') (*Peau noire*: 121; *Black Skin*: 148). It was precisely this feeling of a certain commonality of experience of the colonial order within the 'métropole' that had sparked the critique of the colonial order from black intellectuals and activists in the inter-war period (see below and Dewitte 1985; Sirinelli 1988; Wilder 1999).

Fanon and previous analyses of the colonial racial order in France

Fanon sets out in *Peau noire* to amass a considerable body of evidence to support his claim that 'metropolitan' France is structurally racist. It is as if Fanon feels that the majority (i.e. 'metropolitan' French) reading public, which has not been on the receiving end of this racism, needs convincing of the existence of racism and the harmful effect it has on social relations. *Peau noire* is therefore addressing two distinct reading publics – the white 'metropolitan' French as well as fellow black people – both implicated in the colonial order, albeit in very different ways.

Fanon seems most interested in looking at how the colonial order's culturalist assumptions and racialising processes are internalised by everyone within those societies and then find expression as attitudinal phenomena and in concrete situations as practice. He is also concerned by the effects these processes have on the racialised in terms of *Erlebnis* (lived experience). Fanon establishes a direct link between on the one hand this primarily psychological approach towards the way in which racism is experienced, and, on the other hand, the wider realm of economic and political oppression represented by the colonial order. His concern is with the socio-genic – 'the social origins of human problems' (Gordon 1996: 76) (cf. *Peau noire*: 8–9; *Black Skin*: 12–14). Throughout, Fanon argues that there is a close interaction between structural and individual factors: 'nous sommes renvoyés de l'individu à la structure sociale' ('we are driven from the individual back to the social structure') (*Peau noire*: 172;

Black Skin: 213). For Fanon's psychiatric patients, their health
problems emanate from social structures (*Peau noire*: 81; *Black
Skin*: 100). Yet Fanon also states that 'le problème de la colonisation comporte ainsi non seulement l'intersection de conditions
objectives et historiques, mais aussi l'attitude de l'homme à
l'égard de ces conditions' ('the problem of colonialism includes
not only the interrelations of objective historical conditions but
also human attitudes towards these conditions') (*Peau noire*: 68;
Black Skin: 84).

To explain the causes of the mystification proper to the
colonial order, Fanon uses Jung's concept of the collective
unconscious, which Fanon defines as being 'tout simplement
l'ensemble de préjugés, de mythes, d'attitudes collectives d'un
groupe déterminé' ('purely and simply the sum of prejudices,
myths, collective attitudes of a given group') (*Peau noire*: 152;
Black Skin: 188). However, as Hussein Bulhan (1985: 75–6) and
Ronald Judy (1996: 66–7) have underlined, Fanon uses Jung with
important reservations, since he judges Jung to have failed to
take account of the destructive effects of colonialism, and to have
based his model of the psyche on a natural, quasi-inherited
collective unconscious which failed to consider black people's
specific positionalities (*Peau noire*: 123; *Black Skin*: 151). Fanon
proceeds to historicise Jung's model by stressing how the
collective unconscious is inculcated into all (colonised and
colonisers) through a socialisation that engenders radically distinct
but interlinked outlooks, based around a hierarchy setting White
above Black, and/or coloniser over colonised. Fanon does not see
the French case as specific in the sense that he uses the terms
'l'inconscient européen' ('European unconscious') (*Peau noire*:
153; *Black Skin*: 190) and 'l'inconscient collectif de *l'homo
occidentalis*' ('collective unconscious of *homo occidentalis*') (*Peau
noire*: 154; *Black Skin*: 190) to describe these dominant attitudes
and dispositions. It is this 'imposition culturelle irréfléchie' ('the
unreflected imposition of a culture') (*Peau noire*: 154; *Black Skin*:
191) that is interiorised by both Europeans and (here) Antilleans,
since 'l'Europe a une structure raciste' ('Europe has a racist
structure') (*Peau noire*: 74; *Black Skin*: 92). This historicisation
and re-reading that Fanon gives of Jung is significant since it
introduces the possibility of human agency to resist domination

and opens the door half-wide to a non-racist future. Fanon views racism as being in articulation with and reinforcing dominant political and economic structures: this domination has itself 'colonised' the French collective unconscious.

In order to understand his own facticity, Fanon studies the genealogy of his own alienation and of the alienation of his fellow Antilleans and, more widely, of the colonised. To do so, he uses an at times inaccessible mixture of psychological, psychoanalytic, anthropological, socio-economic and literary texts that form a highly interdisciplinary academic framework (Caute 1970: 37). Fanon starts the text with the affirmation that he is writing about the experiences of Martinicans (and Martinican men in particular), but he moves on to examine the various experiences of Antilleans in general, and then further to the experiences of black people under colonialism (*Peau noire*: 139; *Black Skin*: 172–3), before looking at the case of North Africans in terms of colonial racism. He also considers anti-Semitism. To some extent, Fanon's sources simply cannot 'keep up' with this constant moving out in concentric yet overlapping circles (cf. Robinson 1993: 80–1; Sekyi-Otu 1996: 26, 29).

It is perhaps also important to consider what sources Fanon does not refer to in *Peau noire*, and why this should have been the case. *Peau noire* is marked by an important historical absence since it refers to little of the counter-cultural radicalism developed by black thinkers in France in the inter-war period prior to the late 1930s. *Peau noire* arguably needs to be understood contextually (if not intertextually) as similar (but not identical to) previous interrogations of the colonial order that the inter-war period had brought about. These interrogations had been caused by the experiences of being in large French imperial cities such as Paris or Marseilles and of being in a different racialised climate – that of the 'métropole' – to that in which both black intellectuals and manual workers (whether from French colonies or the USA) had usually been born and brought up (see Dewitte 1985; Jules-Rosette 1998; Miller 1998; Young 2001: 253–73). This movement between different colonial areas fostered a radical comparativism. Both cultures and counter-cultures of colonialism can arguably be usefully explained by this perpetual movement (Gilroy 1993, 2000). The analysis of racism in *Peau noire* is in some respects in line with that of the more radical francophone black campaigning publications such as *La race nègre* and *Le cri des nègres* (The Negroes' Cry) that defined racism as being all pervasive (that is, systemic). Rather than relying on a limited number of vectors (such as the far right), such inter-war publications considered racism as an intrinsic component of the colonial system *qua* system, affecting the attitudes of the 'metropolitan' French (cf. House 2002). Such publications often had recourse to an essentialised black identity.

The relative absence in *Peau noire* of reference to inter-war texts prior to Aimé Césaire's *Cahier d'un retour au pays natal* (*Notebook of a Return to my Native Land*) (1939/1956) and Léon-Gontrand Damas's *Pigments* (1937/1972) has attracted some comment. As David Macey has observed (Macey 2000: 131), Léonard Sainville's review of *Peau noire* pointed out that Fanon seemed unaware of the similarity between *Peau noire* and elements of *Légitime défense* (1932) (see Sirinelli 1988), which provided a sustained critique of pro-assimilationist middle-class Antillean Blacks (intellectuals in particular) coming to the 'métropole' (see the *Légitime défense* reprint, 1970). *Légitime défense* also contains an extract from Claude Mackay's seminal and wide-ranging novel *Banjo* (Mackay 1929/1957), which gave a vivid portrayal of anti-Black racism in France (cf. Fabre 1985, 1991). Like the authors in *Légitime défense*, Fanon complains in *Peau noire* of the lack of radicalism of most of his Antillean predecessors and contemporaries: 'jusqu'en 1940 aucun Antillais n'était capable de se penser nègre' ('as late as 1940 no Antillean found it possible to think of himself as a Negro') (*Peau noire*: 124; *Black Skin*: 153). Of earlier Antillean francophone poets, he says 'ce sont des Blancs' ('these men are Whites'), as they were too fascinated by the mirage of French assimilationism (*Peau noire*: 155; *Black Skin*: 192).

While it is true that in the 1919–39 period Africans in France were usually more radical than Antilleans (Dewitte 1985: 42), there were some exceptions (Dewitte 1985: 98–100). Although politically moderate, *La Revue du monde noir* (*Review of the Black World*) nevertheless produced important interpretations of black people's lived experiences in France (Nicolas 1996: 248). Fanon could not identify fully with assimilationism, Negritude or

Marxism, the three directions between and across which many inter-war and indeed post-war texts seek to understand black experiences (Kruks 1996: 132). Fanon prefers the racial consciousness of Chester Himes's character Robert Jones in *If He Hollers Let Him Go* (1945/1999) to that of many of his francophone contemporaries.[3] We also know that Fanon's relation to the past was extremely complex (cf. *Peau noire*: 181–8; *Black Skin*: 223– 32) and that his project for the future stems from a rejection of being overdetermined by the past (cf. Lucas 1971: 23; Vergès 1999).

However, in *Peau noire*, the conscious rejection of some inter-war sources on Fanon's part (since they do not provide a model for action with which he can fully agree) seems to coincide with a certain (involuntary) unawareness of other sources. The transmission of the memory of those counter-cultural projects that did take place during this period was far from straightforward. The circulation of and publicity attached to *Légitime défense* were assuredly small-scale, and the war and Occupation had intervened (Macey 2000: 132), producing a generational break that only the role played by *Tropiques* (cf. Macey 2000: 76– 7) and Césaire's *Cahiers d'un retour au pays natal* seemed to bridge. We should also remember that in the late 1940s, the colonial order remained hegemonic and its reproduction was predicated on the non-transmission of counter-knowledge and the memory of colonial resistance.[4] In addition, Fanon was not a Paris-based intellectual when he wrote *Peau noire*, and Paris had been the real locus for such earlier radicalism.

One important side effect of this relative absence of reference in *Peau noire* to the context for black people in France prior to the late 1930s is arguably the marginalisation of the place of black women. Intellectuals such as the Nardal sisters (Paulette, Jane and Andrée) from Martinique had played an important role in what Gary Wilder has called 'the colonial public sphere' (1999: 61) through their writing and literary and cross-cultural salons.[5] Paulette Nardal's key article, 'L'Éveil de la conscience de race chez les étudiants noirs', which appeared in *La Revue du monde noir* in 1932, talked specifically of the experiences of black women in France and the different ways in which black women and men were sensitised to the métropole's racial order (Nardal

1932).[6] Indeed, Sharpley-Whiting (2002) has argued that the emergence of Negritude in the 1930s owes much to the largely unrecognised legacy of the Nardal sisters.

In addition, Fanon provides an essentially psychological and sociological reading of his chosen literary sources. Such sources mostly excluded black manual workers.[7] Fanon's text therefore reproduces the contemporary focus on middle-class black (male) experiences: only at the end of *Peau noire* does Fanon turn to the question of other social strata, with a reference to black workers in Abidjan rather than Marseilles or Le Havre (*Peau noire*: 181; *Black Skin*: 223; cf. Lucas 1971: 73–4).[8] *Peau noire* is therefore articulated within Fanon's own gendered, experiential, intellectual and socio-professional preoccupations that both limit and enable an important contribution to the social history of racism in post-war France, a theme to which the discussion here now turns in more detail.

Racisms in the 'métropole'

We have seen in the previous section that one key question Fanon addresses in *Peau noire* is the role of the collective unconscious in informing the attitudes and behaviour of both coloniser and colonised. Fanon assigns a fundamental significance to the way in which the racism that this collective unconscious fosters is then experienced by Antilleans: 'littéralement nous pouvons dire sans crainte de nous tromper que l'Antillais qui va en France afin de se persuader de sa blancheur y trouve son véritable visage' ('Quite literally I can say without any risk of error that the Antillean who goes to France in order to convince himself that he is white will find his real face there' (*Peau noire*: 125 n. 16; *Black Skin*: 153 n. 16). Not only do white people not consider Antilleans their equals, but also for Antilleans – taught to consider themselves superior to black Africans – the 'metropolitan' French cannot distinguish between Antilleans and Africans. Indeed, the French collective unconscious in this respect seems to be based around a Senegalese man with whom all Antillean men are conflated. (Fanon is much less clear on how these stereotypes operate for black women.) Fanon is not only interested in how white negrophobes express racism towards

black people. Central to *Peau noire* is also the devastating effect
anti-Black racism has on black people themselves and their
relations with one another (Sekyi-Otu 1996). Fanon aims not just
to transform white people's attitudes but also to 'de-alienate'
black people (Gibson 2003: 42). Of the former he writes, 'il
importe non pas de les éduquer, mais d'amener le Noir à ne pas
être l'esclave de leurs archétypes' ('what is important is not to
educate them, but to teach the Black not to be the slave of their
archetypes') (*Peau noire*: 27; tr. mod.: 35).

Fanon is explicit about the use to which his multiple examples
of racial stereotypes, phobias and discrimination should be put:
it is not simply a case of listing them but of drawing out the
wider processes that cause them (*Peau noire*: 136; *Black Skin*:
168). Giving anecdotal as well as research-based evidence of the
quotidian manifestations of racism from various social classes,
Fanon looks at French state attitudes and practices, those within
civil society and racism within the private sphere. Indeed, Fanon
insists on the very impossibility of separating the 'private' from
the 'public' since the intimate spheres of sexuality (for example)
have also been colonised. The myriad examples of racism Fanon
provides from the wider popular culture (advertising, journalism,
cinema, fiction) as well as the 'learned' culture (ethnography,
politics) in Martinique and the 'métropole' exemplify just how
these various colonial discourses are mutually reinforcing and
multi-sited.

Fanon argues that

> une société est raciste ou ne l'est pas. [...] Dire, par exemple, que le
> nord de la France est plus raciste que le sud, que le racisme est
> l'oeuvre des subalternes, donc n'engage nullement l'élite, que la
> France est le pays le moins raciste du monde, est le fait d'hommes
> incapables de réfléchir correctement. (*Peau noire*: 69)[9]

This racism is based on presumed knowledge of how black
people think, feel and behave that comes from the collective
unconscious (*Peau noire*: 24–5; *Black Skin*: 31–2). Fanon says that
he has been 'tissé de mille détails, anecdotes, récits' ('woven ...
out of a thousand details, anecdotes, stories') by this racialised
white collective unconscious (*Peau noire*: 90; *Black Skin*: 111).
Thus, on a train, an official replies in 'petit-nègre' ('pidgin

French') even after Fanon has asked him a question in very formal French (*Peau noire*: 28; *Black Skin*: 35–6). The white French 'read' black people according to a pre-written and highly negative script.

This socialisation into 'role-playing' within Europe's 'racist structure' (*Peau noire*: 74; *Black Skin*: 92) takes place from an early age, via the popular imagery of comics, books and films (see *Peau noire*: 27 and 39–40 n. 7; *Black Skin*: 34 and 49–50 n. 7). The school system, while inflicting symbolic violence on the Martinican child (cf. *Peau noire*, Chapter 1), also inculcates a feeling of cultural superiority into 'metropolitan' French children, hence the significance of the young white boy's gaze in the 'train scene' (*Peau noire*: 90–2; *Black Skin*: 111–14). As the boy exclaims 'Tiens, un nègre!' ('Look, a Negro!') he reveals to Fanon the epidermalisation of the black man and the variety of assumed 'knowledge' that this frightened child has of Fanon (*Peau noire*: 90; *Black Skin*: 111). Meanwhile, the boy's mother tries to reassure Fanon by saying that her son 'ne sait pas que vous êtes aussi civilisé que nous' ('does not know that you are as civilized as we') (*Peau noire*: 91; *Black Skin*: 113).[10] Fanon reflects on the various sedimented stereotypes with which the child is already imbued regarding black people: 'l'anthropologie, l'arriération mentale, le fétichisme, les tares raciales, les négriers, et surtout, et surtout: "Y a bon banania"' ('cannibalism, intellectual deficiency, fetishism, racial defects, slave-ships, and above all else, above all: "Sho' good eatin'"') (*Peau noire*: 90; *Black Skin*: 112).[11]

If we are to understand Fanon's text as embodying themes previously explored by black people in France, there is a striking similarity between this scene and one that occurs in the Senegalese writer Ousmane Socé's evocatively entitled novel *Mirages de Paris* (1937). The main character, Fara, has travelled from Senegal to Paris to work at the 1931 Colonial Exhibition (see Hodeir and Pierre 1991; Lebovics 1992; Miller 1998). On his way to the exhibition in the metro, Fara encounters a young white boy accompanied by his mother. There is the same exclamation of surprise from the child as in Fanon's own 'train scene': '"Maman, regarde, le monsieur! Il a oublié de se débarbouiller"', and the same awkward reaction from the mother: '"Il est gentil ce monsieur"' ('"Mum, look – the man! He's forgotten to clean his face"'; '"He's a nice man"'). At his mother's suggestion, the boy shakes Fara's outstretched hand and then checks to see if any black marks have been left on his skin (Socé 1937/1964: 34–5). The tone and Fara's reaction are certainly less angry than Fanon's in *Peau noire*, but Socé's novel contains a critique of the Colonial Exhibition and gives examples of popular assumptions about black people already well sedimented amongst the 'metropolitan' French in the mid-1930s.[12] Socé's text fits in well with the narratives of 'fervent and disappointing' travels from the colonies to France by black people (Jouanny 1984: 338). Public transport arguably provided many examples of the social relations engendered by the colonial racial order since it was one of the very few sites of enforced – albeit transient – spatial co-existence between black and white people.[13]

Fanon's analysis engages with the various socially differentiated racist attitudes he meets. He sees and hears infantilising remarks in relation to black people 'chez les médecins, les agents de police, les entrepreneurs sur les chantiers' ('in physicians, policemen, employers on building sites') (*Peau noire*: 24–5: tr. mod.: 31). Logically, if racism is inherent within the entire social structure, then Fanon should not be surprised to see working-class racism. At the same time, Fanon criticises Octave Mannoni for suggesting that in South Africa only the poor whites rather than the elite could be racist (*Peau noire*: 70–1; *Black Skin*: 86–8). While arguing that, in France, 'en dehors des milieux universitaires subsiste une armée d'imbéciles' ('outside university circles there is an army of fools') (*Peau noire*: 27; *Black Skin*: 35), Fanon does provide examples of racism from his university teachers and fellow students (*Peau noire*: 91, 94–5; *Black Skin*: 113, 116–17). Fanon criticises French academics and writers – Mannoni principally – for spreading misguided assumptions about cultural and social relations, to the detriment of the colonised in whatever setting (*Peau noire*, Chapter 4). He usefully highlights how 'race' and culture were interlinked in the inferiorisation of colonised peoples, a theme to which he would later return (Fanon 1956). He challenges the notion of the stage-theory, that is the developmental discourse which suggested that non-European cultures were behind those of Europe, resulting in a non-synchronicity that it was the colonising mission's 'duty' to 'correct' (*Peau noire*: 104–5; *Black Skin*: 129–30). Influenced by racialising, inferiorising imagery and discourses from a variety of social fields, Fanon argues, it is hardly surprising that all social classes share certain common assumptions, and that this racial order manifests itself in a series of neuroses (*Peau noire*: 123–33; *Black Skin*: 151–65). Fanon saw racism not as 'natural' in the sense of being biologically present in each individual, but 'normal' in the sense of being 'logically' co-substantial with the specific racial order in which social relations took place (Fanon 1956: 48).

This imagery is principally analysed as pertaining to the male black body in the examples Fanon gives of the 'métropole' (as opposed to Martinique or Senegal). Fanon's extensive studies of white Europeans of various nationalities had revealed that, for them, the word 'nègre' evoked 'biologique, sexe, fort, sportif, puissant, boxeur, Joe Louis, Jess Owen [*sic*], tirailleurs sénégalais, sauvage, animal, diable, péché' ('biology, penis, strong, athletic, potent, boxer, Joe Louis, Jesse Owens, Senegalese troops, savage, animal, devil, sin' (*Peau noire*: 134; *Black Skin*: 166). With the probable exception of the postcard (cf. Saada 1995), popular cultural images of black people were concentrated on men (see Blanchard, Deroo and Manceron 2001; Cohen 1980; Nederven Pieterse 1992).

While Fanon does not quote many of the ways in which black women from the colonies in France were represented, we know from other sources that gendered colonial stereotypes and modes of thinking about skin colour were very much in evidence. At the Paris World Fair (1937) there had been a Miss France d'Outre-Mer (Overseas) category that only contained 'métisses' (women of mixed heritage). The lightest-skinned woman won (Ezra 2000: 37). The continuing eroticisation of black women's bodies is seen in Paul Fachetti's 1948 photo collection 'Nus exotiques' ('Exotic nudes') (cf. Blanchard, Deroo and Manceron 2001: 140–1). Such exoticist stereotyping had been attacked from the 1920s onwards by figures such as Jane Nardal (1928).[14] Fanon does list examples of black Antillean women preferring white over black men (*Peau noire*: 38, 40; *Black Skin*: 47–8, 50), just as he uses the female characters in novels by Mayotte Capécia and A. Sadji as examples of women having interiorised the colonial order, although he provides few positive models of black or métisse women resisting such alienating stereotyping.[15]

We can gain a partial glimpse, from other sources, of the context in which the racial discrimination Fanon describes in *Peau noire* operated in the large French cities in the post-war period (cf. McCloy 1973: 271, 281). In early 1952 a tribunal ruled against an employer who refused to hire a black worker.[16] Interestingly, Fanon does not mention one of the major problems that faced black students in France who found that few owners were willing to rent them rooms. Some student associations had to take out adverts in the national press to call for potential non-racist rentals.[17] After having interviewed many students from Martinique and Guadeloupe, some of whom had been in France since the early 1950s, the Guadeloupan medical student Georges-Louis Pétro concluded in his 1959 study (which refers to Fanon's work in many places) that 'les relations entre Antillais et Métropolitains sont (alors) rendues ambiguës sinon difficiles par ce préjugé racial' ('this racial prejudice makes relations between Antilleans and "Métropolitains" ambiguous if not awkward' (Pétro 1959: 89). As one of Pétro's interviewees put it, a black person arriving in the 'métropole' from the Caribbean 'a l'impression de figurer comme une sorte de bête curieuse' ('feels like some kind of freak') (1959: 64).

The examples Fanon quotes of discrimination in Parisian hotels (mostly at the hands of American visitors and French hotel managers) in the summer of 1950 (*Peau noire*: 150; *Black Skin*: 186) had caused considerable emotion amongst Antilleans in Paris.[18] The anti-racist association MRAP (Mouvement contre le racisme, l'antisémitisme, et pour la paix) took up this and similar cases (MRAP 1953: 19).[19] Anti-Black racism in the USA had attracted a considerable amount of publicity in France from the 1920s onwards. The USA had come to represent, along with Germany, a foreign case to which French writers liked to compare France more favourably (House 1997: 216–17; see also Marchand 1953). This trend had continued into the post-war period, aided by wider anti-Americanism on the French left (Makward 1999: 25–6; Stovall 1996: 133), at times in ignorance of what was occurring in the French colonies. Hence, arguably, Fanon's sarcasm at Mannoni's declaration that France was the least racist country in the world: 'beaux nègres, réjouissez-vous d'être français, même si c'est un peu dur, car en Amérique vos congénères sont plus malheureux que vous' ('Be glad that you are French, my fine Negro friends, even if it is a little hard, for your counterparts in America are much worse off than you') (*Peau noire*: 74; *Black Skin*: 92). Against such 'negative comparativism' (one that might declare itself against racism yet not help the construction of opposition to colonial racism), *Peau noire* argues that 'metropolitans' as much as 'colons' and the 'petits blancs' were part of the colonial order (Cherki 2000: 53). Similar to Césaire's argument in *Discours sur le colonialisme* (1950/1955), for Fanon the 'metropolitan' French held collective responsibility for what was being done in their name in the colonies (*Peau noire*: 73; *Black Skin*: 90–1).[20]

With the combined force of the examples of racism that he gathers and the framework within which he analyses them, Fanon in *Peau noire* arguably moves the discussion on colonialism and racism forward. Fanon's text certainly encourages us to analyse racism in the 'métropole' in relation to that in the colonies and overseas departments. However, the basis for this comparison, Fanon seems to be arguing, should not be grounded in terms of a relationship between 'less' and 'more' (i.e. high levels of racism in the colonies as opposed to a 'safe haven' in the 'métropole'). Fanon's text served as a powerful counter-discourse to the reassertion of 'colonial republicanism' in post-war France, where the end of the Vichy regime could be invoked in an attempt to legitimate the more 'benign' paternalism of the French Union.[21] Francis Jeanson, in his introduction to the original edition of *Peau noire* (1952/1965), was right to see Fanon's text as 'offending' those on the French left who thought that racism was on the way to being defeated, or that their own thoughts were entirely free from paternalism. Furthermore, Fanon argues, any analysis of colonial racism and power relations needs to examine the articulation and overlaps, the similarities and dissimilarities that exist between the forms taken by racism of the colonial order in one context and those forms in other contexts.

Rethinking racism in post-war France

The arguments developed in *Peau noire* invite comparison with wider developments taking place within French anti-racist organisations in the period after 1945. The 'Ligue internationale contre l'antisémitisme' (LICA, International League against Antisemitism) had been formed in 1928 and, as its name suggests, had prioritised the fight against anti-Semitism in inter-war France. In the post-war period, the LICA developed a centrist, anti-communist republican discourse and its leader, Bernard Lecache, complained in 1950 that its membership would not consider fighting other forms of racism: 'bien des nôtres restent étrangers aux problèmes anti-racistes intéressant les hommes de couleur et les peuples coloniaux'.[22] The MRAP, on the other hand – a pro-communist anti-racist association formed in 1949 mainly by Jewish war-time Resistance activists – underwent a process of recognising the existence and importance of anti-Black and anti-North African racism in the 'métropole' as well as the colonies (House 1997, 2002; Lloyd 1998). Aimé Césaire was an honorary member of the MRAP and Fanon's friend Marcel Manville was a co-founder. The MRAP developed a wider definition of the many forms racism took, accepting that there was indeed a 'colonial racism', and identified the need for a more transverse politics of resistance, a politics that would not only include Jewish people. Throughout the 1950s, the MRAP was to evolve from a position in which the fight against anti-Semitism had been central, to one where this struggle co-existed alongside the denunciation of colonial-based racism. The MRAP proposed a humanistic argument that racism was 'indivisible' since it was a common offence against humanity. This position fostered solidarity with Algerians and black people in France (cf. House 1997: 207–11 *passim*).

In *Peau noire*, Fanon progresses from a position in which colonial racism (anti-Black racism in particular) was central to a consideration of other forms of racism. For him, the link between different forms of racism seems to reside in their object: 'l'homme' (cf. *Peau noire*: 71; *Black Skin*: 88; Fanon is here referring to a wider determinant – 'exploitation'). He judges racism to be anti-humanist, hence the 'new humanism' that he is out to promote (cf. Bernasconi 1996; Gilroy 2000). Fanon declares that 'le racisme colonial ne diffère pas des autres racismes' ('colonial racism is no different from any other racism') (*Peau noire*: 71; *Black Skin*: 88) and, like the MRAP, surmises that anti-Semites are also anti-Black: 'un antisémite est forcément négrophobe' ('an anti-Semite is inevitably anti-Negro') (*Peau noire*: 98; *Black Skin*: 122). Fanon sympathises with Jews in terms of a fellow racialised group. But, for Fanon, Jews and black people experience the objectifying racist gaze in different ways, since Jews are not targeted via a process of epidermalisation (*Peau noire*: 133–4; *Black Skin*: 162–6).[23] Both Fanon and the MRAP were looking to understand what caused the various forms of racism and what links could then be drawn between them. If the MRAP arrived at a more Marxist reading than Fanon, both nonetheless brought out the political and social (rather than 'natural') causation of racism and used humanistic arguments.

In *Peau noire*, however, Fanon is much less preoccupied with analysing racism as an emanation of an anti-republican far right that was comfortably distant, ideologically speaking, from mainstream republicanism. These far-right vectors of racism were the principal target of the established anti-racist and human rights associations (cf. House 2002). The anti-racist republican left tended to share Jean-Paul Sartre's dismissive position on the use of black identities, which he famously judged as a form of 'anti-racist racism' (1948: 582), as neither Marxism nor republican 'universalism' was likely to welcome any assertion of black identities or racial specificities.[24]

In relation to the wider context of French anti-racist and human rights activism, *Peau noire* was, with hindsight, 'ahead of its time'. Fanon's text articulated a comparativist reflection which attempted to encompass the distinctions and (at times limited) commonalities between different forms of racism, at the same time as describing how one specific form of racism might be experienced in different ways. In 1952, such reflections found a partial echo within what was only an emerging discourse within one specific organisation – the MRAP. As the 1950s progressed, however, such 'comparativist' themes would gain wider currency, and many of these developments help to throw more light on *Peau noire* itself, and on Fanon's subsequent political trajectory.

If the Algerian War of Liberation served to radicalise some sectors of the French left (albeit very late in the day), it was due in part to the noticeable eruption of colonial forms of repression and surveillance in the 'métropole' itself (as opposed to Algeria, where they were already well established).[25] This repression brought the realities of the colonies into the everyday lives of the inhabitants of France's major cities. Such repression heightened the political awareness of Antillean students in France.[26] Writing in a newspaper published for students from Martinique and Guadeloupe, Raoul Capitaine observed that

> les étudiants antillais, même les plus aliénés au départ, ont appris au contact de la vie en France le vrai visage du racisme le plus honteux dans les rues de Paris et d'ailleurs, les arrestations d'Algériens à coups de pieds et de poings, et parfois même d'authentiques ratonnades .... Parfois ils ont été les victimes de ce que les policiers appellent sans humour 'de cruelles méprises'. (1962: 2)[27]

Fanon was not the last Antillean to be mistaken for an Algerian (cf. *Peau noire*: 73; *Black Skin*: 91). Furthermore, many Jewish people were stopped by police on the false assumption they were (Arab-Berber) Algerians. Such practices naturally drew parallels for them with police tactics during the Vichy era.[28]

The Algerian War also provided new insights for those African Americans in France who had previously subscribed to the belief that France was 'colour-blind', since the situation for African Americans in France was less unfavourable than in the USA of the 1940s or 1950s (Hodges 1985: 33; Stovall 1996: 217; Stovall 2000). As Paul Gilroy has shown, African Americans had developed a comparative interest in levels of discrimination due to time spent in various European countries since the First World War (2000: 292–3). The racist gaze visited on Algerians and the question of solidarity from other racialised groups (here African Americans) has recently been examined by Paul Gilroy and Kristin Ross via William Gardner Smith's novel *The Stone Face* (1963), which portrays in vivid detail the 17 October 1961 police repression of Algerians, when police killed many Algerians protesting against an official curfew and in favour of Algerian independence (see Einaudi 2001; House and MacMaster forthcoming). Smith's novel also includes a reflection on anti-Semitism, as parallels are established between different experiences of racism. (On Smith's novel, see Gilroy 2000: 316–24; Hodges 1985; Ross 2002: 44–7.) However, published between *Peau noire* and Smiths' novel, Moroccan writer Driss Chraïbi's novel *Les Boucs* (1955), which contains a barely concealed anger against colonial injustice throughout, had already portrayed anti-Algerian racism in France through many examples of the racist gaze, just as it had established links between anti-North African racism and the anti-Semitism of the Second World War.[29] Robert Antelme's *L'espèce humaine* (1957/1997) (written 1946–7) had earlier encouraged reading the objectifying gaze in terms of racialised power relations. Fanon's decision to compare and contrast different histories of racism as lived experience would therefore become a wider 1950s and early 1960s phenomenon.

Conclusion

This chapter has argued that racism in the 'métropole' plays a key role in *Peau noire*, as Fanon is further reminded of the existence of a colonial order underpinning all racialised social relations from his perspective as a black Martinican francophone man. Whilst it may be tempting to read Fanon's text as saying that racism is not just in the 'periphery', but also at the 'centre', what *Peau noire* arguably does is to break up the distinctions between such notions and allow for more nuanced readings of the sub-cultures of colonial racisms, since these existed in a constant state of cross-fertilisation and evolution. These racisms – at once difference denying and difference creating – make the construction of an agency with which to contest such racisms subject to constant evolution. For Fanon, this agency had to exist outside of Negritude, assimilationism and Marxism taken individually (Cherki 2000: 44–5).

Furthermore, these social relations are shown to articulate 'race' in many different, albeit mutually reinforcing, ways. The analysis of racism in *Peau noire* is constantly pulled between the description of individual experience (Fanon's own) and the need to relate this to the wider, systemic colonial order. On another level, Fanon's acute analysis of the distinctions and parallels between racism as differentially experienced (for example, by

Antilleans and Senegalese) exists alongside the articulation of anti-Black racism with anti-Semitism and anti-North African racism, suggesting the need for the study of racism to exhibit a constant radical comparativism across categories of the individual and the collective (for an example of such an approach, see MacMaster 2001). Such a comparativism should not elide the complex and often problematic space that exists between similar forms of racism that are nonetheless not identical, and may indeed belong to different genealogies within modernity that came to intersect at specific historical moments. At other times, Fanon's text is pulled between a binary analysis of 'white' and 'black' that he implicitly complicates elsewhere, as he discovers 'yet more tangled manifestations of the problems of freedom and community' (Sekyi-Otu 1996: 29) and comes to the view that 'la vérité est que la race nègre est dispersée, (qu')elle ne possède plus d'unité' ('the truth is that the Negro race has been scattered, (that) it can no longer claim unity') (*Peau noire*: 139–40; *Black Skin*: 173). The text works towards an embrace of the socially differentiated ways in which anti-Black racism is experienced and through which de-alienation will take place (cf. Conclusion, *Peau noire*: 181–8; *Black Skin*: 223–32), although the way in which racism and gender are articulated is often unsympathetic towards women (cf. Makward 1999 and Sharpley-Whiting 1998). *Peau noire* also highlights how both black *and* white people are caught up in the racialising process.

Peau noire undermines any reassuring post-war narrative of a non-racist France since it describes a disturbing phenomenon. From the dance hall to the lecture theatre, the dynamics of racial stereotyping are ever present. The text calls today for a new social and cultural history of that period – a resolutely postcolonial history that incorporates and reworks our understanding of the interrelatedness of the 'metropolitan' colonial racial order and the racial orders in the colonies.

Notes

1 Translations other than from *Peau noire* are the author's own.
2 On black people's experiences during Vichy, see Ageron 1992; Monnerville 1975: 269–75 *passim*; Thomas 2002: 676. Mayotte Capécia's

two books (1948, 1950) provide an interesting view on social relations in Martinique during the Vichy period. On Capécia, see Makward 1999.

3 Frantz Duhamel (1984: 66) highlights how Fanon sees only black people in the USA as actively struggling for their freedom at that time.

4 Jeanson's otherwise highly perceptive foreword to the original edition of *Peau noire* shows that he, too, was unaware of the inter-war black experiences (Jeanson 1952/1965).

5 See Louis-Thomas Achille's preface to the 1992 edition (Achille 1992) and Sharpley-Whiting 2002.

6 This text appears in translation in Sharpley-Whiting's study of *Negritude Women* (2002: 119–24). See also Chapter 4, 'Paulette Nardal: Antillean literature and race consciousness' (Sharpley-Whiting 2002: 68–79).

7 See however Albert Londres's piece of reportage (1927/2000).

8 Fanon does state that he has had the chance to talk with a few working-class black people in Paris (*Peau noire*: 182; *Black Skin*: 224).

9 'A given society is racist or it is not. […] Statements, for example, that the north of France is more racist than the south, that racism is the work of underlings and hence in no way involves the ruling class, that France is one of the least racist countries in the world are the product of men incapable of straight thinking' (*Black Skin*: 85).

10 The child in this scene does not talk directly to Fanon (Macey 1999: 9).

11 Banania was a popular drink often advertised using racial stereotyping unsympathetic to black people. This advertising stemmed from images of black men in France from the First World War and (initially at least) referred to Africans more than Antilleans (Dewitte 1985: 12).

12 On Socé's text, see Miller 1998 and Shilton 2001. One of the founders of the anti-colonialist publication *L'Etudiant noir* (The Black Student), Socé became an MP for Senegal in 1937 (Miller 1998: 59, 64).

13 Césaire's *Cahiers d'un retour au pays natal* (1939), from which Fanon quotes extensively, also includes a tram scene set in France and focuses on the white and black gaze on a black man (see Rosello 1993).

14 This text appears in translation in Sharpley-Whiting 2002: 108–13.

15 For a critical reading of this, see Chow 1999: 38. See also Sharpley-Whiting 1998. Owen White has criticised Fanon's portrayal of gender relations in Senegal (1999: 157).

16 *Le Correspondant antillais*, 'Une décision importante en matière de refus d'embauche', n.s., no. 1, Feb. 1952, 2.

17 See Achille's letter 'Logement des étudiants de couleur' in *Alizès*, 3rd year, no. 1, Oct. 1953, 6–7. See also *Lyon étudiant*, 'Solidarité avec les étudiants d'outre-mer', 3rd year, no. 2, Feb. 1955, 1.

18 See *Le Correspondant antillais* (a moderate newspaper), 'Les antillais contre les actes de discrimination raciale', n.s., no. 2, Jan. 1952, p. 3. Manville relates these incidents (1992: 137–8).

19 See also *Droit et liberté*, no. 52 (156), 1–7 Dec. 1950, p. 1.

20 When Fanon's text appeared in 1952, any further colonial reform was off the agenda and independence for the colonies and territories remained unthinkable on the moderate left (Biondi and Morin 1992: 258). On radical anti-colonialists such as Francis Jeanson, see Ulloa 2001.

21 See René Maran's pro-assimilationist article 'Les Français de couleur et la France de Vichy' (Maran 1945). See also Gabriel d'Arbousier's more critical 'Racisme colonial' (1949).

22 'Many of our members do not take on board anti-racist problems affecting men of colour and colonial peoples' ('Rapport politique' to 13th LICA National Congress, 11–12 Feb. 1950, p. 3).

23 See however Gilman (1991), who has highlighted the extent to which anti-Semitic racialising stereotypes have used images of the body and 'blackness'.

24 Fanon's text appeared at a time when UNESCO was revising how the term 'race' should be used – see Taguieff (1995: 329–56).

25 See House and MacMaster forthcoming. In fact, Algerians were, by 1950, already being rounded up on a huge scale in France. According to the police, on 17 September 1950 some 1,127 Algerians were detained in Paris (Archives Nationales, Paris, F1a 5061, Head of Paris Muncipal Police to Interior Ministry, 3 Dec. 1950).

26 Both Guérin (1956: 106–8) and Leiris (1955/1987: 186) argue that by 1954 assertion of Martinican identity was becoming stronger as a reaction against departmentalisation in 1947.

27 'Antillean students – even those who were initially the most alienated – have come to learn through living in France the true nature of the most shameful racism on the streets of Paris or elsewhere. They have seen Algerians kicked and punched when arrested and sometimes even large-scale attacks on Algerians …. Sometimes they themselves have been victims of what the police un-jokingly call "terrible mistakes".'

28 Some MRAP members themselves were also mistakenly stopped by police who thought they had found an 'Algerian' (cf. House 2002: 124). See also Glissant 1981: 74–5.

29 'Boucs' means 'billy goats', but also has a potential secondary meaning since in French the term 'bouc-émissaire' means 'scapegoat'.

References

Achille, L.-T. (1992) 'Préface', in *La Revue du monde noir: facsimile*, Paris: Jean-Michel Place, vii–xvii

Ageron, C.-R. (1992) 'Vichy, les Français et l'Empire', in J.-P. Azéma and F. Bédarida (eds), *Le Régime de Vichy et les Français*, Paris: Fayard, 122–34

Antelme, R. (1957/1997) *L'Espèce humaine*, Paris: Gaillimard

Bernasconi, R. (1996) 'Casting the slough: Fanon's new humanism for a new humanity' in L. R. Gordon, T. D. Sharpley-Whiting and R. T. White (eds), *Fanon: A Critical Reader*, Oxford: Blackwell, 113–21

Biondi, J.-P. and Morin, G. (1992) *Les Anticolonialistes (1881–1962)*, Paris: Hachette

Blanchard, P., Deroo, É. and Manceron, G. (2001) *Le Paris noir*, Paris: Éditions Hazan

Bonniol, J.-L. (1992) *La Couleur comme maléfice: une illustration créole de la généalogie des Blancs et des Noirs*, Paris: Albin Michel

Bulhan, H. A., (1985) *Frantz Fanon and the Psychology of Oppression*, New York and London: Plenum Press

Capécia, M. (1948) *Je suis martiniquaise*, Paris: Éditions Corrêa

—— (1950) *La Négresse blanche*, Paris: Éditions Corrêa

Capitaine, R. (1962) 'Après l'Algérie, les Antilles', *Matouba (Revue des étudiants antillais de la Guadeloupe et de la Martinique)*, 2, Apr., 1–2

Caute, D. (1970) *Fanon*, London: Fontana/Collins

Césaire, A. (1939/1956) *Cahier d'un retour au pays natal*, Paris: Présence Africaine

—— (1950/1955) *Discours sur le colonialisme*, Paris: Présence Africaine

Cherki, A. (2000) *Frantz Fanon, portrait*, Paris: Seuil

Chow, R. (1999) 'The politics of admittance: female sexual agency, miscegenation, and the formation of community in Frantz Fanon', in A. C. Alessandrini (ed.), *Frantz Fanon: Critical Perspectives*, London and New York: Routledge, 34–56

Chraïbi, D. (1955) *Les Boucs*, Paris: Denoël

Cohen, W. B. (1980) *The French Encounter with Africans: White Responses to Blacks, 1530–1880*, Bloomington: Indiana University Press

D'Arbousier, G. (1949) 'Racisme colonial', *Droit et liberté*, 27 (95), 1 May, 2

Damas, L.-G. (1937/1972) *Pigments*, Paris: Présence Africaine

Dewitte, P. (1985) *Les Mouvements nègres en France, 1919–1939*, Paris: L'Harmattan

Dornel, L. (1995) 'Les usages du racialisme: le cas de la main-d'œuvre coloniale en France pendant la première guerre mondiale', *Genèses*, 20, 48–72

Duhamel, F. (1984) 'Frantz Fanon: l'odysée de la conscience dominée' in *Mémorial International Frantz Fanon*, Paris: Présence Africaine, 51–70

Einaudi, J.-L. (2001) *Octobre 1961: un massacre à Paris*, Paris: Fayard

Ezra, E. (2000) *The Colonial Unconscious: Race and Culture in Inter-war France*, Ithaca, NY and London: Cornell University Press

Fabre, M. (1985) *La Rive noire: de Harlem à la Seine*, Paris: Lieu Commun

Fabre, M. (1991) *From Harlem to Paris: Black American Writers in France, 1840–1980*, Urbana and Chicago: University of Chicago Press

Fanon, F. (1956) 'Race et culture', *Présence Africaine*, n.s., 8-9-10, 237–51

Gibson, N. C. (2003) *Fanon: The Postcolonial Imagination*, Cambridge: Polity

Gilman, S. (1991) *The Jew's Body*, London and New York: Routledge

Gilroy, P. (1993) *The Black Atlantic: Modernity and Double Consciousness*, London and New York: Verso

—— (2000), *Between Camps: Race, Identity and Nationalism at the End of the Colour Line*, London: Allen Lane/The Penguin Press, 2000

Glissant, É. (1981) *Le Discours antillais*, Paris: Seuil

Gordon, L. R. (1996) 'The Black and the body politic: Fanon's existential phenomenological critique of psychoanalysis' in L. R. Gordon, T. D. Sharpley-Whiting and R. T. White (eds), *Fanon: A Critical Reader*, Oxford: Blackwell, 74–84

Guérin, D. (1956) *Les Antilles décolonisées*, Paris: Présence Africaine

Guillaumin, C. (1972) *L'Idéologie raciste: genèse et langage actuel*, Paris and The Hague: Mouton

Himes, C. (1945/1999) *If He Hollers Let Him Go*, London: Serpent's Tail

Hodeir, C. and Pierre, M. (1991) *L'Exposition coloniale*, Brussels: Éditions Complexe

Hodges, L. S. Jr. (1985) *Portrait of an Expatriate: William Gardner Smith, Writer*, Westport, CT and London: Greenwood Press

House, J. (1997) 'Antiracism and antiracist discourse in France from 1900 to the present day', Ph.D. thesis, University of Leeds

—— (2002) 'Anti-racism in France, 1898–1962: modernity and beyond', in C. Lloyd and F. Anthias (eds), *Re-thinking Antiracisms: From Theory to Practice*, London and New York: Routledge, 111–27

House, J. and MacMaster, N. (forthcoming) *Paris 1961: Algerians, State Terror and Post-colonial Memories*, Oxford: Oxford University Press

Jeanson, F. (1952/1965) 'Préface', in F. Fanon, *Peau noire, masques blancs*, Paris: Seuil, 7–22

Jouanny, R. (1984) 'Des Nègres à Paris', in *Paris et le phénomène des capitales littéraires: carrefour ou dialogue des cultures*, Actes du premier colloque du Centre de recherche en littérature comparée, Paris: Université de Paris-Sorbonne (Paris IV), 327–42

Judy, R. A. T. (1996) 'Fanon's body of black experience', in L. R. Gordon, T. D. Sharpley-Whiting and R. T. White (eds), *Fanon: A Critical Reader*, Oxford: Blackwell, 53–73

Jules-Rosette, B. (1998) *Black Paris: The African Writers' Landscape*, Urbana and Chicago: University of Illinois Press

Kruks, S. (1996) 'Fanon, Sartre and identity politics', in L. R. Gordon, T. D. Sharpley-Whiting and R. T. White (eds), *Fanon: A Critical Reader*, Oxford: Blackwell, 122–33

Lebovics, H. (1992) *True France: The Wars over Cultural Identity, 1900–1945*, Ithaca, NY and London: Cornell University Press

Légitime défense (1932/1970), Liechenstein: Nendeln Klaus

Leiris, M. (1955/1987) *Contacts de civilisations en Martinique et en Guadeloupe*, Paris: Gallimard/UNESCO

Lloyd, C. (1998) *Discourses of Antiracism in France*, Aldershot: Ashgate

Londres, A. (1927/2000) *Marseille, porte du Sud*, Paris: Le Serpent à Plumes

Lucas, P. (1971) *Sociologie de Frantz Fanon: contribution à une anthropologie de la libération*, Algiers: SNED

Macey, D. (1999) 'Fanon, phenomenology, race', *Radical Philosophy*, 95, 8–14

—— (2000) *Frantz Fanon: A Life*, London: Granta

Mackay, C. (1929/1957) *Banjo: A Story Without a Plot*, New York: Harcourt Brace Jovanovich

MacMaster, N. (1997) *Colonial Migrants and Racism: Algerians in France, 1900–62*, Basingstoke: Macmillan

—— (2001) *Racism in Europe 1870–2000*, Basingstoke: Palgrave

Makward, C. P. (1999) *Mayotte Capécia ou l'aliénation selon Fanon*, Paris: Karthala

Manville, M. (1992) *Les Antilles sans fard*, Paris: L'Harmattan

Maran, R. (1945) 'Les Français de couleur et la France de Vichy', *Fraternité*, 44, 9 Apr., 3–4

Marchand, J. (1953) 'L'antiracisme à l'école et dans la vie', *Droit et liberté*, 121 (225), Apr., 2

McCloy, S. T. (1973) *The Negro in France*, New York: Haskell Books

Miller, C. L. (1998) *Nationalists and Nomads: Essays on Francophone African Literature and Culture*, Chicago and London: University of Chicago Press

Monnerville, G. (1975) *Témoignage: de la France equinoxiale au Palais de Luxembourg*, Paris: Plon

MRAP (1953) *Halte à l'antisémitisme et au racisme!*, Paris: MRAP

Nardal, J. (1928) 'Pantins exotiques', *La Dépêche africaine*, 1: 8, 15 Oct., 2

Nardal, P. (1932) 'L'Éveil de la conscience de race chez les étudiants noirs', *La Revue du monde noir*, 6, Apr., 25–31

Nederven Pieterse, J. (1992) *White on Black: Images of Africa and Blacks in Western Popular Culture*, New Haven and London: Yale University Press

Nicolas, A. (1996) *Histoire de la Martinique. De 1848 à 1939. Tome II*, Paris: L'Harmattan

Pétro, G.-L. (1959) 'Les étudiants antillais. I Incidence de la tuberculose. II Problèmes d'adaptation psycho-sociale', MD thesis, Bordeaux: Librairie Delmas

Robinson, C. (1993) 'The appropriation of Frantz Fanon', *Race and Class*, 35: 1, 79–91

Ross, K. (2002) *May '68 and Its Afterlives*, Chicago and London: University of Chicago Press

Rosello, M. (1993) '"One more sea to cross": exile and intertextuality in Aimé Césaire's *Cahier d'un retour au pays natal*', *Yale French Studies*, 83:2, 176–85

Saada, E. (1995) 'Le poids des mots, la routine des photos: photographies de femmes martiniquaises 1880–1930', *Genèses*, 21, 134–47

Sartre, J.-P. (1948) 'Orphée noir', *Les Temps modernes*, 38, 577–606

Sayad, A. (1999) *La Double Absence: des illusions de l'émigré aux souffrances de l'immigré*, Paris: Seuil

Sekyi-Otu, A. (1996) *Fanon's Dialectic of Experience*, Cambridge, MA and London: Harvard University Press

Sharpley-Whiting, T. D. (1998) *Frantz Fanon: Conflicts and Feminism*, New York and Oxford: Rowman and Littlefield

—— (2002) *Negritude Women*, Minneapolis and London: University of Minnesota Press

Shilton, S. (2001) 'Journeys between cultures, journeys within cultures: understanding exile and travel in Ousmane Socé and Azouz Begag', in C. Forsdick (ed.), *Travel and Exile: Postcolonial Perspectives*, ASCALF Critical Studies in Postcolonial Literature 1, 31–47

Sirinelli, J.-F. (1988) 'Deux étudiants "coloniaux" à Paris à l'aube des années trente', *Vingtième siécle: revue d'histoire*, 18, 77–87

Smith, W. G. (1963) *The Stone Face*, New York: Farrar, Straus

Socé, O. (1937/1964) *Mirages de Paris*, Paris: Nouvelles Éditions Latines

Stoler, A. and Cooper, F. (1997) 'Between metropole and colony: rethinking a research agenda', in F. Cooper and A. Stoler (eds), *Tensions of Empire: Colonial Cultures in a Bourgeois World*, Los Angeles and London: University of California Press, 1–56

Stovall, T. (1993) 'Colour-blind France? Colonial workers during the First World War', *Race and Class*, 35:2, 35–55

—— (1996) *Paris Noir: African Americans in the City of Light*, Boston and New York: Houghton Mifflin

—— (2000) 'The fire this time: black American expatriates and the Algerian War', *Yale French Studies*, 98, 182–200

Taguieff, P.-A. (1987) *La Force du préjugé: essai sur le racisme et ses doubles*, Paris: La Découverte

—— (1995) *Les Fins de l'antiracisme*, Paris: Michalon

Thomas, M. C. (2002) 'The Vichy government and French colonial prisoners of war, 1940–1944', *French Historical Studies*, 25:4, 657–92

Tosquelles, F. (2001) 'Frantz Fanon et la psychothérapie institutionnelle', *Sud/Nord: folies et cultures*, 14, 166–74

Ulloa, M.-P. (2001) *Francis Jeanson: un intellectuel en dissidence de la Résistance à la guerre d'Algérie*, Paris: Berg International

Vergès, F. (1999) '"I am not the slave of slavery": the politics of reparation in (French) postslavery communities', in A. C. Alessandrini (ed.), *Frantz Fanon: Critical Perspectives*, London and New York: Routledge, 258–75

White, O. (1999) *Children of the French Empire: Miscegenation and Colonial Society in French West Africa 1895–1960*, Oxford: Clarendon Press

Wilder, G. (1999) 'Practicing citizenship in Imperial Paris', in J. L. and J. Comoroff (eds), *Civil Society and the Political Imagination in Africa: Colonial Perspectives*, Chicago and London: University of Chicago Press, 44–71

Young, R. J. C. (2001) *Postcolonialism: An Historical Introduction*, Oxford: Blackwell

4

Frantz Fanon and the Black–Jewish imaginary[1]

BRYAN CHEYETTE

In his posthumously published essays on the Algerian revolution, *L'An V de la révolution algérienne* (1959), Frantz Fanon characterises Algerian Jewry, which made up 'le cinquième de la population non musulmane d'Algérie' ('one-fifth of the non-Moslem population of Algeria') (Fanon 2001: 142; Fanon 1989: 153), as containing three distinct strands. First, 'les commerçants juifs' ('Jewish tradesmen') who are mainly invested in French rule and therefore do not favour the setting up of an Algerian national authority; secondly, 'les fonctionnaires juifs (qui) imaginent eux aussi avec effroi la naissance d'un Etat algérien' ('Jewish civil servants (who) look upon the birth of an Algerian state with fear and trembling') (Fanon 2001: 143 and 144; Fanon 1989: 154); finally, the majority of Jews, three-quarters of the Jewish population, who for the most part serve or aid the militias. The latter group makes 'peu importante' ('unimportant') the minority of Jews 'engagé(s) activement dans les rangs du colonialisme' ('actively engaged in the ranks of colonialism') (Fanon 2001: 145; Fanon 1989: 155). This is especially true when the majority of Algerian Jews fulfilled their role of becoming 'au sein du dispositif ennemi … "les yeux et les oreilles de la Révolution"' ('"the eyes and ears of the Revolution" inside the enemy apparatus') (Fanon 2001: 145; Fanon 1989: 155). Fanon's nuanced account of Algerian Jewry echoes his representation of French Jews in *Peau noire* who were considered to be both the victims and beneficiaries of European modernity. As Fanon notes in the later work, 'leur comportement [des Juifs algériens] face à la lutte du peuple algérien n'est évidemment pas univoque' ('the attitude of Algerian Jewry toward the struggle of the Algerian people is obviously not a homogenous one') (Fanon 2001: 142; Fanon 1989: 153). The subject of this essay is precisely such heterogeneous juxtapositions which bring together diasporic Jewry and the history of anti-Semitism with the colonial struggle and anti-Black racism.

While such historical intersections tend to be missing from present-day accounts of postcolonialism, they were very much part of Fanon's post-war perspective. What is more, as David Macey argues, *Peau noire* is a form of 'bricolage' (Macey 2000: 162) whose content and form brings together disparate cultural and racial histories. Fanon compared assimilated European Jews and Blacks in *Peau noire* as examples of racial groups which internalised racist structures. In his *L'An V de la révolution algérienne*, he similarly notes that Jews, especially when part of the bourgeoisie, colluded with the colonial apparatus in Algeria. However, as he goes on to contend, 'la masse imposante, arabisée à l'extrême, parlant mal le français' ('the great majority, a floating, highly Arabized mass having only a poor knowledge of French') (Fanon 2001: 144–5; Fanon 1989: 155) tended to oppose colonialism. Robert Young has related this 'cultural inbetween-ness' – Jews as both colonial and anti-colonial – to the Derridean roots of postcolonial theory which arises out of the Algerian Jewish community (Young 2001: 422). However, as Fanon argues, it was not assimilated Algerian Jews, such as Jacques Derrida, who tended actively to oppose French colonialism, but the unassimilated Jewish majority. As Gillian Rose has shown, Jews within French post-structuralism are invariably essentialised as the ineffable alterity within western metaphysics (Rose 1993: 14–24). Rather than reading Algerian Jews back in relation to these contemporary formulations, Fanon helps us to understand post-war Jewry in relation to the colonial struggle in less abstract and more historically grounded terms. To this end, I will read Frantz Fanon's *Peau noire* alongside Jean-Paul Sartre's *Réflexions sur la question juive* (1946) which had a profound impact on Fanon's thinking while writing his first book.

That Fanon drew specifically and in detail on Sartre's *Réflexions sur la question juive* while formulating his seminal account of the effects of colonial racism on himself and others is under-represented in accounts of his life and work. This essay will look in detail at the intertextual relationship between Fanon's and Sartre's works and will read one against the other to show, especially, the ways in which Fanon both resisted and rewrote Sartre. This is not a straightforward question of Sartrean influence on Fanon but, more accurately, a case study in the anxiety of influence as Fanon incorporated many of Sartre's ideas and thought processes only to reject or modify them. I will argue that both Sartre and Fanon slip between actuality and discourse in a bid to understand the impact of a dominant racial imaginary on Blacks and Jews. As we will see, Fanon understood his own status as a Europeanised colonial subject, belittled by a dominant French culture, partly in relation to assimilated but racially abused metropolitan Jews.

Whereas Sartre desires to bring together Jews and Blacks unproblematically within a wider dialectic concerning the repressions of western humanism, Fanon preserved the differences between Jews and Blacks so as to stress the specific acts of resistance needed by particular groups to overcome racism and anti-Semitism. The tension between the particular and the universal informs Fanon's understanding of Jews both as fellow victims of European modernity and as irrelevant to his specific struggle with anti-Black colonial racism. I will conclude by arguing that Fanon's heterogeneous perspective helps us to rethink the astonishing number of texts (imaginative, critical and historical) which bring together the black body and the Jewish mind as part of a racial imaginary. This is a long-standing aspect of American popular culture, as can be seen in Hollywood films from *Home of the Brave* (1949) to *Independence Day* (1996). Fanon's rejection of the Americanisation of the black-Jewish imaginary in his response to *Home of the Brave* is particularly noteworthy in this regard. My reading of *Peau noire* is designed, finally, to help us rethink the kind of histories that are being constructed – both in a European and in an American context – when we focus on Blacks and Jews in the name of liberal assimilationism.

At one point in *Peau noire*, Frantz Fanon describes Jean-Paul

Sartre's *Réflexions sur la question juive* as containing some of 'les plus belles [pages] que nous ayons jamais lues. Les plus belles, parce que le problème qu'elles expriment nous prend aux entrailles' ('the finest [pages] that I have ever read. The finest, because the problem discussed in them grips us in our guts') (*Peau noire*: 146; *Black Skin*: 181). It is worth noting this gut-wrenching response, although, as we will see, Fanon is elsewhere rather more considered when reading Sartre. Sartre was certainly an abiding presence for Fanon, especially during the period when he was writing *Peau noire*, since, along with Maurice Merleau-Ponty, Sartre was at the heart of radical French political debate in the 1940s, which influenced much of Fanon's intellectual thinking (Macey 2000: 27). 'Portrait de l'antisémite', the first chapter of *Réflexions sur la question juive*, was initially published in *Les Temps modernes* in November 1945 and was a key point of reference for those who opposed the resurgence of French anti-Semitism immediately after the war. Although Fanon was an avid reader of *Les Temps modernes*, this was not merely a matter of textual influence. Fanon had served as part of the Free French forces in a war against racism and fascism and had lived through Nazi discrimination against the handful of Jews in Martinique and the larger Jewish population in Algeria (Macey 2000: 83–4, 94–7). These experiences informed much of *Peau noire*.

Not unlike a great many black soldiers who fought for the allies during the Second World War, Fanon's appreciation of the horrors of fascism impinged directly on his understanding of European colonialism and the racism of the United States. Robert Young has argued that anti-colonial French thinkers especially understood the history of Nazism and fascism as 'European colonialism brought home to Europe' (Young 1990: 8). In this francophone tradition, Fanon 'semble encore entendre' ('can still hear') his friend and compatriot Aimé Césaire in his *Discours politiques* commenting on the electoral campaign in Martinique in 1945:

> Quand je tourne le bouton de ma radio, que j'entends qu'en Amérique des nègres sont lynchés, je dis qu'on nous a menti: Hitler n'est pas mort; quand je tourne le bouton de ma radio, que j'apprends que des Juifs sont insultés, méprisés, pogromisés, je dis

qu'on nous a menti: Hitler n'est pas mort; que je tourne enfin le
bouton de ma radio et que j'apprenne qu'en Afrique le travail forcé
est institué, légalisé, je dis que, véritablement, on nous a menti:
Hitler n'est pas mort. (*Peau noire*: 71–2)[2]

Fanon quotes Césaire as part of his extended critique of
Octave Mannoni, who argued in his *Psychologie de la colonisation*
(1950, trans. 1956) that colonial racism was essentially unique.
Mannoni states contentiously that those who are colonised are
psychologically predisposed to this condition and therefore
'"l'exploitation coloniale ne se confond pas avec les autres formes
d'exploitation, le racisme colonial diffère des autres racisms"'
('"colonial exploitation is not the same as other forms of
exploitation, and colonial racialism is different from other kinds
of racialism"' (*Peau noire*: 71; *Black Skin*: 88). Fanon's response to
Mannoni follows Césaire's *Discours politiques* in making no
distinction between different kinds of racisms and his rebuttal is
especially powerful:

> Le racisme colonial ne diffère pas des autres racismes. L'anti-
> sémitisme me touche en pleine chair, je m'émeus, une contestation
> effroyable m'anémie, on me refuse la possibilité d'être un homme.
> Je ne puis pas me désolidariser du sort réservé à mon frère. Chacun
> de mes actes engage l'homme. Chacune de mes réticences, chacune
> de mes lâchetés manifeste l'homme. (*Peau noire*: 71)[3]

Here, in exemplary fashion, Fanon is articulating a sense of
injustice which is universalised beyond racial difference and so
undermines an essentialised notion of black victimhood. To this
end he employs Karl Jaspers's concept of 'culpabilité méta-
physique' ('metaphysical guilt') (*Peau noire*: 71; *Black Skin*: 89)
and the words of Maryse Choisy who argues that all those who
remained 'neutral' during the Nazi occupation of France 'se
sentaient confusément responsables de tous ces morts et de tous
les Buchenwald' ('felt that they were responsible for all the
deaths and all the Buchenwalds') (*Peau noire*: 72; *Black Skin*: 89).

Fanon confirms his common humanity or 'whiteness' precisely
at the point where he feels most complicit with European anti-
Semitism. Those who did not oppose fascism and Nazism are
'white' in the same way as those who align themselves with
colonialism (either passively or actively). Fanon is initially

responding to Mannoni's misguided belief that '"la civilisation
européenne et ses représentants les plus qualifiés ne sont pas
responsables du racisme colonial"' ('"European civilization and
its best representatives are not responsible for colonial racialism"') (*Peau noire*: 73; *Black Skin*: 91) by showing that racism and
anti-Semitism are absolutely at the centre of European culture.
As Paul Gilroy has noted, these Fanonian 'knotted intersections
of histories' help to deracialise the differing strands of violence
and oppression within western modernity (Gilroy 2000: 78–9).
Césaire was a particularly important influence on Fanon as he
understood the complicity of European humanism with the worst
racial atrocities. Fanon cites an extraordinary passage from
Césaire's *Discours sur le colonialisme* (1956) which notes that
those who did not oppose Nazism were responsible for it, 'et qu'il
sourd, qu'il perce, qu'il goutte, avant de l'engloutir dans ses
eaux rougies, de toutes les fissures de la civilisation occidentale
et chrétiennne' ('and it drips, it seeps, it wells from every crack
in western Christian civilization until it engulfs that civilization
in a bloody sea') (*Peau noire*: 73; *Black Skin*: 90–1). Césaire's potent
mixture of Negritude and communism gives a sense of the range
of reference, both particularist and universalist, which Fanon
wished to encompass.

Like so much of *Peau noire*, the response to Mannoni and the
citation of Césaire both has a considerable theoretical weight and
is also taken directly from Fanon's experience as an Antillean
serving in the Free French forces. Fanon begins Chapter 1 with
what he regards as a central 'problem', which is that 'le Noir
Antillais sera d'autant plus blanc ... qu'il aura fait sienne la
langue française' ('the Negro of the Antilles will be propor-
tionately whiter ... in direct ratio to his mastery of the French
language') (*Peau noire*: 14; *Black Skin*: 18). The chapter ends with
a French acquaintance telling Fanon enthusiastically that '"au
fond, tu es un blanc"' ('"At bottom you are a white man"') due
to his mastery of 'la langue du Blanc' ('white man's language')
which in turn gives him 'droit de cité' ('honorary [French]
citizenship') (*Peau noire*: 30; *Black Skin*: 38). Antillean solders,
Fanon notes, often acted as interpreters 'à transmettre à leurs
congénères les ordres du maître' ('to convey the master's orders
to their fellows') and so have 'une certaine honorabilité' ('a

certain position of honor') (*Peau noire*: 14; *Black Skin*: 19). He also explains at some length the nature of the racial hierarchy in the army, which is summarised in the following terms: 'Les originaires méprisent les tirailleurs et l'Antillais règne sur toute cette négraille en maître incontesté' ('The Europeans despise the Senegalese, and the Antilles Negro rules the black roost as its unchallenged master') (*Peau noire*: 20; *Black Skin*: 26).

Fanon's enforced position as one of a group of racialised middle-men in the Free French army enables him to understand what he later calls 'la répartition raciale de la culpabilité' ('the racial distribution of guilt'): 'Le Français n'aime pas le Juif qui n'aime pas l'Arabe, qui n'aime pas le nègre' ('The Frenchman does not like the Jew, who does not like the Arab, who does not like the Negro' (*Peau noire*: 83; *Black Skin*: 103). But it is precisely the ambiguity of 'the Frenchman' as an ethno-national category, defined by his anti-Semitism, which Fanon grapples with throughout *Peau noire*. As we will see, Fanon's book both foregrounds a fluid set of racial classifications and, at the same time, understands the world in Manichaean terms (after Mayotte Capécia) as 'deux pôles [blanc et noir] d'un monde, pôles en lutte perpétuelle' ('two [white and black] poles in perpetual conflict') (*Peau noire*: 36; *Black Skin*: 44). The critique of Mannoni is, above all else, an attack on the particularism of his 'dependency' theories of colonialism and the absolute distinctions between different kinds of racisms. Fanon deploys Sartre and the 'Jewish question' in a bid to disprove Mannoni's account of colonial racism which lets French culture as a whole off the hook. To this end, Fanon asks Mannoni 's'il ne pense pas que pour un Juif les différences entre l'antisémitisme de Maurras et celui de Goebbels sont impalpables' ('whether he does not think that for a Jew the differences between the [French] anti-Semitism of Maurras and that of Goebbels are imperceptible') (*Peau noire*: 69; *Black Skin*: 86). He then goes on to quote *Réflexions sur la question juive* – '"la plupart des riches *utilisent* cette passion (antisémite)"' ('"the rich for the most part *exploit* this (anti-Semitic) passion for their own uses"') (*Peau noire*: 70; *Black Skin*: 87; Fanon's emphasis) – so as to clinch the argument, *contra* Mannoni, that colonial racism has an economic basis which crosses all national boundaries.

As David Marriott has rightly maintained, the rhetoric of

war or 'perpetual conflict' is a key motif in *Peau noire*, not least in relation to the 'appalling (European) battle' which bleeds Fanon 'white' and culminates in the death camps (Marriott 2000: 69–70). Echoing Fanon's critique of Mannoni's theories of racial uniqueness, the exemplary pages of Sartre's *Réflexions sur la question juive*, which Fanon claims 'nous prend aux entrailles' ('grips us in our guts'), end with Sartre claiming that '"le sang juif que les Nazis ont versé retombe sur toutes nos têtes"' ('"the Jewish blood that the Nazis shed falls on all our heads"' (*Peau noire*: 147, note 45; *Black Skin*: 182). Marriott identifies Fanon's war rhetoric with both an internal struggle, the 'imago' of the black man that has to be defeated from within, and an external anti-colonial struggle between Black and White. But this rhetoric is crucially carried over from the Second World War, as Sartre demonstrates: 'Le Juif d'aujourd'hui est en pleine guerre' ('The Jew of today is in full war') (Sartre 1954: 182; Sartre 1948: 150). The figure of the Jew, in these terms, is a means by which Fanon can reflect upon his own status as a Europeanised victorious Antillean soldier who is nonetheless racially abused and belittled by a dominant French culture (Macey 2000: 104–5). His extensive discussion of *Réflexions sur la question juive*, and Jews and Jewishness more generally, is also a way of resolving often irresolvable questions concerning the nature of racial difference and the impossibility of assimilation in contemporary France.

There are, in these terms, two incommensurable narratives in *Peau noire* concerning Blacks and Jews that revolve around the uncertainty of whether Jews should be regarded as 'black' or 'white'. Fanon's hybrid text, that is, simultaneously rewrites and resists Sartre's *Réflexions sur la question juive*, sometimes explicitly, often implicitly, in a bid to make a range of contradictory points about both the particularity of black experience and the universality of racist and anti-Semitic discourse. The 'persistent instabilities' in Fanon's writings, in the words of Benita Parry, are therefore often figured in terms of a competing discussion of Jews and anti-Semitism (Parry 1994: 186). In other words, the references to Jews and anti-Semitism in *Peau noire* are part of a wider tension concerning the relationship between a particularist anti-colonial nationalism (which excludes 'the Jew') and more universalist or transnational theories of racial oppression (which include 'the Jew') (McCulloch 1983: 214; Parry 1994: 186–7). Sartre's *Réflexions sur la question juive* revealed, in part, a generalised anti-racism to complement his universalising *Orphée noir* (1948). But *Orphée noir* was to be famously resisted by Fanon until he published *Les Damnés de la terre* (1961) as it 'a détruit l'enthousiasme noir' ('destroyed black zeal') (*Peau noire*: 109; *Black Skin*: 135) by placing black cultural nationalism in the context of a supposedly all-encompassing Hegelian dialectic. This fear of being assimilated back into a set of 'pré-existant' ('pre-existing') Eurocentric paradigms (*Peau noire*: 109; *Black Skin*: 134) – however ostensibly progressive – also plays itself out in relation to Sartre's *Réflexions sur la question juive*. For this reason Fanon both brings together the history of 'Negrophobia' with the history of 'anti-Semitism' while, at the same time, resisting a too easy assimilation between these two racisms which he dismisses as 'les erreurs d'analyse' ('errors of analysis') (*Peau noire*: 148; *Black Skin*: 183).

Towards the beginning of Chapter 5, mistakenly translated as 'The Fact of Blackness',[4] Fanon speaks of listening to a drunken Frenchman on a train who, after spouting some anti-Semitic vitriol, turns to Fanon and states, 'face aux étrangers ... quels qu'ils soient"' ('"let's face up to the foreigners ... no matter who they are"') (*Peau noire*: 98; *Black Skin*: 121). His conclusions from this incident are echoed throughout the following chapters:

> De prime abord, il peut sembler étonnant que l'attitude de l'antisémite s'apparente à celle du négrophobe. C'est mon professeur de philosophie, d'origine antillaise, qui me le rappelait un jour: 'Quand vous entendez dire du mal des Juifs, dressez l'oreille, on parle de vous.' Et je pensais qu'il avait raison universellement, entendant par-là que j'étais responsable, dans mon corps et dans mon âme, du sort réservé à mon frère. Depuis lors, j'ai compris qu'il voulait tout simplement dire: un antisémite est forcément négrophobe. (*Peau noire*: 98)[5]

This process of working through the acknowledged strangeness of associating anti-Semitism with Negrophobia – which culminates in the simplicity of his eventual conclusion that anti-Semites are inevitably anti-Negro – is more troubled than at first appears. Does his final straightforward sentence mean that he is no longer 'responsable, dans mon corps et dans mon âme, du sort réservé à mon frère' ('answerable in my body and in my heart for what was done to my brother')? That the question of anti-Semitism should be eventually disembodied and become a mere cerebral matter is repeated on a larger scale throughout *Peau noire*. Sartre's pages on anti-Semitism are 'masterful' precisely because 'le problème qu'elles expriment nous prend aux entrailles' ('the problem discussed in them grips us in our guts') (*Peau noire*: 146; *Black Skin*: 181). The shift towards a disembodied response to anti-Semitism is therefore significant as it lessens its importance for Fanon.

There is an uneasy intimacy between Fanon and Sartre's *Réflexions sur la question juive*, and it is significant that the latter book ends with the following: 'il conviendra de représenter à chacun que le destin des Juifs est *son* destin' ('what must be done is to point out to each one that the fate of the Jews is *his* fate' (Sartre 1954: 185; 1948: 153). This statement echoes the Antillean philosophy professor: '"Quand vous entendez dire du mal des Juifs, dressez l'oreille, on parle de vous"' ('"Whenever you hear anyone abuse the Jews, pay attention, because he is talking about you"'). But, just as Fanon resists the universalising dialectic of *Orphée noir*, he also resists particularising gestures in *Réflexions sur la question juive*, especially with regard to the 'caractère somatique' ('somatic characteristic') of Jews (Sartre 1954: 77; Sartre 1948: 63). Unlike Fanon, Sartre relies upon an all-embracing dialectic, and not particularist acts of resistance, to defeat racism. At the same time, he does not distinguish between the 'somatic characteristics' of Blacks and Jews. But, as McCulloch notes, Fanon pointedly chose to ignore the Marxist tenor of *Réflexions sur la question juive* in his early writings and therefore stressed increasingly the racial differences between Blacks and Jews (McCulloch 1983: 80).

At his best, Fanon makes it possible to run together both black and Jewish oppression in relation to the 'manichéisme délirant' ('manicheism delirium') of western metaphysics which divides the world into 'Bien-Mal, Beau-Laid, Blanc-Noir' ('Good-Evil, Beauty-Ugliness, White-Black') (*Peau noire*: 148; *Black Skin*: 183). Sartre's understanding of anti-Semitism as 'originellement un Manichéisme' ('at bottom a form of Manichaeism') is relevant in this regard (Sartre 1954: 47; 1948: 40). There are a number of notable moments in *Peau noire* when Fanon dramatically brings home the implications of this broader, inclusivist analysis. At his most inclusive, Fanon can argue that 'ce que d'autres ont décrit dans le cas des Juifs s'applique parfaitement au négre') ('what others have described in the case of the Jew applies perfectly in that of the Negro') (*Peau noire*: 148; *Black Skin*: 183). Earlier in the chapter, Fanon is quite explicit about what he calls the 'point commun' ('one point in common') that Jews and Blacks have: 'Tous deux', he says 'nous représentons le Mal' ('both of us stand for Evil') (*Peau noire*: 145; *Black Skin*: 180). Once again, Sartre says much the same thing: 'l'antisémitisme est une conception du monde manichéiste et primitive où la haine du Juif prend place à titre de grand mythe explicatif' ('anti-Semitism is a conception of the Manichaean and primitive world in which hatred for the Jew arises as a great explanatory myth') (Sartre 1954: 179; Sartre 1948: 148). But this facile point of identification is quickly qualified by Fanon as he goes on to state, 'le noir davantage, pour la bonne raison qu'il est noir' ('the black man more so, for the good reason that he is black') (*Peau noire*: 145; *Black Skin*: 180). Fanon has gone back to his memory of the Antilles. As one Antillean said of another, '"son corps est noir, sa langue est noire, son âme aussi doit être noire." Cette logique, le Blanc la réalise quotidiennement' (*Peau noire*: 145).[6]

The overarching logic of racial Manichaeism, which brings together Blacks and Jews, is countered by the stark and ever-present fact of the black body in relation to the white colonialist. Fanon grapples with this tension throughout his work. Not that the Jewish body is entirely absent from *Peau noire*. Towards the beginning of Chapter 6, which is entitled 'Le Nègre et la psycho-pathologie' ('The Negro and psychopathology'), Fanon speaks of the oppression of 'le nègre', who, when he first experiences the look of 'le Blanc', is made to feel what he calls 'le poids de sa mélanine' ('the whole weight of his blackness') (*Peau noire*: 122; *Black Skin*: 150). Immediately after this statement Fanon goes on to refer, in a footnote, to Sartre's *Réflexions sur la question juive*, which cites the example of a young Jewish girl who discovered her Jewishness after being racially abused at the age of fifteen. Sartre draws a more general conclusion from this episode which clearly influenced Fanon:

Plus tardive est la découverte, plus violente est la secousse: tout d'un coup ils s'aperçoivent que les autres savaient sur eux quelque chose qu'ils ignoraient, qu'on leur appliquait ce qualificatif louche et inquiétant ('juif') qui n'est pas employé dans leur famille. (*Peau noire*: 122)[7]

Much of Fanon's response to Sartre takes place in the footnotes to *Peau noire*, which often act as a kind of Möbius strip which enables him to tell the differing stories of colonial racism and anti-Semitism simultaneously. The brutal application of 'ce qualificatif louche et inquiétant' ('this ugly and upsetting term') echoes Fanon's chilling and often cited sense, at the beginning of Chapter 5, of 'une hémorragie qui callait du sang noir sur tout mon corps' ('a hemorrhage that spattered my whole body with black blood') (*Peau noire*: 91; *Black Skin*: 112) as he begins to think of himself for the first time as an 'ugly' object after a child sees him and is immediately frightened by his skin colour. At this point, Fanon has an overriding sense of being '(un) corps au sein d'un monde spatial et temporel' ('a body in the middle of a spatial and temporal world') which in turn 's'installe entre mon corps et le monde une dialectique effective' ('creates a real dialectic between my body and the world' (*Peau noire*: 89; *Black Skin*: 111). However, his 'schéma épidermique racial' ('racial epidermal schema') (*Peau noire*: 90; *Black Skin*: 112) is precisely what makes it impossible for Fanon to identify fully with the abused Jew, who is always 'white', that is disembodied, in his work. But this construction of 'the Jew' as being identified, at one and the same time, with both abused 'Blacks' and 'white' oppressors clearly creates a good deal of anxiety which Fanon must eventually resolve.

On the one hand, much of Fanon's experiential evidence, taken from his psychiatric case studies, explicitly echoes Sartre's *Réflexions sur la question juive*. Fanon's belief that the greatest fear of many of his patients is that they cannot escape being formed by the racial imagination reinforces Sartre's definition of the inauthentic Jew as someone who fears that they will conform to the anti-Semitic image of them. In other words, as Fanon vehemently argues in response to Mannoni's *Psychologie de la colonisation*, 'c'est le raciste qui crée l'infériorisé' ('it is the racist who creates his inferior') (*Peau noire*: 75; *Black Skin*: 93), whoever happens to be the object of his gaze. At this point of absolute identification with 'the Jew', insofar as he or she is created by racial discourse, Fanon most explicitly disrupts any too easy equivalence between black and Jewish victimhood and, most especially, the black and Jewish body. This can be seen with regard to the frequently cited incident on the train when Fanon, immediately after hearing the racist and anti-Semitic diatribe of a drunken passenger, comments as follows: 'Une honte! Le Juif et moi: non content de me racialiser, par un coup heureux du sort, je m'humanisais. Je rejoignais le Juif, frères de malheur' (*Peau noire*: 98).[8]

After Fanon is brought together with 'the Jew', as part of the brotherhood of the racially abused, there is a fateful, if paradoxical, form of humanisation. This can only be because 'the Jew' in these terms is unequivocally 'white'. Such supposed humanisation is opposed to the experience of being 'racialised' which is associated, in Fanon's mind, exclusively with Negrophobia. The main point of difference, that is, between Fanon and Sartre is with regard to the nature of the Jew's body. Sartre argues contentiously that 'nous envisageons ... les caractères somatiques et héréditaires du Juif comme un facteur parmi d'autres de sa situation, non comme une condition déterminante de sa nature' ('we must ... envisage the hereditary and somatic characteristics of the Jew as one factor among others in his situation, not as a condition determining his nature') (Sartre 1954: 77; Sartre 1948: 64). Later on, Sartre contends that 'les seuls caractères ethniques du Juif sont physiques. L'antisémite s'est emparé de ce fait et l'a transformé en mythe' ('the sole ethnic characteristics of the Jews are physical. The anti-Semite has seized upon this fact and has transformed it into a myth') (Sartre 1954: 144; Sartre 1948: 118). Sartre therefore speaks of 'les cheveux noirs et un peu frisés' ('the black and curly hair') and beard of the Jew in several places (Sartre 1954: 74–5; Sartre 1948: 62–3) and it is this aspect of Sartre's work – drawn from wartime anti-Semitic sources – that Fanon rightly rejects (Nochlin and Garb (eds) 1995: 201–18). Rather than the ethnic blackness of the Jew, in Sartre's terms, Fanon argues that:

> Le juif peut être ignoré dans sa juiverie. Il n'est pas intégralement ce qu'il est. On espère, on attend. Ses actes, son comportement

décident en dernier ressort. C'est un Blanc et, hormis quelques traits assez discutables, il lui arrive de passer inaperçu. Il appartient à la race de ceux qui de tout temps ont ignoré l'anthropophagie. Quelle idée aussi de dévorer son père! C'est bien fait, on n'a qu'à ne pas être nègre. (*Peau noire*: 93)[9]

Once again, it is the body, or to be precise the eating of other bodies, that is to the fore, not unlike Jews who, since the medieval period, have been accused of eating Christian bodies. The key point for Fanon, as we will see, is that it is possible for Jews, in their essentialised whiteness, to assimilate or pass unnoticed in European society whereas it is impossible for Blacks, in their essentialised blackness, to do so. Fanon spends much of his book recounting the failed assimilation of other black intellectuals such as the Antillean Jean Veneuse who, in France, is 'incapable de s'intégrer, incapable de passer inaperçu' ('unable to be assimilated, unable to pass unnoticed' (*Peau noire*: 52; *Black Skin*: 65).

Like Fanon, Sartre also places the question of the body at the heart of European racism, but he notes that, given their self-evident ethnicity, some Jews are led to 'nier ce corps qui le trahit' ('deny the body that betrays them') (Sartre 1954: 144; Sartre 1948: 119) and thus seek 'désincarnation' ('disincarnation') (Sartre 1954: 135; Sartre 1948: 111). Here Fanon learned a great deal from Sartre in terms of his representation of the Jew. For Sartre argues that 'le rationalisme auquel le Juif adhère si passionnément, c'est d'abord un exercice d'ascèse et de purification, une évasion dans l'universel' ('the rationalism to which the Jew adheres so passionately is first of all an exercise of asceticism and of purification, an escape into the universal' (Sartre 1954: 136; Sartre 1948: 112). In other words, '(s)i la Raison existe, il n'y a point une vérité française et une vérité allemande; il n'y a pas une vérité nègre ou juive. Il n'y a qu'une vérité' ('if reason exists, then there is no French truth or German truth; there is no Negro truth or Jewish truth. There is only one Truth') (Sartre 1954: 135; Sartre 1948: 111). In a passage which Fanon cites at length, Sartre calls this assimilatory logic 'une sorte d'impérialisme passionné de la raison' ('a sort of impassioned imperialism of reason'):

> Car [le Juif] ne veut pas seulement convaincre qu'il est dans le vrai, son but est de persuader à ses interlocuteurs qu'il y a une valeur absolue et inconditionnée du rationalisme. Il se considère comme un missionnaire de l'universel; en face de l'universalité de la religion catholique, dont il est exclu, il veut établir la 'catholicité' du rationnel, instrument pour atteindre le vrai et lien spirituel entre les hommes. (Sartre 1954: 137, cited in *Peau noire*: 95)[10]

There is a telling slippage throughout *Réflexions sur la question juive* as Sartre argues that the characterisation of 'the Jew' as 'un pur raisonneur' ('a pure reasoner') is both an aspect of French anti-Semitism – where 'les termes d'abstrait, de rationaliste et d'intellectuel prennent un sens péjoratif' ('the terms *abstract, rationalist, intellectual* here take on a pejorative sense') (Sartre 1954: 133; Sartre 1948: 109) – and also applies to real Jews: 'il réalise sur un plan (intellectuel) supérieur cet accord et cette assimilation qu'on lui refuse sur le plan social'; 'il a le goût de l'intelligence pure'; 'ce que le Juif veut détruire est strictement localisé' (Sartre 1954: 136–8).[11] Sartre's overdetermined characterisation of the disembodied Jewish mind, eliding discourse and reality, is repeated by Fanon. In fact, Fanon utilises this model of Jewish universalism to see the extent to which it can be applied to his own situation as a 'Negro' in metropolitan France. Soon after quoting Sartre, he attempts to 'rationaliser le monde, montrer au Blanc qu'il était dans l'erreur' ('rationalize the world and to show the white man that he was mistaken') and to this end 'je me mis à inventorier, à sonder l'entourage' ('I set to cataloguing and probing my surroundings') (*Peau noire*: 95–6; *Black Skin*: 118–19). But he is quickly disillusioned and has to change his tune (*Peau noire*: 96; *Black Skin*: 119). After this, Fanon encounters the drunkard on the train whose irrational prejudices taught him the following: 'puisque, sur le plan de la raison, l'accord n'était pas possible, je me rejetais vers l'irrationalité' ('since no agreement was possible on the level of reason, I threw myself back toward unreason') (*Peau noire*: 99; *Black Skin*: 123).

The shift from reason to unreason and back again is figured crucially in relation to the Jewish mind and the black body. Jewish universalism, the absolute promise of liberal assimilation, results in the denial of what is local and particular: 'à mon irrationnel, on opposait le rationnel. A mon rationnel, le "véritable rationnel". A tous les coups, je jouais perdant [...] Je voulais être typiquement nègre, – ce n'était plus possible. Je voulais être blanc, – il valait mieux en rire. Et quand j'essayais ... de revendiquer ma négritude, on me l'arrachait' (*Peau noire*: 107).[12] Fanon's ambivalent positioning, somewhere between Sartre's 'white' dialectical reasoning and the unreason of Negritude, leads in Chapter 6 to a contagion of rigid antitheses with regard to Jews and Blacks: 'Pour le Juif, on pense à l'argent et à ses dérivés. Pour le nègre, au sexe. L'antisémitisme est susceptible de rationalisation sur le plan foncier. C'est parce que les Juifs s'annexent le pays qu'ils sont dangereux' (*Peau noire*: 130).[13] Or, again:

> Il ne viendrait ... à l'idée d'aucun anti-Sémite de castrer le Juif. On le tue ou on le stérilise. Le nègre, lui, est castré [...] On aperçoit la différence entre les deux attitudes. [...] (C)haque fois qu'un Juif est persécuté, c'est toute la race qu'on persécute à travers lui. Mais c'est dans sa corporéité que l'on atteint le nègre. C'est en tant que personnalité concrète qu'on le lynche. C'est en tant qu'être actuel qu'il est dangereux. Le péril juif est remplacé par la peur de la puissance sexuelle du nègre. (*Peau noire*: 132–3)[14]

Given the stark differences between anti-Semitism and Negrophobia, it is difficult at times for Fanon to account adequately for the depth of European violence against Jews:

> Bien entendu, les Juifs sont brimés, que dis-je, ils sont pourchassés, exterminés, enfournés, mais ce sont les petites histoires familiales. Le Juif n'est pas aimé à partir du moment où il est dépisté. Mais avec moi tout prend un visage *nouveau*. Aucune chance ne m'est permise. Je suis sur-déterminé de l'extérieur. Je ne suis pas l'esclave de "l'idée" que les autres ont de moi, mais de mon apparaître. (*Peau noire*: 93)[15]

The particularising logic of Fanon's essentialising oppositions – that Jews are overdetermined from the inside and Blacks from the outside – means that he is able, eventually, to reduce anti-Jewish and anti-Black racism to the following formula: 'Le nègre représente le danger biologique. Le Juif, le danger intellectuel' ('The Negro symbolizes the biological danger; the Jew, the intellectual danger') (*Peau noire*: 134; *Black Skin*: 165). These epigrammatic formulae, dotted throughout the book, clearly show the absence of a more universalising vocabulary that, as Edward Said puts it in *Representations of the Intellectual*, can give 'greater human scope to what a particular race or nation suffered' (Said 1994: 33). But Fanon is here following Sartre, who regards an assimilatory universalism as essentially inauthentic as it denies the reality of ethnicity – that there is such a person as a Jew or Negro – and therefore concludes that 'l'éveil à la raison est ... la mort au corps, aux particularités du caractère' ('the awakening to reason is ... death of the body, to particularities of character') (Sartre 1954: 135; Sartre 1948: 111). It is in these terms that the oppositions between reason and the body, inner and outer, Jew and Black, help resolve the irresolvable contradiction (in Said's statement) that European humanism is both complicit with and yet transcends racial violence.

Once 'the Jew' is thought of as being determined by his 'comportement' ('behaviour') (*Peau noire*: 93; *Black Skin*: 115) and Blacks by their 'corporéité ('corporeality') (*Peau noire*: 133; *Black Skin*: 163), then the discursive dimension of racial discourse is lost. When Fanon states that '(l)'antisémitisme est susceptible de rationalisation sur le plan foncier. C'est parce que les Juifs s'annexent le pays qu'ils sont dangereux' ('anti-Semitism can be rationalized on a basic level. It is because he takes over the country that the Jew is a danger') (*Peau noire*: 130; *Black Skin*: 160), he is referring worryingly, not unlike Sartre, *both* to the supposed actions of Jews and to the 'idea' of Jewish behaviour. At the same time, the first chapter of *Réflexions sur la question juive*, which Fanon read in *Les Temps modernes*, stresses that it is '*l'idée* qu'on se fait du Juif qui semble déterminer l'histoire, non la "donnée historique" qui fait naître l'idée' ('the *idea* of the Jew that one forms for himself which would seem to determine history, not the "historical fact" that produces the idea' (Sartre 1954: 18; Sartre 1948: 16). It is for this reason that Sartre argues that 'les caractères somatiques et héréditaires du Juif' are not 'une condition déterminante de sa nature' ('the hereditary and somatic characteristics of the Jew' are not 'a condition determining his nature') (Sartre 1954: 77; Sartre 1948: 64). For much of his work, Fanon also emphasises the determining impact of ideas and images on minority consciousness: 'Mais quand nous disons que la culture européenne possède une *imago* du nègre responsable de tous les conflits qui peuvent naître, nous ne dépassons pas le réel' ('But when we assert that European culture has an *imago* of the Negro which is responsible for all the conflicts that may arise, we do not go beyond reality') (*Peau noire*: 136–7; *Black Skin*: 169). An essentialist and an anti-essentialist Fanon come into conflict when he argues in a footnote that 'aux Antilles la perception se situe toujours sur le plan de l'imaginaire' ('in the Antilles perception always occurs on the level of the imaginary') (*Peau noire*: 132; *Black Skin*: 163 n. 25) and, on the same page, distinguishes absolutely between Negrophobia and anti-Semitism.

On several occasions, Fanon pulls himself up short so as not to identify too closely with 'the Jew'. After understanding black identity in diasporic as opposed to nationalistic terms – '[l]a vérité est que la race nègre est dispersé, qu'elle ne possède plus d'unité' ('[t]he truth is that the Negro race has been scattered, that it can no longer claim unity') (*Peau noire*: 139–40; *Black Skin*: 173) – he states tentatively that '[p]ar là il rejoint en quelque sorte le Juif' ('[t]his in a way places [the Negro] beside the Jew') (*Peau noire*: 140; *Black Skin*: 173). But, immediately after making this statement, he notes categorically that '[c]ontre les obstacles allégués ci-dessus, nous ferons appel à une evidence: *où qu'il aille, un nègre demeure un nègre*' ('[a]gainst all the arguments I have just cited, I come back to one fact: *Wherever he goes, the Negro remains a Negro*') (*Peau noire*: 140; *Black Skin*: 173; Fanon's emphasis). This constant play of identity/differentiation with 'the Jew' relates especially to the issue of universalising out black particularity with 'the Jew', in his disembodied rationality, on the side of universality. Fanon is aware that Sartre makes no distinction between Blacks and Jews: 'Sartre disait: ici c'est le Juif, ailleurs c'est le nègre. Ce qu'il faut, c'est un bouc émissaire' ('Sartre said: Here it is the Jew, somewhere else it is the Negro. What is essential is a scapegoat') (*Peau noire*: 148; *Black Skin*: 183). By creating a third category, that of 'scapegoat', to encompass both Blacks and Jews Sartre is engaging in a form of dialectical reasoning which destroys 'l'enthousiasme noir' ('black zeal') (*Peau noire*: 109; *Black Skin*: 135). According to Fanon, 'assimiler l'antisémitisme à la négrophobie' ('assimilating anti-Semitism to Negrophobia') is one of those 'erreurs d'analyse' ('errors of analysis') (*Peau noire*: 148; *Black Skin*: 183) precisely because it universalises difference and places it in a synthetic Eurocentric framework.

After Fanon rejects Sartre's dialectics he argues, significantly, that 'la conscience noire est immanente à elle-même. Je ne suis pas une potentialité de quelque chose, je suis pleinement ce que je suis. Je n'ai pas à rechercher l'universel' (*Peau noire*: 109).[16] Later on, he speaks about being drowned in the universal (*Peau noire*: 151; *Black Skin*: 186) and of valuing his own subjectivity in relation to 'l'inconscient collectif de cette Europe' ('the collective unconscious of that Europe') in which, as he emphasises, '*le Mal est représenté par le Noir*' ('*the black man is the symbol of Evil*') (*Peau noire*: 152; *Black Skin*: 188). It is precisely because the question of a specifically black unconscious is at the heart of Fanon's thinking that the figure of the Jewish psychologist, the embodiment of the Jewish mind, has an overdetermined role in *Peau noire*. As Fanon reminds us, 'ni Freud, ni Adler … n'ont pensé aux Noirs, dans le cours de leurs recherches' ('neither Freud nor Adler … thought of the Negro in all their investigations') (*Peau noire*: 123; tr. mod.: 151). These Jewish psychologists are therefore unqualified to restore a healthy black subjectivity. Because 'un nègre à tout instant combat son image' ('a Negro is forever in combat with his own image') (*Peau noire*: 156; *Black Skin*: 194), this restorative work is particularly crucial to Fanon, who practised as a psychologist so as to help combat such deeply ingrained and damaging self-representations. Jewish psychologists, on the other hand, are dismissed with increased anger as being wholly unworthy of combating Negrophobia. Take Michel Salomon, for example:

> Quoiqu'il s'en défende, il pue le raciste. Il est Juif, il a une 'expérience millénaire de l'antisémitisme', et pourtant il est raciste. Ecoutez-le: 'Mais nier que, du fait de sa peau et de sa chevelure, de cette aura de sensualité qu'il (le nègre) dégage, il n'y a pas, spontanément, une certaine gêne, attractive ou répulsive, c'est se refuser à l'évidence au nom d'une pruderie absurde qui n'a jamais rien résolu …' Plus loin, il va jusqu'à nous parler de la 'prodigieuse vitalité du Noir'. (*Peau noire*: 162–3)[17]

To this extent, Fanon in part defines a specifically black psychoanalysis by opposing a 'racist' Jewish practitioner who essentialises the black body. In the case of the Eurocentric Alfred Adler, Fanon explicitly devises a strategy to 'nous dégager de la ventouse adlérienne' ('shak[e] off the Adlerian leech') (*Peau noire*: 174; *Black Skin*: 215) from his thoughts. By assimilating 'the Negro' into an empty universalism at the deepest level, Jewish psychologists are said to 'leech' on their black counterparts. This can be seen specifically with regard to Fanon's vituperative response to the Hollywood film *Home of the Brave* (1949), which positions the Jewish psychiatrist next to the traumatised black soldier.

As both Michael Rogin and David Marriott have argued, *Home of the Brave* confirmed Fanon's distrust of the ways in which mainstream psychoanalysis has been applied to Blacks (*Peau noire*: 123; *Black Skin*: 151) and is also a significant moment of the history of Black–Jewish relations in the United States. The film was based on a Broadway play by Arthur Laurents which originally had a Jewish soldier, Peter Coen, as the protagonist. The film's producer and writer, Stanley Kramer and Carl Foreman, however, decided to 'black up' Coen after the release of *Crossfire* (1947) and *Gentleman's Agreement* (1947), both of which exposed American anti-Semitism, as it would be better 'box office … to shift from Jews to blacks' (Rogin 1996: 228). Peter Coen, therefore, was transformed into Peter Moss, a young black GI who in a series of flashbacks describes to a sympathetic doctor his emotional breakdown during the war. Although this could not in fact have happened in the segregated 'Jim Crow American army of World War Two' (Rogin 1996: 231–2), Moss has suffered 'partial amnesia and a hysterical paralysis after his best friend, white, is killed' (Marriott 2000: 75). As Rogin has shown, the film not only 'Blacks up' Peter Moss but turns his psychiatrist into a Jew by giving him a 'Jewish nose', photographing him so as to emphasise his 'facial look' and having him allude to his own experience of anti-Semitism (Rogin 1996: 231–3). The unnamed psychiatrist's 'cathartic cure' (Marriott 2000: 72) takes the form of subjecting Moss to the wartime racism which has traumatised him so that he can finally overcome it.

Fanon objected principally to the ending of the film, which concluded on a note of absolute recognition between Black and White. Moss leaves the military hospital fully cured. An easygoing white soldier called Mingo, whom Moss knew during the war, approaches him and asks him to become a partner in a bar and restaurant which he wants to open. Mingo has lost an arm and a wife, and in the final scenes of the film asks Moss to 'take my coward's hand' in a 'powerful gesture of solidarity' (Marriott 2000: 76). Moss takes his hand, accepts his offer, and mouths the assimilatory liberalism of Kramer and Foreman: 'I am different,' he says. 'We all are. But underneath we're the same' (Bogle 1989: 145). As Fanon comments: 'L'estropié de la guerre du Pacifique dit à mon frère: "Accommode-toi de ta couleur comme moi de mon moignon; nous sommes tous deux des accidentés"' ('The crippled veteran of the Pacific war says to my brother, "Resign yourself to your color the way I got used to my stump; we're both victims"') (*Peau noire*: 113; *Black Skin*: 140). It is this easy universalisation of victimhood which makes Fanon weep (*Peau noire*: 114; *Black Skin*: 140) and relates back to his earlier rejection of Blacks and Jews as undifferentiated scapegoats (*Peau noire*: 148; *Black Skin*: 183).

In the end, *Home of the Brave* undermines itself, as transcendence of the difference between Black and disabled, Black and White, Black and Jew is only possible by 'the Negro' acting out his deep-seated racial inferiority. It is significant that such contradictions are figured in terms of the black-Jewish imaginary: 'Assimilated to the Jew at the high level of the mind, Moss is made emotion-ridden and female at the level of the body' (Rogin 1996: 235). To adapt to the values of Jewish liberals such as Kramer and Foreman, and his unnamed doctor, Moss must parade his abject blackness in the name of a 'shared humanity'. The play of sameness and difference conforms to how his Jewish analyst sees him, which is, essentially, as a crippled victim. *Home of the Brave*, the first of the post-war Hollywood 'problem pictures' (Bogle 1989: 144), dissolves 'black rage' (Rogin 1996: 238) and represents the black psyche as nothing more or less than an extension of the white imago. But, as the popular movie *Independence Day* (1996) demonstrates, the coming together of the black body and the Jewish mind is an essential Hollywood myth in the self-definition of American white liberalism (Rogin 1998: 2).

At one point in *Peau noire*, Fanon speaks of 'the Negro' as 'un objet phobogène, anxiogène' ('a phobogenic object, a stimulus to anxiety') (*Peau noire*: 123; *Black Skin*: 151). This is an identical formulation to Zygmunt Bauman's concept of 'proteophobia', which he defines as the apprehension or anxiety caused by those who do not fall easily into any established categories (Bauman 1998: 144). Bauman is referring to racial discourses concerning Jews but, as Fanon shows, he could just as easily have been referring to Blacks. In *The Black Atlantic: Modernity and Double Consciousness* (1993), Paul Gilroy challenges Bauman's Judeo-centric and Eurocentric construction of racial ambivalence and includes the history of slavery and anti-Black racism within Bauman's conceptual framework (Gilroy 1993: 213–14). In this way, Gilroy shows that Bauman's location of modernity, as the site *par excellence* which produced racial ambivalence, can be read back into the work of Fanon. After all, Fanon argued that 'toute ontologie est rendue irréalisable dans une société colonisée et civilisée' ('every ontology is made unattainable in a colonized and civilized society') (*Peau noire*: 88; *Black Skin*: 109) due to the 'impureté' ('impurity') of the colonised people which 'interdit toute explication ontologique' ('outlaws any ontological explanation') (*Peau noire*: 88; *Black Skin*: 110). Bauman maintains similarly that the impure ambivalence of 'the Jew' disrupts the ordering, classifying nature of modernity which was signified, above all, by the rise of the nation-state.

In the end, Fanon's distrust of a facile liberal assimilationism, whether in France or the United States, meant that he was to qualify his critique of a modernising colonialism in relation to other histories, including the history of European fascism. Because anti-Black racism is understood simultaneously as a function both of European 'civilising' discourse and of individual psychopathology, it was not always possible for him to go beyond his immediate case studies. For this reason, 'the Jew' and 'the Negro' were brought together in relation to the oppressive potentiality of European humanism, but were irrevocably separated in relation to Fanon's particularising theories of racial pathology and colonial resistance. As the appropriating ending of *Home of the Brave* illustrated, Fanon feared for good reason the too easy universalisation of the victims of modernity. For this reason,

Fanon for the most part chose to oppose the Jewish mind and the black body rather than to bring them together in the name of liberal assimilationism. To this extent, he rejected the Sartrean formulation which rewrites American or democratic liberalism in the name of ethnic particularity:

> Ce que nous proposons ici est un libéralisme concret [...] Cela signifie donc que les Juifs, comme aussi bien les Arabes ou les Noirs, dès lors qu'ils sont solidaires de l'entreprise nationale, ont droit de regard sur cette entreprise; ils sont citoyens. Mais ils ont ces droits à titre de Juifs, de Noirs, ou d'Arabes, c'est-à-dire comme personnes concrètes. (Sartre 1954: 177; Sartre's emphasis)[18]

Perhaps it was the spectre of American liberalism, but Fanon in the end refused all such universalising gestures in Sartre's *Réflexions sur la question juive* and chose instead to concretise only one victim of European modernity: 'chaque fois qu'un Juif est persécuté, c'est toute la race qu'on persécute à travers lui. Mais c'est dans sa corporéité que l'on atteint le nègre. C'est en tant que personnalité concrète qu'on le lynche. C'est en tant qu'être actuel qu'il est dangereux' (*Peau noire*: 133).[19]

Notes

1   I am most grateful to Max Silverman for his help and advice on this essay.

2   'When I turn on my radio, when I hear that Negroes have been lynched in America, I say that we have been lied to: Hitler is not dead; when I turn on my radio, when I learn that Jews have been insulted, mistreated, persecuted, I say that we have been lied to: Hitler is not dead; when, finally, I turn on my radio and hear that in Africa forced labour has been inaugurated and legalized, I say that we have certainly been lied to: Hitler is not dead' (*Black Skin*: 90).

3   'Colonial racism is no different from any other racism. Anti-Semitism hits me head on: I am enraged, I am bled white by an appalling battle, I am deprived of the possibility of being a man. I cannot disassociate myself from the future that is proposed for my brother. Every one of my acts commits me as a man. Every one of my silences, every one of my cowardices reveals me as a man' (*Black Skin*: 88–9).

4   David Macey translates the title of Chapter 5 as 'The lived experience of the black man' (Macey 2000: 26).

5   'At first thought it may seem strange that the anti-Semite's outlook should be related to that of the Negrophobe. It was my philosophy professor, a native of the Antilles, who recalled the fact to me one day: "Whenever you

hear anyone abuse the Jews, pay attention, because he is talking about you." And I found that he was universally right – by which I meant that I was answerable in my body and in my heart for what was done to my brother. Later I realized that he meant, quite simply, an anti-Semite is inevitably anti-Negro' (*Black Skin*: 122).

6 '"His body is black, his language is black, his soul must be black too". This logic is put into daily practice by the white man' (*Black Skin*: 180).

7 '"The later the discovery, the more violent the shock. Suddenly they perceive that others know something about them that they do not know, that people apply to them an ugly and upsetting term ['Jew'] that is not used in their own families"' (*Black Skin*: 150).

8 'An outrage! The Jew and I: Since I was not satisfied to be racialized, by a lucky turn of fate I was humanized. I joined the Jew, my brother in misery' (*Black Skin*: 122).

9 'The Jew can be unknown in his Jewishness. He is not wholly what he is. One hopes, one waits. His actions, his behavior are the final determinant. He is a white man, and apart from some rather debatable characteristics, he can sometimes go unnoticed. He belongs to the race of those who since the beginning of time have never known cannibalism. What an idea, to eat one's father! Simple enough, one has only not to be a nigger' (*Black Skin*: 115).

10 'For ['the Jew'] wishes not only to convince others that he is right; his goal is to persuade them that there is an absolute and unconditional value to rationalism. He feels himself to be a missionary of the universal; against the universalism of the Catholic religion, from which he is excluded, he asserts the "catholicity" of the rational, an instrument by which to attain to the truth and establish a spiritual bond among men' (Sartre 1948: 112–13, cited in *Black Skin*: 118–19).

11 'On a superior (intellectual) level he realizes that accord and assimilation which is denied him on a social level'; 'he has a taste for pure intelligence'; 'what the Jew wishes to destroy is strictly localized' (Sartre 1948: 112–14).

12 'My unreason was countered with reason, my reason with "real reason". Every hand was a losing hand [...] I wanted to be typically Negro – it was no longer possible. I wanted to be white – that was a joke. And, when I tried ... to reclaim my Negritude, it was snatched away from me' (*Black Skin*: 132).

13 'In the case of the Jew, one thinks of money and its cognates. In that of the Negro, one thinks of sex. Anti-Semitism can be rationalized on a basic level. It is because he takes over the country that the Jew is a danger' (*Black Skin*: 160).

14 'No anti-Semite ... would ever conceive of the idea of castrating the Jew. He is killed or sterilized. But the Negro is castrated [...] The difference between the two attitudes is apparent. [...] [E]very time that a Jew is persecuted, it is the whole race that is persecuted in his person. But it is in his corporeality that the Negro is attacked. It is as a concrete personality

that he is lynched. It is as an actual being that he is a threat. The Jewish menace is replaced by the fear of the sexual potency of the Negro' (*Black Skin*: 162–4).

15   'Granted, the Jews are harassed – what am I thinking of? They are hunted down, exterminated, cremated. But these are little family quarrels. The Jew is disliked from the moment he is tracked down. But in my case everything takes on a *new* guise. I am given no chance. I am over-determined from without. I am the slave not of the "idea" that others have of me but of my own appearance' (*Black Skin*: 115–16).

16   '[B]lack consciousness is immanent in its own eyes. I am not a potentiality of something, I am wholly what I am. I do not have to look for the universal' (*Black Skin*: 135).

17   'Although he defends himself against the charge, he stinks of racism. He is a Jew, he has a "millennial experience of anti-Semitism," and yet he is a racist. Listen to him: "But to say that the mere fact of his skin, of his hair, of that aura of sensuality that he [the Negro] gives off, does not spontaneously give rise to a certain embarrassment, whether of attraction or of revulsion, is to reject the facts in the name of a ridiculous prudery that has never solved anything ..." Later he goes to the extreme of telling us about the "prodigious vitality of the black man"' (*Black Skin*: 201).

18   'What we propose here is a concrete liberalism [...] This means, then, that the Jews – and likewise the Arabs and Negroes – from the moment that they are participants in the national enterprise, have a right in that enterprise; they are citizens. But they have these rights *as* Jews, Negroes, or Arabs – that is, as concrete persons' (Sartre 1948: 146; Sartre's emphasis).

19   'every time that a Jew is persecuted, it is the whole race that is persecuted in his person. But it is in his corporeality that the Negro is attacked. It is as a concrete personality that he is lynched. It is as an actual being that he is a threat' (*Black Skin*: 163).

References

Bauman, Z. (1998) 'Allosemitism: premodern, modern, postmodern' in B. Cheyette and L. Marcus (eds), *Modernity, Culture and 'the Jew'*, Cambridge: Polity Press, 143–56

Bogle, D. (1989) *Toms, Coons, Mulattoes, Mammies and Bucks: An Interpretive History of Blacks in American Films*, New York: Continuum Books, 2nd edn

Fanon, F. (1961) *Les Damnés de la terre* (*The Wretched of the Earth*, trans. C. Farrington, Harmondsworth: Penguin)

—— (2001) *L'An V de la révolution algérienne*, Paris: La Découverte (first pub. 1959; *A Dying Colonialism*, trans. H. Chevalier, London: Earthscan Publications, 1989)

Gilroy, P. (1993) *The Black Atlantic: Modernity and Double Consciousness*, London: Verso

—— (2000) *Between Camps: Nations, Cultures and the Allure of Race* Harmondsworth: Penguin

McCulloch, J. (1983) *Black Soul, White Artifact: Fanon's Clinical Psychology and Social Theory*, Cambridge: Cambridge University Press

Macey, D. (2000) *Frantz Fanon: A Life*, London: Granta

Mannoni, O. (1950) *Psychologie de la colonisation*, Paris: Seuil (*Prospero and Caliban: the Psychology of Colonisation*, trans. P. Powesland, London: Methuen, 1956)

Marriott, D. (2000) *On Black Men*, Edinburgh: Edinburgh University Press

Nochlin, L. and Garb, T. (eds) (1995) *The Jew in the Text: Modernity and the Construction of Identity*, London: Thames and Hudson

Parry, B. (1994) 'Resistance theory/theorising resistance, or two cheers for nativism', in F. Barker, P. Hulme and M. Iverson (eds), *Colonial Discourse, Postcolonial Theory*, Manchester: Manchester University Press

Rogin, M. (1996) *Blackface, White Noise: Jewish Immigrants in the Hollywood Melting Pot*, Berkeley: University of California Press

—— (1998) *Independence Day*, London: BFI Publishing

Rose, G. (1993) *Judaism & Modernity: Philosophical Essays*, Oxford: Blackwell

Said, E. (1994) *Representations of the Intellectual*, London: Chatto and Windus

Sartre, J.-P. (1954) *Réflexions sur la question juive*, Paris: Gallimard (first pub. 1946; *Anti-Semite and Jew*, trans. G. J. Becker, New York: Schocken Books, 1948)

Young, R. J. C. (1990) *White Mythologies: Writing History and the West*, London and New York: Routledge

—— (2001) *Postcolonialism: An Historical Introduction*, Oxford: Blackwell

5

The European knows and does not know: Fanon's response to Sartre

ROBERT BERNASCONI

Jean-Paul Sartre's 'Orphée noir', his introduction to Leopold Sédar Senghor's *Anthologie de la nouvelle poésie nègre et malgache de langue française*, explicitly raises the question of how Whites should respond to the poems included there (Sartre 1948: ix; Sartre 2001: 115). He concedes that a white man can hardly speak suitably of Negritude (Sartre 1948: xxix; Sartre 2001: 129), and yet he offers to explain to Whites what Blacks already know: why Blacks attain self-consciousness through poetry and why at this juncture black poetry is the only great revolutionary poetry (Sartre 1948: xi–xii; Sartre 2001: 117). In *Peau noire* Fanon contests the appropriateness of certain aspects of Sartre's essay. It seemed to Fanon that Sartre, in ways I shall explain, had said more than it was legitimate for him as a white man to say. But this leaves the question of how white readers should approach *Peau noire*. To address this question, I take Fanon's response to Sartre as my guide.

Peau noire is difficult for Whites to read because of the intensity with which Fanon describes his personal experience of racism. His phenomenological description of the lived experience of the Black in Chapter 5 presents an extraordinary challenge to his white readers at many levels, but not least because it obliges white readers, like myself, to consider what we prefer to ignore and what we too easily dismiss as beyond our understanding: the impact of racism, both personal and structural, on Blacks. But

how much *can* Whites understand? Fanon sought to address the
misery of Blacks and in this context insisted that a subjective
experience can be understood by others (*Peau noire*: 69; *Black
Skin*: 86). He wrote this in part in response to the restrictions that
some members of the Negritude movement placed on the ability
of Whites to understand the cosmic message of Negritude, a
position he paraphrases as follows: 'Seul le nègre est capable de le
transmettre, d'en déchiffrer le sens, la portée' ('Only the Negro
has the capacity to convey it, to decipher its meaning, its scope')
(*Peau noire*: 100; tr. mod.: 124). However, elsewhere in *Peau noire*
Fanon underwrites the view that Whites cannot understand
Louis Armstrong (*Peau noire*: 36; *Black Skin*: 45). I shall argue in
this paper that Fanon's considered opinion, which today might
be understood as a version of standpoint theory or the epistem-
ology of provenance, but which was in its own time developed
by him in terms of existential phenomenology, is that 'l'Européen
sait et ne sait pas' ('The European knows and he does not know')
(*Peau noire*: 161; *Black Skin*: 199).

The original title of *Peau noire, Essai sur la désaliénation du
Noir* (Cheriki 2000: 42),[1] together with an enigmatic reference in
the Introduction to those people to whom the book is directed
(*Peau noire*: 5; *Black Skin*: 7), raises a question about the place of
the book's white readers: is it a book about Blacks for Blacks?
That question is given its clearest answer in the Introduction,
where Fanon announces that he wants to persuade his brother,
whether black or white, 'à secouer le plus énergiquement la
lamentable livrée édifée par des siècles d'incompréhension') ('to
shake off most energetically, the lamentable livery set up by
centuries of incomprehension') (*Peau noire*: 10; tr. mod.: 14). The
passage allows for white readers and, indeed, seems to be
directed to the dissolution of racial identities. But throughout the
book Fanon addresses Blacks and Whites very differently. He
writes: 'J'ai constamment essayé de révéler au Noir, qu'en un
sens il s'anormalise; au Blanc, qu'il est à la fois mystificateur et
mystifié' ('I have constantly tried to show the Black that he is in a
sense abnormalised; I have tried to show the White that he is at
the same time a mystifactor and mystified') (*Peau noire*: 182; tr.
mod.: 225). Although *Peau noire* has attracted a growing number
of white commentators eager to use it as a basis for discussions of

blackness, it has not, so far as I am aware, played a prominent role in discussions of whiteness. Here I will be concerned specifically with white *men* reading and writing about Fanon. I believe there is clear evidence that Fanon anticipated the importance of the question of whether the reader was white or black and wrote accordingly. However, it seems that in spite of his frequent references to the man or woman of colour, he did not always think as deeply about the response of a reader who was neither white nor black. He was perhaps even less concerned with the sensitivities of women readers, as the secondary literature on the second and third chapter confirm.

One passage from Chapter 6 gives a clear indication of what Fanon thought of Whites obsessed with black themes, that is to say, the kind of white person who would choose to read his book carefully. The context is the question of whether or not Whites and Blacks can behave healthily toward one another, a question imposed on him by virtue of his claim that European culture has an *imago* of the Negro that is responsible for all the conflicts that may arise (*Peau noire*: 136–7; *Black Skin*: 169). Fanon believed that just as Blacks often identify with Whites, Whites sometimes identify with Blacks (see for example *Peau noire*: 140; *Black Skin*: 173–4). He cites as evidence Whites who play in 'hot orchestras', who sing the blues and spirituals, and who write novels in which the black men talk of their suffering, and even Whites who paint themselves black (*Peau noire*: 143n; *Black Skin*: 177n). Citing Bernard Wolfe's essay on the myth of Uncle Remus, Fanon focuses on the claim that it is unconscious masochism that leads Whites to read books where black men make love to white women, where Whites discover that they are in fact black, and where Whites are strangled by Blacks (Wolfe 1949: 898). Fanon explains that behind this masochism is the acknowledgement by Whites that, if they were black, they would not show any pity to their oppressors (*Peau noire*: 143n; *Black Skin*: 177n). That is to say, Whites believe that, if they were in the place that Blacks are, they would respond differently.

The question then becomes the following: did Fanon see another possibility for Whites? On Fanon's analysis, alongside economic factors, the myth of the Negro as entertained by Whites plays a major role in causing Black alienation (*Peau noire*: 165;

Black Skin: 204). It seems, therefore, that the project of the disalienation of the Black depends in part on Whites abandoning their unconscious image of Blacks. But how might that happen? Only in the Conclusion does Fanon even hint at the possibility of Whites being freed from their complexes. He writes that all those who refuse to let themselves be enclosed in the substantialised tower of the past will be disalienated, whether they are black or white (*Peau noire*: 183; *Black Skin*: 226). But he immediately adds that disalienation can come to Blacks in other ways, if they refuse to regard actuality as they find it as definitive. In other words, Fanon proclaims that there are many ways for Blacks to be disalienated, but only one way for Whites. Furthermore, there is no indication of how Whites might take the one path open to them, whereas the various obstacles facing Blacks are repeatedly discussed. White readers of *Peau noire* are therefore in an uncomfortable and uncertain position. If Fanon is right about white masochism, they are probably enjoying this discomfort, wallowing in white guilt. But that cannot be the end of the matter. When in Chapter 4 Fanon makes a sustained effort to alter the racial distribution of guilt so that it no longer sits on black shoulders but is transferred to Whites where it belongs, he is not proposing white guilt as a solution (*Peau noire*: 185; *Black Skin*: 228). Fanon's white patient who is discussed at some length at the end of Chapter 6 is left unable to resume social life (*Peau noire*: 169; *Black Skin*: 209).

Fanon not only advocates a restructuring of the world (*Peau noire*: 66; *Black Skin*: 82); he recognises that Whites cannot be left behind. A unilateral solution would be incomplete (*Peau noire*: 9; *Black Skin*: 11). In the remainder of this paper I want to explore Fanon's response to Sartre in order to highlight what it shows about the role Fanon was willing to give to this 'ami des peuples de couleur' ('friend of the colored peoples') (*Peau noire*: 108; *Black Skin*: 133).[2] Fanon does not object to Sartre speaking on the subject of racism: not only does he find certain pages of *Réflexions sur la question juive* (*Anti-Semite and Jew*) among the most powerful he has ever read (*Peau noire*: 146; *Black Skin*: 181), he also asked Sartre to write the Preface to *Les Damnés de la terre* (*The Wretched of the Earth*). But I will show that he insists that Sartre should acknowledge his limitations as a white man.

When Sartre, at the beginning of 'Orphée noir', raises the question of the response of Whites reading books by Blacks, he says to his white readers 'je vous souhaite de ressentir comme moi le saisissement d'être vus' ('I hope that you – like me – will feel the shock of being seen') (Sartre 1948: Sartre 2001: 115). In other words, the structure of the gaze is reversed by the poets anthologised by Senghor. Blacks are no longer merely the object of the white gaze. But even though Fanon constantly reaffirms black agency, Chapter 5 offers a powerful confirmation of Sartre's original account of the white gaze. Fanon came into the world wanting to be a subject but discovers himself locked up in an 'objectivité écrasante' ('crushing objecthood') (*Peau noire*: 88; *Black Skin*: 189). Even after an extensive dose of the Negritude poets, this problem is not resolved by the end of the chapter and he is left feeling guilty, although he does not know for what (*Peau noire*: 112; *Black Skin*: 139).

Previous commentators have tended to focus on Fanon's complaint that Sartre destroyed black enthusiasm by locating the Negritude movement within the dialectic in which the Black – and the Black alone – was asked to renounce his or her race: 'Jean-Paul Sartre, dans cette étude, a détruit l'enthousiasme noir. Contre le devenir historique, il y avait à opposer l'imprévisibilité. J'avais besoin de me perdre dans la négritude absolument' (*Peau noire*: 109).[3] However, in the Introduction to *Peau noire*, Fanon celebrates at some length – and in no way mourns – this loss of enthusiasm: '(l)'enthousiasme est par excellence l'arme des impuissants' ('enthusiasm is par excellence the weapon of the powerless') (*Peau noire*: 7; tr. mod.: 9). He explains that he no longer trusts enthusiasm because wherever it is released it brings fire, famine, misery and contempt for man in its wake. That Fanon's objection to Sartre is rather more complicated than it at first appears is confirmed when he explains that the problem is not that Sartre was wrong, but rather that he, Fanon, does not need to be told this: 'En tout cas *j'avais besoin* d'ignorer' ('In any case I *needed* to be oblivious') (*Peau noire*: 109; tr. mod.: 135). What Fanon needed to be oblivious of are the essences and determinations of the being of consciousness: 'La conscience engagée dans l'expérience ignore, doit ignorer les essences et les déterminations de son être' ('Consciousness, when committed to experience, is oblivious and must be oblivious of the essences and determination of its being') (*Peau noire*: 108; tr. mod.: 134). By the same token, Fanon later complains not that Sartre misleads him, but that he shatters his illusions (*Peau noire*: 111; *Black Skin*: 137).

Sartre located Negritude in a dialectical history that has white racism for its first term. Despite its liberatory intent, it is in a certain sense a philosophy of white history, a white philosophy of history. Furthermore, although Sartre identified Negritude as 'an anti-racist racism', a phrase that Fanon later employed for himself (Fanon 1961: 177; Fanon 1991: 139), by declaring that Negritude gives way to the idea of the proletariat, Sartre located Negritude as a stage in the dialectic and thereby robbed Fanon of his Negritude. This is why, even though Sartre looked forward to a raceless society, Fanon responded '(p)as encore blanc, plus tout à faire noir, j'étais un damné' ('not yet white, no longer wholly black, I was damned') (*Peau noire*: 112; *Black Skin*: 138). This 'born Hegelian' – not the most precise phrase to describe Sartre perhaps, but a fine riposte – had forgotten that 'la conscience a besoin de se perdre dans la nuit de l'absolu, seule condition pour parvenir à la conscience de soi' ('consciousness has to lose itself in the night of the absolute, the only condition able to attain consciousness of self') (*Peau noire*: 108; tr. mod.: 133–4). What Fanon seems to have had in mind is the distinction in the *Phénoménologie de l'esprit* (*Phenomenology of the Spirit*) between natural consciousness, which understands itself as free, and absolute consciousness, which recognises the necessity governing the dialectic. Fanon's objection was not so much that Sartre looked beyond the conditions which spawned the Negritude movement to a time after it. Fanon himself did so incessantly. Indeed, one of the ways to secure disalienation lay in refusing to take present realities as definitive (*Peau noire*: 183; *Black Skin*: 226). Furthermore, in Chapter 6, Fanon, thinking of Aimé Césaire's *Discours sur le colonialisme* (*Discourse on Colonialism*), acknowledges that he understands that a Marxist position is the logical conclusion of the Negritude movement (*Peau noire*: 159; *Black Skin*: 197; see also Bernasconi 2002: 74), although in the concluding pages Fanon appears to endorse the struggle against exploitation rather than the Marxist analysis that is sometimes imposed on it (*Peau noire*: 101–2; *Black Skin*: 224).

Fanon's response to Sartre must be understood in context. It takes place precisely at the point where Sartre, having moved from the essentialisation of race in terms of a 'black soul' to the existentialisation of race, thereby turning the idea of Negritude from a state into an existential attitude, then turned to Hegel and dissolved Negritude in the Hegelian dialectic. One needs to be clear that it is in the name of an existential account of race that Fanon criticised Sartre's appeal to the dialectic. The objections that Fanon levels against Sartre at this point are Sartrean, that is to say, existentialist: the dialectic 'rompt ma position irréfléchie' ('shatters my non-reflective position') (*Peau noire*: 109; tr. mod.: 135). Fanon described 'Orphée noir' as marking 'une date dans l'intellectualisation de l'*exister* noir' ('a date in the intellectualization of Black existing') (*Peau noire*: 108; tr. mod.: 134). The phrase subtly corrects a comment in Ch. André Julien's foreword to the *Anthologie de la nouvelle poésie nègre et malgache de langue française*, where he predicted, '*Orphée noir* marquerait une date dans l'analyse de la négritude' ('*Black Orpheus* will mark a date in the analysis of Negritude') (Senghor 1948: viii). Fanon's formulation is not only more precise than Julien's, but also prefigures his critique of Sartre. Sartre, the philosopher of existence, intellectualised black existence; he did so through his desire 'à vouloir *dire* l'orientation de mon action' (by 'saying the orientation of my action') (Fanon 1951: 674; Fanon 2001: 196).[4] It is of the utmost significance that Fanon specifically focused on the fact that it is his intellectual commitment to Negritude, not his existential commitment, that Sartre destroyed: 'Et quand j'essayais, sur le plan de l'idée et de l'activité intellectuelle, de revendiquer ma négritude, on me l'arrachait' ('When I tried, on the level of ideas and intellectual activity, to reclaim my Negritude, it was snatched away from me') (*Peau noire*: 107; *Black Skin*: 132). Sartre, in the context of a reading of the poem 'Black Soul' by the Haitian poet Jean-F. Brière, had announced the transition by which race became historicity by being inserted into Universal History: 'La race n'est plus un *état* ni même une attitude existentielle, c'est un Devenir' ('Race is no longer a *state*, nor even an existential attitude, it is a Becoming') (Sartre 1948: xxxix; Sartre 2001: 136). By contrast, Fanon attempted to leave the future open: in place of becoming, he announced the unforeseeable (*Peau noire*: 109; *Black Skin*: 135).

When Sartre pronounced the transformation of Negritude
from an existential attitude into a moment in the philosophy of
history by saying that 'la notion subjective, existentielle, ethnique
de *négritude* "passe", comme dit Hegel, dans celle – objective,
positive, exacte – de *prolétariat*' ('the subjective, existential, ethnic
notion of Negritude "passes", as Hegel says, into the objective,
positive and precise notion of the proletariat') (Sartre 1948: xl;
Sartre 2001: 137), we should not forget that he did so not on his
own initiative, but on the basis of the contents of Senghor's
Anthologie. Sartre quoted from Senghor's introductory note on
Aimé Césaire the observation that 'à travers les hommes à peau
noire de sa race, c'est la lutte du prolétariat mondial qu'il chante'
('over and beyond the black-skinned men of his race, he sings
about the worldwide proletarian struggle') (Senghor 1948: 55;
cited in Sartre 1948: xl; Sartre 2001: 137). Sartre also quoted
Jacques Roumain from Haiti, who wrote that the only race he
wanted to belong to was that of the peasant workers of all
countries (Senghor 1948: 116; cited in Sartre 1948: xli; Sartre
2001: 137). Nor has this escaped Fanon, who acknowledges in
Chapter 6 of *Peau noire* that he understands why Sartre regarded
Marxism as 'la fin logique de la négritude' ('the logical conclusion of Negritude') (*Peau noire*: 159; tr. mod.: 197). Fanon's
immediate objection in Chapter 5 is that 'l'expérience nègre est
ambigue, car il n'y a pas *un* nègre, mais *des* nègres' ('the Negro
experience is ambiguous, for there is not merely *one* Negro, but
several Negroes') (*Peau noire*: 110; tr. mod.: 136). In other words,
Sartre had no right to privilege the Marxist voices in the Negritude movement over the other voices: it was not for him to
choose Césaire over Senghor.

But the underlying objection against Sartre is that he forgot
that 'le nègre souffre dans son corps autrement que le Blanc' ('the
Negro suffers in his body differently than the White') (*Peau
noire*: 112; tr. mod.: 138). This is not merely 'an individual failure
of judgment', as one commentator has recently insisted (Krucks
2001: 103). If Sartre had not been white, he could not have
forgotten. That he forgot suggests that he knew, but yet did not
know. Sartre's race is the issue for Fanon. However, this is not to
be understood in an essentialist way: Fanon's account of racial
identity is profoundly existentialist. Fanon wrote: 'Ce qui est

certain, c'est qu'au moment où je tente une saisie de mon être, Sartre, qui demeure l'Autre, en me nommant m'enlève toute illusion' ('What is certain is that, at the very moment when I was trying to grasp my own being, Sartre, who remained The Other, gave me a name and thus shattered my last illusion') (*Peau noire*: 111; *Black Skin*: 137). The reference to Sartre as the other is a reference to Sartre's whiteness: Fanon is clear that alterity for the Black lies in whiteness (*Peau noire*: 78 and 125; *Black Skin*: 97 and 154). But Sartre as white is not only the other. Fanon explains in a note that the application of Sartre's studies on the existence of the other in *L'Être et le néant* (*Being and Nothingness*) to 'une conscience nègre' ('a Negro consciousness') proves fallacious. This is because the White is not only the other, but also the master, whether real or imaginary (*Peau noire*: 112n; *Black Skin*: 138n). Sartre's proclamations about the meaning of Negritude keep intact the structure that serves to produce the problem, when he, a white man, asks Blacks unilaterally to renounce the pride of their colour (Sartre 1948: xlii; Sartre 2001: 138). There is a problem about proposing a solution to a freedom (*Peau noire*: 50; *Black Skin*: 62).

However, Fanon makes a further point. The lived experience of Blacks is different from that of Whites. Fanon says it most clearly when, as we have seen, he comments that Sartre has forgotten that the Black suffers bodily differently from the White (*Peau noire*: 112; *Black Skin*: 138), but this is already fore-shadowed earlier in the chapter when he explains that black consciousness is immanent to itself and is not a potentiality, because black consciousness is not a lack but adheres to itself (*Peau noire*: 109; *Black Skin*: 135). The situation is such that the facticity of race presents itself differently to Blacks than to Whites, which is why Sartre cannot make his demand. To renounce his race is not an option for Fanon, who endorses the Sartrean framework of facticity and transcendence, that is to say, of a solidarity with Being through which one surpasses Being (*Peau noire*: 186; *Black Skin*: 229), but who experiences the weight of the social constraints on freedom differently from the way Sartre presents them in *L'Être et le néant*.

Although Fanon had a strong notion of racial identity, it was, like Sartre's account of the Jew, one that gave little or no place to

ethnicity and relied heavily on the racist gaze. Referring to
Sartre's *Réflexions sur la question juive*, Fanon explains that the
racist creates his inferior (*Peau noire*: 75; *Black Skin*: 93). That is
to say, what is often called the black soul is a white construction
(*Peau noire*: 11; *Black Skin*: 14). This conception of the construction of racial identities in principle allows for their end, but that
end comes only with an end to racism, and Fanon presents a
vicious circle that offers no way out. So long as there is no
solution to racism, racial identities are here to stay. As I have
argued elsewhere, *Peau noire* does not offer a clear solution, only
a diagnosis (Bernasconi 2001: 17–19). But Fanon's book, properly
understood, impacts the white reader differently from the black
reader, because the white reader can live for long periods
forgetful that there is a problem to be addressed, whereas the
black reader cannot.

On the basis of much of the secondary literature, one could
easily have formed the impression that Fanon was concerned
exclusively with black identity. In fact, his insistence that there
are no unilateral solutions together with his theory of the role
played by the Negro myth in sustaining racism obliges him also
to address Whites and white identity. Those who focus on
Fanon's statements of the fraternity or solidarity of all humanity
tend to ignore his consistent charge that Whites are dehumanised.
We read in the Introduction that '(l)e Noir veut être Blanc. Le
Blanc s'acharne à réaliser une condition d'homme' ('the Black
wants to be White. The White works hard to realize a human
condition') (*Peau noire*: 7; tr. mod.: 11). That is to say, those
Blacks who want to be white may aspire to human dignity, but
they are looking in the wrong place because Whites are themselves far from 'human': we fail to behave in a human way,
which is the one thing one can legitimately ask of another (*Peau
noire*: 185; *Black Skin*: 228). As Fanon insists, the inhumanity of
the White is to have killed Man somewhere (*Peau noire*: 187;
Black Skin: 231).

I have written this chapter in response to what I see as a too
easy appropriation of Fanon by white philosophers and cultural
critics. That his texts resist domestication is part of his greatness:
he marked the limits of what white men can legitimately say on
the basis of our own experience. He told white men what we

need to know, while at the same time reminding us that we will never really know it. Racism is inscribed on Fanon's body. Hence, at the end of the book, his prayer is that he become a body that questions (*Peau noire*: 188; *Black Skin*: 232). Whites have a different relation to their bodies for this very reason. There are things, therefore, that Whites need to be told. The achievement of *Peau noire* is that even after fifty years nobody has done a better job of telling white men what we continue to do both individually and through our institutions, and how our understanding of the full effects of this situation will inevitably remain limited. Fanon knew he had the power to disturb, but he also knew that that was not enough. It was also necessary for Blacks and Whites to break with the past. But how this was to be done was addressed by Fanon only in his subsequent works (Bernasconi 2001: 21–2).

Notes

1 See also *Peau noire*: 30 and 148. The title *Peau noire, masques blancs* was apparently Frances Jeanson's idea.

2 Space unfortunately does not allow a full consideration of this intriguing and important exchange, so I must postpone it for another occasion.

3 'Jean-Paul Sartre, in this work, has destroyed black enthusiasm. The unforeseeable should have been opposed to historical becoming. I felt the need to lose myself absolutely in Negritude' (tr. mod.: 135).

4 The sentence in which this last phrase appeared was omitted when the 1951 essay, 'L'Expérience vécue du noir', was turned into Chapter 5 of *Peau noire*.

References

Bernasconi, R. (2001) 'Eliminating the cycle of violence: the place of a dying colonialism within Fanon's revolutionary thought', *Philosophia Africana*, 4:2, 17–25
—— (2002) 'The assumption of Negritude: Aimé Césaire, Frantz Fanon, and the vicious circle of racial politics', *Parallax*, 23, 68–83
Cheriki, A. (2000) *Frantz Fanon, portrait*, Paris: Seuil
Fanon, F. (1951) 'L'Expérience vécue du noir', *Esprit*, 19:179, 657–79
—— (1961) *Les Damnés de la terre*, Paris: François Maspero (*The Wretched of the Earth*, trans. C. Farrington, New York: Grove Weidenfeld, 1991)
—— (2001) 'The lived experience of the Black', trans. V. Moulard in R. Bernasconi (ed.), *Race*, Oxford: Blackwell, 184–201

Krucks, S. (2001) *Retrieving Experience: Subjectivity and Recognition in Feminist Politics*, Ithaca, NY: Cornell University Press

Sartre, J.-P. (1948) 'Orphée noir' in L. Senghor (ed.), *Anthologie de la nouvelle poésie nègre et malgache de langue francaise*, Paris: Presses Universitaires de France, ix–xliv

—— (1954) *Réflexions sur la question juive*, Paris: Gallimard (first pub. 1946; *Anti-Semite and Jew*, trans. G. J. Becker, New York: Schocken Books, 1948)

—— (2001) 'Black Orpheus', trans. J. MacCombie, in R. Bernasconi (ed.), *Race*, Oxford: Blackwell, 115–42

Senghor, L. S. (ed.) (1948) *Anthologie de la nouvelle poèsie nègre et malgache de langue française*, Paris: Presses Universitaires de France

Wolfe, B. (1949) 'L'oncle Remus et son lapin', *Les Temps Modernes*, 4:43, 888–913

6

Reflections on the human question

MAX SILVERMAN

J'appartiens irréductiblement à mon époque (I belong irreducibly to my time) (*Peau noire*: 10; *Black Skin*: 15)

Sameness and difference: Fanon, Antelme, Lévi-Strauss

Peau noire, masques blancs was published only seven years after the end of the Second World War. There is no mention of the war in the text. Neither is there any mention of the Holocaust, even though Fanon discusses the situation of the Jew via his engagement with Sartre's *Réflexions sur la question juive* (1946). These are strange omissions in a text which deals passionately with the power of racialised difference to alienate men and women from their true selves. Early testimonies from survivors of the Nazi concentration camps were available.[1] Robert Antelme's *L'Espèce humaine* (1947) and David Rousset's *L'Univers concentrationnaire* (1946) both reappraised the human condition in light of the catastrophe of the previous years. In a different arena, in 1952 (the year of publication of *Peau noire*) Unesco published a series of essays on racism. An important product of this project was Claude Lévi-Strauss's *Race et histoire*, which turned out to be not only a critique of racism but a more sustained reflection on western culture and the nature of civilisation. In this chapter I would like to situate *Peau noire* within this broader post-war reassessment of race and the human condition. I will argue that, although there are no overt references in *Peau noire* to any of the works mentioned above, we can nevertheless see how the general reflections on humanity that they contain inform the deep structure of the text.

Robert Antelme's testimony of his time spent in the Gandersheim concentration camp describes an episode in which he is given a piece of mirror by a fellow inmate. He has not seen his own reflection for a long time and is struck, first of all, by the simple realisation that he has a face. For the SS he has no face; in its place is simply 'un poids sur les épaules' ('a weight on my shoulders') (Antelme 1957: 60; Antelme 1992: 51). Moreover, it is dangerous for the inmate to contradict this negation of a face by the SS since anything that reminds the SS of the inmate's humanity is likely to lead to worse treatment than if he remains anonymous. Easier by far, then, 'à faire soi-même un effort de négation de son propre visage, parfaitement accordé à celui du SS' ('to make an effort to negate our faces ourselves, an effort which perfectly matched the negation practised by the SS' (Antelme 1957: 60; Antelme 1992: 52 (tr. mod.)). Antelme then reflects as follows:

> Niée, deux fois niée, ou alors aussi risible et aussi provocante qu'un masque – c'était proprement provoquer le scandale en effet, que de porter sur nos épaules quelque chose de notre visage ancien, le masque de l'homme –, la figure avait fini pour nous-mêmes par s'absenter de notre vie. (Antelme 1957: 60)[2]

In this passage Antelme highlights not only the way in which the mask of anonymity is imposed on the inmates, hence reducing the human to a thing, but also the way in which this mask is adopted by the inmate to hide the human face. The mirror shatters this mask, shatters the look of the SS and reveals the human distinctiveness of the face, 'ce morceau de solitude éclatant' ('this bit of brilliant solitude') (Antelme 1957: 61; Antelme 1992: 52–3).[3]

Although there are no references to Antelme in *Peau noire* (indeed, there is, to the best of my knowledge, no indication that Fanon had even come across his testimony), there are nevertheless all sorts of echoes of this scene in Fanon's text: the mask which is imposed on the Black by the look of the white master ('le noir n'a plus à être noir, mais à l'être en face du Blanc'; 'not only must the black man be black; he must be black in relation to the

white man', *Peau noire*: 88; *Black Skin*: 110), the Black's adoption
and internalisation of the mask which is the sign of his own
alienation ('Après avoir été esclave du Blanc, il (le Nègre)
s'autoesclavagise'; 'After having been the slave of the white man,
he enslaves himself', *Peau noire*: 155; *Black Skin*: 192[4]) and the
passionate and tenacious faith in the eventual retrieval of the
human face beneath the mask. In both cases, racialised difference
objectifies the other and negates his individuality; in both cases,
the master's power over the other is expressed through the look
which detaches the other's body from his sense of self; and in
both cases, human freedom ultimately lies in resisting systems
which alienate human beings from their selves in this way. Do
the similarities between these two works regarding the objectifying look of the other therefore suggest the same humanist message:
differences alienate humans and divide humanity into unequal
parts? Disalienation, freedom and equality must therefore reside
in restoring our individuality and shared humanity.

Claude Lévi-Strauss's *Race et histoire* apparently presents a
very different version of freedom and equality in the aftermath
of the war and the Holocaust. These are not necessarily achieved
through the pursuit of common goals and a belief in a shared
humanity but through the recognition of difference. Indeed,
Lévi-Strauss's text is one of the most important critiques in the
post-war period of the humanism at the heart of the western
Enlightenment version of civilisation and progress. 'Les grandes
déclarations des droits de l'homme', he suggests, pronounce 'un
idéal trop souvent oublieux du fait que l'homme ne réalise pas sa
nature dans une humanité abstraite, mais dans des cultures
traditionnelles' ('The grand declarations of the Rights of Man
[pronounce] an ideal which too often forgets the fact that Man's
true nature is not to be found in an abstract humanity but in
traditional cultures') (Lévi-Strauss 1987: 23; my trans.). He exposes
the ethnocentrism underpinning western universalism, demonstrates how it denies differences by measuring them against a
single European yardstick and argues ultimately for the diversity
of cultures.

Once again there are profound echoes of Lévi-Strauss's
critique of the West in Fanon's text. In the universalising
language and culture of the European master are the traps posed

for the colonial subject whose own culture is devalued when measured against the values of 'humanity'. It is true that Fanon and Lévi-Strauss arrive at this position via different routes. Fanon comes to the critique of the West via the route of personal experience in Martinique and then metropolitan France, the Negritude writers and Sartrean phenomenology, while Lévi-Strauss comes to it via the developing awareness among western anthropologists and ethnologists of their own subjective and situated observer status when analysing other peoples and cultures. Where Lévi-Strauss talks of Europe's ethnocentrism, Fanon is more direct and names it clearly as racism ('L'Europe a une structure raciste'; 'Europe has a racist structure', *Peau noire*: 74; *Black Skin*: 92). Nevertheless, their challenge to the West's propensity to reduce the other to the same is comparable.

If the analogy with Antelme appears to highlight Fanon's Enlightenment perspective on the destructive force of racialised difference, the analogy with Lévi-Strauss highlights, instead, his desperate plea for a difference which will not already be incorporated in the binary and Manichaean divide determining the western look. This apparent contradiction – between sameness and difference, universalism and particularism – situates Fanon's text at a crucial moment in the post-war reappraisal of humanity and civilisation, both inside and outside Europe, with whose repercussions we are still grappling today. However, Fanon does not simply slide between these two poles in *Peau noire*: it is also the dualistic structure itself which is under attack. The comparison with Antelme and Lévi-Strauss demonstrates that, in this, as Fanon himself states in the quotation used as an epigraph to this chapter, he is an integral part of his era.

Seeking the human

Fanon's opening statements in *Peau noire* are indicative of the tension between the universal ('Homme') and the particular ('le Noir'): 'Nos frères de couleur ... je crois en toi, Homme' ('Our coloured brothers ... Mankind, I believe in you') (*Peau noire*: 5; tr. mod.: 9); 'Que veut l'homme? Que veut l'homme noir?' ('What does Man want? What does the black man want?) (*Peau noire*: 6; tr. mod.: 10). He says that he comes 'point armé de vérités

décisives' ('without certain truths') but hopes that his text will
point the way towards 'un nouvel humanisme' ('a new humanism') (*Peau noire*: 5; tr. mod.: 9). If, by the end of the text, this has
been achieved, then it is more through having implicitly exposed
the shortcomings of the old humanism, via the ambivalent nature
of his own argument, than through the explicit proclamation of a
new programme.[5] I will consider three moments in the text when
this ambivalence is particularly visible. Here we see, as Fanon
suggests, no clear delineation of truths but a restless narration
grappling with western constructions of the human in its search
for 'un nouvel humanisme'.

The first moment is Fanon's engagement with Sartre. At one
stage in *Peau noire* Fanon remarks, 'certaines pages de *Réflexions
sur la question juive* sont les plus belles que nous ayons jamais
lues. Les plus belles, parce que le problème qu'elles expriment
nous prend aux entrailles' (*Peau noire*: 146).[6] Fanon's references
to *Réflexions sur la question juive* (first published in 1946) are not
his only engagement with Sartre in *Peau noire*. Elsewhere he
discusses 'Orphée noir', the preface Sartre wrote for the *Anthologie
de la poésie nègre et malgache* (see especially *Peau noire*: 107–12;
Black Skin: 133–8), Sartre's philosophical work *L'Etre et le néant*
and his play *La Putain respectueuse*. In a more general sense, it is
Sartrean phenomenology and existentialism which, to a large
extent, inform the theoretical approach adopted in the text. The
last pages of *Peau noire*, which I will discuss later, are a hymn to
disalienation, authenticity and freedom which could have been
written by a pure disciple of Sartre.

Sartre's *Réflexions sur la question juive* is itself a powerful
exposé of the trap for the Jew posed by the universalising and
particularising mechanisms at work in modern French society:
either the Jew attempts to assimilate to the norms of 'civilised'
society (hence confirming his or her Jewish particularity as a
stigma which must be eradicated) or the Jew indulges his or her
particular practices and customs (hence confirming the very
stereotype that the anti-Semite has of the Jew). Either way the
Jew is trapped by the gaze of the non-Jew. Fanon can see the
many parallels between the situation of the Jew under conditions
of modernity and the situation of the Black under conditions of
colonialism. He uses Sartre's model to great effect in explaining

how the Black has become alienated from himself under the controlling colonial gaze.

However, Fanon is also aware of the drawbacks of Sartre's approach. In his discussion of Sartre's 'Orphée noir' he objects bitterly to the way in which Sartre devalues blackness by defining it as simply oppositional to whiteness. Whiteness is the primary term against which blackness comes into being and reacts, in the same way that, for Sartre, Jewishness is simply a secondary product of the projection of the non-Jew. Fanon understands how, for Sartre, blackness is simply an element in the dialectic (that is, a *European* perception of the teleological unfolding of history) which will eventually see the disappearance of both black and white in a raceless and classless society. This discussion appears in Chapter 5 of *Peau noire* ('L'Expérience vécue du noir', 'The lived experience of the Black') and it is precisely Fanon's sense that Sartre's intellectualising formula (or what Ato Sekyi-Otu (1996: 17) describes as 'Sartre's allegorizing reading of Negritude') has robbed him of his lived experience of blackness ('l'intellectualisation de l'*exister* noir', 'the intellectualization of the experience of being black', *Peau noire*: 108; *Black Skin*: 134) that leads him to complain so bitterly of being betrayed by this 'ami des peuples de couleur' ('friend of people of colour') (*Peau noire*: 108; tr. mod.: 133).

Fanon's critique is devastating. In a sense, it prefigures the more recent criticisms that have been made of Sartre's perception of the Jew in *Refléxions sur la question juive* (see for example Grosz 1990; Kritzman 1995; Suleiman 1995; Wolitz 1994). Yet it makes its challenge to Sartre's blind spots not from the point of view of the outraged critic but from the position of the young black man struggling to define himself in a white world. In *Refléxions sur la question juive*, Sartre's proposition that the Jew is constructed by the look of the anti-Semite, and is therefore simply a by-product of the anti-Semite's 'mauvaise foi' ('bad faith'), implies, first, that Jewishness and Judaism have no ontological existence of their own and, secondly, that the Jew is destined to disappear with the eventual elimination of anti-Semitism.[7] Fanon understands how this sort of reasoning, when applied to blackness, transforms his very real sense of lived experience of that blackness into a chimera of the white imagination. Fanon is also intensely aware of the universalist foundations of Sartre's Hegelianism whose master narrative – the dialectical unfolding of history – situates 'race' as simply a stage on the path of progress towards a disalienated society. Fanon seems to understand that this vision of history is simply another version of the western Enlightenment vision of Man: ethnic attachments are a sign of parochialism and backwardness which must be removed in the pursuit of freedom.

However, in his effort to retrieve his sense of self from the universalising historical discourse in which Sartre has situated the Black, Fanon proclaims 'Je ne suis pas une potentialité de quelque chose, je suis pleinement ce que je suis (…) Ma conscience nègre ne se donne pas comme manque. Elle *est*. Elle est adhérente à elle-même' (*Peau noire*: 109).[8] This is a bold form of resistance to Sartre's negative perspective on blackness. Yet it begs the question what is this blackness that seems to precede its contact with the white world and is subsequently shattered by its normalisation within the white 'intellectualising' gaze? 'Pas encore blanc, plus tout à fait noir, j'étais un damné' ('Not yet white, no longer wholly black, I was damned') (*Peau noire*: 112; *Black Skin*: 138).[9] What, then, was this blackness that is now no longer whole? Does Fanon imply (as Jock McCulloch's ultimately reductionist account of Fanon (1983) seems to suggest) that there was a self-presence which constituted an essential black self prior to its fragmentation within the objectifying white gaze (a position which would actually be in contradiction to his critique of the wholeness and self-presence of the white self at the heart of the Hegelian dialectic and of his critique elsewhere of the essentialism of Negritude). Or does he imply, instead, that that 'blackness' is a perception of somatic otherness whose recognition is fundamental for the establishment of disalienated human relations?

Rather than provide answers to these questions, Fanon will later present blackness in a very different way. 'L'Antillais ne se pense pas Noir; il se pense Antillais [...] Or, c'est un nègre. Cela, il s'en apercevra une fois en Europe, et quand on parlera de nègres il saura qu'il s'agit de lui aussi bien que du Sénégalais' (*Peau noire*: 120–1).[10] Here blackness is, once again, simply a European social construction. Before contact with the objectifying and racialising gaze of the European, the Antillean is unaware of the coded language of colour. This is the lesson that Fanon has already learnt when, in metropolitan France, he is objectified as a demonic black figure in the eyes of a white boy (*Peau noire*: 90–2; *Black Skin*: 111–14).

In the first example, the white gaze shatters a sense of blackness; in the second example, it imposes a sense of blackness which objectifies and alienates the colonised man. Blackness slides between lived experience and racial term. It is through this language that the real drama is played out: namely, the sense of self held between inchoate experience and social construction, between a state prior to or outside the European dialectic (imaginary because unattainable, or rather only attainable through the normalising framework of dialectical thinking) and the assigned position within that signifying system. As Benita Parry rightly argues, in *Peau noire* there is 'both an intellectual apprehension of blackness as a construct … and a visceral attachment to the powerful fiction of black identity' (Parry 1994: 187).

The second moment in the text that I would like to consider is the brief section at the end of Chapter 7 ('Le Nègre et la reconnaissance') entitled 'Le Nègre et Hegel'. Here Fanon engages with the Hegelian dialectic not through the intermediary of Sartre but directly through a reflection on Hegel's *Phenomenology of the Spirit* and its relevance to the situation of the colonised Black. Fanon discusses the idea of reciprocal recognition at the heart of the Hegelian dialectic. In order to go beyond the 'natural' world of things, in order to respect the other's freedom and desire for being, in order to realise being for itself ('être pour soi') in oneself and in the other, there has to be mutual recognition:

> Je me demande qu'on me considère à partir de mon Désir. Je ne suis pas seulement ici-maintenant, enfermé dans la choséité. Je suis pour ailleurs et pour autre chose. Je réclame qu'on tienne compte de mon activité négatrice en tant que je poursuis autre chose que la vie; en tant que je lutte pour la naissance d'un monde humain, c'est-à-dire d'un monde de reconnaissances réciproques. (*Peau noire*: 177)[11]

However, the problem for the black slave, according to Fanon, is that his recognition by the white master, and consequently the freedom and justice he has attained, have come about not through his own struggle but through the liberal conscience of the white master himself, to whom the Black must be eternally grateful: 'il se bat pour la Liberté et la Justice, mais il s'agit toujours de liberté blanche et de justice blanche, c'est-à-dire de valeurs sécrétées par les maîtres' ('he fights for Liberty and Justice but these are always white liberty and white justice, that is values imposed by the masters') (*Peau noire*: 179; tr. mod.: 221). The universal fraternity of men into which the Black has been welcomed is a false universalism, with no genuine reciprocity of recognition, precisely because it is regulated by the white master who controls the rules of the game.

As we noted above, Fanon's interpretation of the Hegelian dialectic is that it is established on the terms of the white master. The self seeks recognition as a free being and, instead, finds itself locked into the prison of thing-ness. In such circumstances the Black is always fixed in the position of the object of the master's gaze and recognition of his human desire and freedom is denied (see Gibson 2003: 33–7). The dissatisfaction expressed towards Sartre in Chapter 5 derives from the understanding that the Hegelian dialectic he is employing implicitly endorses a European 'I' (or eye). Once again, Fanon's search for freedom brings him up against the central conflict between his desire for recognition of his otherness and the harsh gaze cast back at him which fixes him as an object. Yet, as I suggested above, a more profound tension in the text springs from Fanon's own slippages between this critical perspective on the false universalism of the Hegelian dialectic and the adoption of that very universalism which he has exposed.

The concluding chapter of *Peau noire* ('En guise de conclusion') – the third moment in the text that I would like to consider – highlights this well. These pages are a strange conclusion to what has gone before, for Fanon seems to forget the tension established beforehand between otherness and racialisation and opts wholeheartedly for a Sartrean version of freedom. He makes it clear that the path to freedom does not lie in a return to an essentialist vision of blackness which he believes underlies Negritude: 'En aucune façon je ne dois m'attacher à faire revivre une civilisation nègre injustement méconnue. Je ne me fais l'homme d'aucun passé. Je ne veux pas chanter le passé aux dépens de mon présent et de mon avenir' (*Peau noire*: 183). By opposing all forms of essentialism ('Ce n'est pas le monde noir qui me dicte ma conduite. Ma peau noire n'est pas dépositaire de valeurs spécifiques' (*Peau noire*: 184)), by dismissing the determinations of History ('Je ne suis pas prisonnier de l'Histoire. Je ne dois pas y chercher le sens de ma destinée' (*Peau noire*: 186); 'La densité de l'Histoire ne détermine aucun de mes actes' (*Peau noire*: 187)), and by embracing his freedom and humanity rather than the burden of his race ('Il y a ma liberté qui me renvoie à moi-même. Non, je n'ai pas le droit d'être un Noir' (*Peau noire*: 185); 'Le nègre n'est pas. Pas plus que le Blanc' (*Peau noire*: 187)), Fanon ultimately adopts the very existentialist humanism which he had previously criticised in 'Orphée noir'.[12] What has been lost is that other sense of blackness as lived experience *in its singularity and difference* which Fanon opposed to Sartre's negative appropriation and intellectualising of blackness from the outside in Chapter 5. In other words, Fanon adopts the binary vision of the master's dialectical and teleological unfolding of History which, at another (more profound?) level, he knows to be part of the problem for the colonised rather than the solution to his or her alienation.

Towards a post-humanism?

Recent interest in Antelme's *L'Espèce humaine* has focused on its challenge to a humanist approach to the human in the wake of the camps. The residual humanity which resists (and must always resist) all attempts at annihilation is not the self-present self of humanism but rather the indefinable otherness beyond the Enlightenment assimilation or exclusion of the other. Antelme's text has been reinvented as a precursor of a Levinasian ethics of the other and thus recruited for the promotion of a new post-war and post-humanist approach to otherness and ethics.[13] Although Lévi-Strauss's *Race et histoire* has not been adopted in the same way in contemporary post-Levinasian criticism, nevertheless we might also see it in the context of a post-war reappraisal of otherness and difference. The study of Lévi-Strauss written by Jean Pouillon in 1956 (Pouillon 1987) is an early recognition of Lévi-Strauss's effort to think otherness beyond the straitjacket of a western binary framework of sameness and difference.[14]

Despite my sceptical attitude towards some recent Antelme criticism (which often anachronistically decontextualises and sometimes plainly misreads Antelme) and my awareness of the danger of conflating very different approaches by different thinkers, I would suggest (as I did in the introduction to this chapter) that Antelme's *L'Espèce humaine*, Lévi-Strauss's *Race et histoire* and Fanon's *Peau noire* can be usefully aligned to highlight the renewed attention to the question of the human in the aftermath of the Second World War and the Holocaust and at a time of the crisis of the West. I do not believe that any of these texts openly embraces a post-humanist perspective, in the way, for instance, that some critics suggest of *L'Espèce humaine* (see for example Cohen 2002) and that some critics suggest of Fanon himself (see for example Bhabha 1986). The interest of each of them derives especially from their search for a redefinition of the human which frequently highlights (if only unconsciously at times) the problematic nature of the Enlightenment values underpinning the western invention of 'Man'.

In *Peau noire*, the real tension springs not so much from the contradictions between a universalist and a particularist perspective but from the slippages between, on the one hand, this dualistic framework and, on the other hand, the sense of a different perspective which would break with the binary opposition of universalism and particularism itself. I have attempted to highlight this tension by considering Fanon's ambivalent engagement with Sartre and Hegel. At times Fanon's insertion of the lived experience of the Black into dialectical and teleological thinking allows him to deconstruct their implicit dualist assumptions. At others, Fanon is caught up in the very dualist assumptions from which he is trying to extricate himself (just as Sartre's *Réflexions sur la question juive* is a brilliant exposé of the pitfalls of western dualist thinking and the trap it poses for the Jew, yet ultimately proposes the very universalism which the author has criticised in the figure of the 'democrat'). Fanon seems to forget his own initial response to Sartre's 'Orphée noir' (cf. Parry 1994: 190 and Kruks 1996: 132). When Sartre asks rhetorically of the White whether, on giving the Black language after having oppressed him for centuries, he expects to 'lire l'adoration dans les yeux' ('find adoration in their eyes'), Fanon replies, 'je dis que celui qui cherchera dans mes yeux autre chose qu'une interrogation perpétuelle devra perdre la vue; ni reconnaissance ni haine. Et si je pousse un grand cri, il ne sera point nègre' (*Peau noire*: 23).[15] The 'interrogation perpétuelle' and the refusal to confirm the binary of 'reconnaissance' or 'haine' troubles the position of the white look with a cry that shall not be contained either by tacit approval of white universalism or by a retreat into a black essentialism. However, at other times in the text, it is precisely this dualism which is allowed to re-establish its determining point of view.

One of the many fascinations of *Peau noire* lies in the way in which the conscious and unconscious demands of the pheno-menology of lived experience coupled with the teleology of dialectical thinking establish an overdetermined text in which the concepts of humanity and freedom are never clearly defined. I would propose that these contradictions and slippages are symptomatic of Fanon's engagement with, and attempt to disentangle himself from, the Enlightenment version of the human. Rather than assume that Fanon opts ultimately for difference over sameness, particularism over universalism (cf. Finkielkraut 1987), or vice versa, we might instead read the contradictions in the text as an unconscious symptom of a search beyond the constraining logic of the binary itself. We can agree with Ethan Kleinberg when he says, 'Fanon anticipates a new way of trying to understand the Other by making a space for the Other prior to the restrictive classifications of the Western epistemological structure' (Kleinberg 2003: 127). We can also agree with Robert Bernasconi when he argues (*contra* Robert Young in *White Mythologies*) that Fanon's 'new humanism' is not simply a variation of western humanism (Bernasconi 1996). What we see in *Peau noire* is not so much a new humanism as a passionate, and often confused, struggle to redefine the human; that is, a text both implicated in the western construction of Man and constituting 'a radical posing of the question of Man' (Gordon 1995: 10) from the point of view of Man's ambivalent other. By aligning Fanon's *Peau noire* with Antelme's *L'Espèce humaine* and Lévi-Strauss's *Race et histoire* we might also view these in the same light. The apparent differences between these works regarding the question of sameness and difference would then be transformed into a convergence around a new concern with otherness. Should we, then, see these post-war texts neither as simple restatements of humanism or as straightforward proclamations of difference but rather as attempts to refashion the human in the wake of racialising systems of power and violence?

Notes

1 Despite the popular myth that there was a complete silence around the question of the camps until the late 1960s while France got on with the more serious business of reconstructing a divided nation, many survivor testimonies were in fact available in the immediate post-war period. Whether anyone wanted to listen was another question (see Wieviorka 1992).

2 'Denied, doubly denied, or else as laughable and as provocative as a mask – for indeed it was nothing else than to provoke a scandal, this carrying of our one-time face, the mask of a human being – our face had, for us, finally become absent from our life' (Antelme 1992: 52).

3 For other references in the text to the objectifying look of the SS, see esp. pp. 84, 124–6, 152, 239 and 252.

4 See also 'Ce jour-là, désorienté, incapable d'être dehors avec l'autre, le Blanc, qui, impitoyable, m'emprisonnait, je me portai loin de mon être-là, très loin, me constituant objet … Pourtant, je ne voulais pas cette reconsidération, cette thématisation. Je voulais tout simplement être un homme parmi d'autres hommes' ('On that day, completely dislocated, unable to be abroad with the other, the white man, who unmercifully imprisoned me, I took myself far off from my own presence, far indeed, and made myself an object … But I did not want this revision, this thematization. All I wanted was to be a man among other men') (*Peau noire*: 91; *Black Skin*: 112).

5 Cf. 'the very nature of humanity becomes estranged in the colonial condition and from that "naked declivity" it emerges, not as an assertion of will nor as an evocation of freedom, but as an enigmatic questioning' (Bhabha 1986: xi).

6 'Certain pages of *Anti-Semite and Jew* are the finest that I have ever read. The finest, because the problem discussed in them grips us in our guts' (*Black Skin*: 181).

7 Sartre's view that a Jewish 'reality' stems from the perception of the Jew from outside leads to the following strange reflection when he considers what happens to Jews when that outside perception is absent: 'Or, lorsqu'ils se retrouvent entre eux dans l'intimité de leurs appartements, en éliminant le témoin non-juif, ils éliminent du même coup la réalité juive' ('When, therefore, they are by themselves in the intimacy of their

apartments, by eliminating the non-Jewish witness they eliminate Jewish reality at the same time') (Sartre 1954: 122–3; Sartre 1948: 101).

8 'I am not a potentiality of something, I am wholly what I am. [...] My Negro consciousness does not present itself as a lack. It *is*. It is sufficient unto itself' (tr. mod.: 135).

9 Cf. Fanon's discussion in Chapter 3 of Jean Veneuse, the hero of René Maran's semi-autobiographical novel *Un homme pareil aux autres*. He, too, is 'pas encore blanc, plus tout à fait noir ... un damné'.

10 'The Antillean does not think of himself as a black man; he thinks of himself as an Antillean [...] But he is a Negro. That he will learn once he goes to Europe; and when he hears Negroes mentioned he will recognize that the word includes himself as well as the Senegalese' (*Black Skin*: 148).

11 'I ask that I should be considered as a being who desires. I am not merely here-and-now, sealed into thingness. I am for elsewhere and for something else. I demand that notice be taken of my negating activity insofar as I pursue something other than life, insofar as I struggle for the birth of a human world, that is to say a world of reciprocal recognitions' (tr. mod.: 218).

12 'In no way should I dedicate myself to the revival of an unjustly misunderstood Negro civilization. I will not make myself the man of any past. I do not want to exalt the past at the expense of my present and my future'; 'It is not the black world that dictates my behaviour. My black skin is not the repository of specific values'; 'I am not a prisoner of History. I do not have to look there for the meaning of my destiny'; 'The weight of History does not determine a single one of my actions'; 'My freedom returns me to myself. No, I do not have the right to be a Black'; 'The Negro is not. Any more than the white man' (tr. mod.: 226–31).

13 This approach is inspired in large part by the essay on Antelme by Maurice Blanchot, first published as an article in 1962 and then republished as part of his book *L'entretien infini* (1969).

14 'c'est en tant qu'essentiellement autre que l'autre doit être vu' ('it is as essentially other that the other should be seen') (Pouillon 1987: 92); 'l'essentiel est la différence, qu'il s'agit de comprendre sans céder à la tentation de la réduire' ('the fundamental principle is difference. It is this that must be understood without giving in to the temptation to reduce it') (Pouillon 1987: 93); 'juxtaposer les différences ou les effacer à l'aide de vagues ressemblances ou d'une idée apriori de l'homme, tels sont les deux défauts à éviter' ('to juxtapose differences or to efface them, either by employing vague resemblances or a preconceived idea of Man – these are the two mistakes to avoid') (Pouillon 1987: 95; my trans.).

15 'I say that he who looks into my eyes for anything but a perpetual questioning will have to lose his sight; neither recognition nor hate. And if I cry out, it will not be a black cry' (tr. mod.: 29).

References

Antelme, R. (1957) *L'Espèce humaine*, Paris: Gallimard (first pub. 1947; *The Human Race*, trans. J. Haight and A. Mahler, Marlboro, VT: The Marlboro Press, 1992)

Bernasconi, R. (1996) 'Casting the slough: Fanon's new humanism for a new humanity' in L. R. Gordon, T. D. Sharpley-Whiting and R. T. White (eds), *Fanon: A Critical Reader*, Oxford: Blackwell, 113–21

Bhabha, H. (1986) 'Remembering Fanon: self, psyche and the colonial condition', 'Foreword' in F. Fanon, *Black Skin, White Masks*, trans. C. L. Markmann, London: Pluto Press, vii–xxvi

Blanchot, M. (1969) *L'Entretien infini*, Paris: Gallimard

Cohen, J. (2002) *Interrupting Auschwitz: Art, Religion and Philosophy*, London and New York: Continuum

Finkielkraut, A. (1987) *La Défaite de la pensée*, Paris: Gallimard

Gibson, N. C. (2003) *Fanon: The Postcolonial Imagination*, Cambridge: Polity

Gordon, L. R. (1995) *Fanon and the Crisis of European Man: An Essay on Philosophy and the Human Sciences*, New York and London: Routledge

Grosz, E. (1990) 'Judaism and exile: the ethics of otherness', *New Formations*, no. 12, Winter, 77–88

Kleinberg, E. (2003) 'Kojève and Fanon: the desire for recognition and the fact of blackness' in T. Stovall and G. van den Abbeele (eds), *French Civilization and its Discontents: Nationalism, Colonialism, Race*, Oxford and New York: Lexington Books, 115–18

Kritzman, L. D. (1995) 'Critical reflections: self-portraiture and the representation of Jewish identity in French' in L. Kritzman (ed.), *Auschwitz and After: Race, Culture and "the Jewish Question" in France*, London and New York: Routledge, 98–118

Kruks, S. (1996) 'Fanon, Sartre and identity politics' in L. R. Gordon, T. D. Sharpley-Whiting and R. T. White (eds), *Fanon: A Critical Reader*, Oxford: Blackwell, 122–33

Lévi-Strauss, C. (1987) *Race et histoire*, Paris: Denoel (first pub. 1952)

McCulloch, J. (1983) *Black Soul White Artifact: Fanon's Clinical Psychology and Social Theory*, Cambridge: Cambridge University Press

Parry, B. (1994) 'Resistance theory/theorizing resistance or two cheers for nativism' in F. Barker, P. Hulme and M. Iverson (eds), *Colonial Discourse/Postcolonial Theory*, Manchester: Manchester University Press, 172–96

Pouillon, J. (1987) 'L'Oeuvre de Claude Lévi-Strauss' in *Race et histoire*, Paris: Denoel (first pub. in *Les Temps Modernes*, no. 126, 1956), 87–127

Rousset, D. (1965) *L'Univers concentrationnaire*, Paris: Minuit (first pub. 1946)

Sartre, J.-P. (1954) *Réflexions sur la question juive*, Paris: Gallimard (first pub. 1946; *Anti-Semite and Jew*, trans. G. J. Becker, New York: Schocken Books, 1948)

Sekyi-Otu, A. (1996) *Fanon's Dialectic of Experience*, Cambridge, MA: Harvard University Press

Suleiman, S. R. (1995) 'The Jew in Jean-Paul Sartre's *Réfléxions sur la question juive*: an exercise in historical reading' in L. Nochlin and T. Garb (eds), *The Jew in the Text: Modernity and the Construction of Identity*, London: Thames and Hudson, 201–18

Wieviorka, A. (1992) *Déportation et génocide: entre la mémoire et l'oubli*, Paris: Plon

Wolitz, S. L. (1994) 'Imagining the Jew in France: from 1945 to the present', *Yale French Studies*, 'Discourses of Jewish Identity in Twentieth Century France', ed. A. Astro, no. 85, 119–34

7

Children of violence[1]

VICKY LEBEAU

In the course of the public inquiry into the murder of Stephen Lawrence – the black teenager stabbed to death by a white racist gang in Eltham on 22 April 1993 – three terms come to the fore of British politics in a renewed and controversial way: institution, racism, unconscious. Announced by Home Secretary Jack Straw on 31 July 1997 and chaired by Sir William Macpherson, the Lawrence Inquiry took place over sixty-nine days of public hearings, taking evidence from eighty-eight witnesses on the death of Stephen Lawrence and, in particular, police investigation into and public prosecution of the murder. A dismal story emerges, one in which police negligence and incompetence merge into the grotesque behaviour of the five suspects in the case (notably, their infamous, if fully legal, response to the questions put to them at the inquest held in February 1995: 'I claim privilege'). In his opening statement to the inquiry on 24 March 1998, Michael Mansfield QC identified the core of the Lawrences' grievance against the police in terms that would resonate through public discussion of the case:

> The magnitude of the failure in this case, we say, cannot be explained by mere incompetence or a lack of direction by senior officers or a lack of execution and application by junior officers, nor by woeful under resourcing. So much was missed by so many that deeper causes and forces must be considered.
>
> We suggest these forces relate to two main propositions. The first is, dealing with the facts themselves, that the victim was black and there was as a result a racism, both conscious and unconscious,

that permeated the investigation. Secondly, the fact that the
perpetrators were white and were expecting some form of provocation and protection. More particularly, obviously, protection. (*The
Stephen Lawrence Inquiry, Volume II*, appendices pp. 116–18)

The struggle to think racism as a force exceeding individual
and institutional consciousness has come to distinguish the
Lawrence Inquiry, part of its legacy to the history and interpretation of race relations in Britain. For a brief moment, it was
impossible to separate racism from an idea of the unconscious,
albeit vaguely invoked; equally, the unconscious entered the
debate as a force at work in the institution, in the realm of
collective (as opposed to individual) life. Perhaps predictably,
such a focus has proved difficult to sustain, with contributors to
the debate hesitating between unconscious, institutional and
cultural racism – terms charged with the task of finding a way to
think about a racism that will out despite every democratic
commitment to equality and protection before the law ('the white
experience, the white beliefs, the white values', in the words of
one representative of the Metropolitan Police Service Black
Police Association (*The Stephen Lawrence Inquiry, Volume II*: ch.
6, para. 6.28)). From violence to complicity, racism describes a
'whole climate of opinion' (to borrow Auden's phrase), perverting
the very institutions supposed to offer protection from its effects.
Mansfield insists that, far from being a question of protection,
this amounts to murder, that is, enforcement of the law as protection for racist murder. He recalls Doreen Lawrence's description
of the first few days of the police investigation into her son's
death: 'My son was stereotyped by the police. He was black and
he must be a criminal and they set about investigating him and
us. … Our crime is living in a country where the justice system
supports racist murderers against innocent people' (*The Stephen
Lawrence Inquiry, Volume II*, ch. 42, para. 42.13).

It is a stark and painful claim, one of several in which Doreen
Lawrence draws together the fact of violent racism and the
failure to protect – to value the life of – black men, women and
children in contemporary British culture. In a direct challenge to
the Metropolitan Police following the close of the inquest, she
insisted the following:

> What I was hearing was none of the police officers attending the
> scene made any attempts to see if there was anything they could
> do. They just stood there while my son bleeds to death. None of
> them check to see where the blood was coming from ... There are
> two questions I would like the police to answer, are all officers
> trained in basic first aid, or was it because they just did not want to
> get their hands dirty with a black man's blood? (*The Stephen
> Lawrence Inquiry, Volume II*, ch. 42, para. 42.37)

Black blood, dirty blood: what, if anything, does that association
have to do with the question of unconscious racism at the heart
of the Lawrence Inquiry? An entire chapter of Macpherson's
published report is devoted to the issue of first aid, to the
confusing, often contradictory, reports of who did what – more
precisely, who did nothing – to help Stephen Lawrence as he
bled to death by the side of the road. On whether or not police
officers are adequately trained in first aid, the Lawrence Inquiry
is finally equivocal; nowhere does it (can it?) directly address the
possibility of a profoundly irrational response to the black body
driving the actions of the officers called to the scene of Stephen
Lawrence's death.[2] Yet that possibility is there for Doreen
Lawrence, whose disappointment on publication of *The Stephen
Lawrence Inquiry* was widely publicised. 'It has only scratched
the surface,' she said, during a news conference at the Home
Office, 'and has not gone to the heart of the problem.' Her unease
is palpable and pervasive: racism as a force, a resistance to change,
racism as the problem that will not budge: 'I believe black
youngsters will never be safe on the streets. Nothing has changed.'

> Où qu'il aille, le nègre demeure un nègre
> (Wherever he goes, the Negro remains a Negro) (*Peau noire*: 140;
> *Black Skin*: 173)

'Le nègre est un objet phobogène, anxiogène' ('The Negro is a
phobogenic object, a stimulus to anxiety') (*Peau noire*: 123; *Black
Skin*: 151). First published in 1952, Frantz Fanon's *Peau noire*
remains one of the most persuasive and controversial attempts to
think the unconscious in relation to the institution of racist
violence. 'Nous l'avons dit, il existe des négrophobes' ('I have
said that Negrophobes exist') (*Peau noire*: 43; *Black Skin*: 53) is
how Fanon introduces the concepts of Negrophobia and

Negrophobogenesis which will run a psychoanalysis of phobia into a phenomenology of racism. This is part of Fanon's struggle against the confabulation between fear and knowledge, and between anxiety and reason, at the heart of racist culture. 'Maman, regarde le nègre, j'ai peur!' ('Mummy, look at the Negro! I'm frightened') (Peau noire: 90; tr. mod.: 112): a white child's fright echoes through Peau noire, breaking through to Fanon, breaking *into* him. Letting that fear speak through his writing, Fanon brings his readers up against the question that drives Peau noire: the origins of racist hatred, its role as a destructive force in collective life. Slavery, lynching, segregation: with a child's looking and pointing, Fanon associates some of the most virulent expressions of that hatred, as if discovering the foundations of racism – its passions, its politics – in the figure of a child. 'Mon corps me revenait étalé, disjoint, rétamé, tout endeuillé dans ce jour blanc d'hiver' ('My body came back to me spread out, disconnected, wiped out, cast into mourning on that white winter's day') (Peau noire: 91; tr. mod.: 113), Fanon recalls, taking his readers into a compelling and, by now, canonic scene that runs the 'trembling' of a terrified child into the object of his terror, a black man:

> Le nègre est une bête, le nègre est mauvais, le nègre est méchant, le nègre est laid; tiens un nègre, il fait froid, le nègre tremble, le nègre tremble parce qu'il a froid, le petit garçon tremble parce qu'il a peur du nègre, le nègre tremble de froid, ce froid qui vous tord les os, le beau petit garçon tremble parce qu'il croit que le nègre tremble de rage, le petit garçon blanc se jette dans les bras de sa mère: maman, le nègre va me manger. (Peau noire: 91–2)[3]

Animal, bad, nasty, ugly: black. Fanon knows this child's fear; his writing inhabits it, gives voice to it. A black man trembles, a white child trembles – as if something dreadful is passing between the two: the imago, or fantasm, of the Black. 'Mais quand nous disons', Fanon is about to insist, 'que la culture européenne possède une *imago* du nègre responsable de tous les conflits qui peuvent naître, nous ne dépassons pas le réel' ('But when we say that European culture possesses an *imago* of the Negro responsible for all the conflicts that may arise, we do not go beyond the real') (Peau noire: 136–7; tr. mod.: 169). One white winter's day, on the streets of Lyons, Fanon is confronted by that image of himself in the voice and gesture of a child: a child's appeal to his mother first to look and then to shelter him. From looking to holding, the emergence of the imago sustains the passage between the two, the child acting as if he has been exposed to the mythic discovery of the 'Dark Continent', its overwhelming difference – for which, as Hannah Arendt points out, the 'emergency explanation' is 'race' (Arendt 1973: 185). Trying to calm her son, his mother hastens to reassure Fanon: 'Ne faîtes pas attention, monsieur, il ne sait pas que vous êtes aussi civilisé que nous' ('Pay no attention, sir, he does not know that you are as civilised as we') (*Peau noire*: 91; tr. mod.: 113).

If those words cast Fanon into mourning, it may be because part of what is destructive in the child's fear is the reasons found for it: the black as natural source and respository of fright; fear of blackness as what the child grows out of rather than *into*. Situated at the very heart of the book, the encounter between Fanon, a white mother and her child has become one of the primal scenes of reading *Peau noire*. 'Little more than a footnote to scopophilia' is Nigel Gibson's rebuff to a limited and, on his view, thoroughly institutionalised reading of Fanon established via that 'Look, a Negro!': the scene standing in for *Peau noire*; *Peau noire* standing in for Fanon's oeuvre as such (Gibson 1999: 121).[4] But if this scene has come to symbolise the force, the *resistance*, of racism in European and Anglo-American culture, it is, I want to suggest, because it condenses and, perhaps, contains the upheaval that accompanies Fanon's struggle to open up the concept, and concrete experience, of racism to the unconscious life of the mind. In other words, part of the challenge of a child's 'Look, a Negro!' is as a fragment of theory struggling to find a place in *Peau noire*, a psychoanalysis of racism in which a young boy's ties to his mother, the transference of fear from subject to object, comes right to the fore.

'Le beau nègre vous emmerde, madame!' ('Kiss the handsome negro's ass, madam!') is Fanon's response to that transference, his jarring retort to the woman, still trying to pacify her child – 'Regarde, il est beau, ce nègre' ('Look how handsome that Negro is …') – with a civility that reveals her to be an active participant in her child's fear (*Peau noire*: 92; *Black Skin*: 114). Towards the end of Chapter 6, 'Le Nègre et la psychopathologie', Fanon muses, 'J'ai toujours été frappé par la rapidité avec laquelle on passe de "beau jeune Noir" à "jeune poulain, étalon"' ('I have always been struck by the rapidity with which one travels from "handsome young Black man" to "young colt, stallion"') (*Peau noire*: 135; tr. mod.: 167). What Fanon hears in this woman's words, it seems, is the volatile mix of fascination and repulsion, sexuality and aggression, articulated in the typical forms of phobic fantasy about to be identified through *Peau noire*. 'Qui dit viol dit nègre' ('Whoever says rape says Negro') (*Peau noire*: 134; *Black Skin*: 166), 'Un nègre me viole' ('A Negro is raping me') (*Peau noire*: 144; *Black Skin*: 178) are Fanon's privileged examples of phobia in *Peau noire*: Negrophobia as symptom of sexualized anxiety, as sign of the hallucinatory sexual presence of black men in a phobic imaginary. 'Au fond, cette *peur* du viol n'appelle-t-elle pas, justement, le viol?' ('Basically, does this *fear* of rape not itself cry out for rape?') he wonders, in one of the most provocative moments of the book, 'ne pourrait-on pas décrire des femmes à viol? ('could one not speak of women who ask to be raped?') (*Peau noire*: 127; tr. mod.: 156).

'A means to reify the myth of femininity as masochism' is Jean Walton's response to this passage, one that summarises a pervasive unease that, in displacing the stereotype of the black man as always and ever a rapist, Fanon has invested in a no less troubling version of the feminine (Walton 1995: 792; see also, for example, Doane 1991; Edelman 1994; Fuss 1994). Certainly, it is with this vision of feminine fantasy that Fanon attempts to settle the issue of Negrophobia, the connivance between infantile fantasy and a cultural institutionalisation of hatred. In this sense, part of the work of *Peau noire* is to shift the provenance of phobia from the object (its 'natural' and nauseating properties) to the phobic subject, a struggle that, as Jacques André points out, helps to determine Fanon's characteristic presentation of psycho-analysis as, at once, absolutely indispensable and perfectly useless (André 1982: 111).[5] Fanon's controversial reading of sexuality and sexual difference, his description of the negrophobic woman driven by a complex mix of desire and revulsion belonging to her *own* libidinal life, enables precisely that shift. 'Le phantasme du viol par le nègre', Fanon concludes, 'est une variante de cette représentation: "Je souhaite que le nègre m'éventre comme moi

je l'aurais fait d'une femme"' ('The fantasy of rape by a negro is a
variant of this representation: "I wish that the negro would rip
me open as I would have done to a woman"') (*Peau noire*: 144–5;
tr. mod.: 179). Living the fantasy of being raped by a black man,
the white woman rapes herself raping a woman, a coalition that
underlines the conceptual turmoil accompanying any attempt to
distinguish between activity and passivity at the level of the
drive (masochists, as Jean Laplanche has put it, 'are very active
in getting their masochistic satisfaction' (quoted in Fletcher and
Stanton (eds) 1992: 80)).

Drawing on the psychoanalysis of female sexuality put
forward through the 1940s by Helene Deutsch and Marie
Bonaparte, Fanon writes his way into that turmoil via the figure
of the young white girl, oscillating between clitoris (activity,
sadism, masculinity) and vagina (passivity, masochism, femininity), between infantile and oedipal fantasy. But if we are back
with the problem of the origins of phobia, the black man as
predestined depositary of a young girl's aggression, Fanon is also
shifting the burden of phobic provocation from object to
structure, to the dynamics of desire and transgression internal to
the psychoanalytic concept of the Oedipus complex. Put this
way, (Negro)phobia returns as a question of cultural investiture,
a symptom marking the child's transition into the sexual and
symbolic life of culture. Is this a form of sacrifice, perhaps?[6] As
both Fanon and Deutsch suggest in their various reflections on
the 'terrible penalties' (Deutsch's phrase) inflicted on black men
accused of raping white women, if 'a negro is raping me' exhibits
a form of feminine masochism, its unelaborated appeal to the law,
to violent retribution, can also function as a death threat against
the black man identified with rape in a racist culture.[7] In other
words, the collective representation of the infant's fantasy of
disemboweling the mother sustains its fusion of passivity and
aggression; the cultural stereotype – the 'Negro myth', the black
imago – displaces *and* re-enacts the drama of self–other violation
that Fanon discovers in the white girl's unconscious: '"Je souhaite
que le nègre m'éventre comme moi je l'aurais fait d'une femme".'

Part of what is at issue is an understanding of conscious, and
collective, fantasy driven by the wishful-shameful intimacies of
the infant self, by the transposition and projection of unbearable

drive out into the world. But, read alongside the scene that unfolds from a child's 'Look, a Negro!', the work of Fanon's interpretation of negrophobic fantasy goes further than that insofar as it attempts (and, given its critical notoriety, largely achieves) a displacement of the question of phobia in *Peau noire* – a displacement clarified by Fanon's response to the felt pressure of the negrophobic stereotype in Lyons. In particular, his reply to the child's mother, that rebuke to a white woman, is described by Fanon himself as a moment of liberation from thinking – 'Enfin, j'étais libéré de ma rumination' ('Finally, I had been liberated from my thinking') (*Peau noire*: 92; tr. mod.: 114) – from the painful reflections on the meaning of blackness precipitated by this mother and her child. In place of thought, there is a white woman's shame: 'La honte lui orna le visage' ('Shame flooded her face') (*Peau noire*: 92; *Black Skin*: 114).

Such an acknowledgement – a projection of thought, of painful thought, on to the white woman – is remarkable not least because it begins to draw attention to the overdetermination of the interpretation of sexuality and phobia about to be put forward in 'Le Nègre et la psychopathologie'. In other words, that model of phobia – Fanon's attention to the trauma of sexuality, to sexuality as trauma – is bound to his struggle *not to think* the transfer of a white boy's fear, his mother's reason, into the black body, to refuse the fraught opening to the world that the Black comes to represent in *Peau noire*. That opening is explored throughout the book, nowhere more poignantly than in Fanon's visceral response to his sudden identification with the black imago on the streets of Lyons, his reflections on the uncanny black body composed of, and so subject to, the words and images of a racist culture. 'J'avais créé au-dessous du schéma corporel un schéma historico-racial' ('I had created below the corporeal schema a historical-racial schema'), Fanon writes (*Peau noire*: 90; tr. mod.: 111), a schema forged through a narrative and visual imaginary of the Black: anthropophagy, mental retardation, fetishism, racial defects, slavers. '[L]e Blanc', he continues, ' ... m'avait tissé de mille détails, anecdotes, récits' ('[T]he White ... had woven me from a thousand details, anecdotes, stories') (*Peau noire*: 90; tr. mod.: 111) – details, anecdotes, stories which interrupt the sensible life of the black body, its capacity for touch, sight, hearing. That body, the black subject's being in his or her body, gives way at this point. More precisely, on contact with the white world of the black, a potential to give way, to crumble, becomes a way of being. 'Le Noir n'a pas de résistance ontologique aux yeux du Blanc' ('The black man has no ontological resistance in the eyes of the white man'), Fanon insists (*Peau noire*: 88: *Black Skin*: 110); 'Alors le schéma corporel, attaqué en plusieurs points, s'écroula, cédant la place à un schéma épidermique racial' ('Then the corporeal schema, attacked on several points, crumbled, giving way to a racial epidermal schema') (*Peau noire*: 90; *Black Skin*: 112).

The very surface of the body, Fanon seems to be saying, is inhabited by history, by hatred; its skin, its protective layer, vulnerable to an other already there, and agitating. As resistance crumbles, so the work of subjectivity – agency, creativity – becomes that of putting oneself together from the words, phrases, images invested in that body by (white) others. It is not, for Fanon, a question of hearing oneself spoken about, of discovering the self, in the third person; rather, the othering at issue here involves a type of rupture, the self broken between the corporeal and the epidermal, between body and history, between I and the *White*. Not being spoken of but being spoken *by*, as it were. In this instance, a child's words – 'Tiens, un nègre!' – cue that rupture, Fanon's representation of himself torn open, spattered with black blood, as if his body is erupting from within. At risk is his capacity for being human – 'Je voulais être homme, rien qu'homme' ('I wanted to be a man, nothing but a man') – in a world which uses the black body to mark the limits of the civilised community: 'Ne faîtes pas attention, monsieur, il ne sait pas que vous êtes aussi civilisé que nous' ('Pay no attention, sir, he does not know that you are as civilized as we') (*Peau noire*: 91; tr. mod.: 113).

'Qu'est-ce que la phobie?' ('What is phobia?') (*Peau noire*: 125; *Black Skin*: 154). Fanon's question comes in response to that passage from (white) fear to (black) mourning, from phobic to phobic object. In fact, from beginning to end of *Peau noire*, the question of phobia will be thought from the side of the object, Negrophobia as a means to explore not only the articulation between anxiety and object (Freud's question) but the fact, or fate, of *being* that object: animal, bad, nasty, ugly, black. 'Naturellement,' Fanon notes ironically in an initial response to that question, 'cet objet devra revêtir certains aspects. Il faut, dit Hesnard, qu'il éveille la crainte et le dégoût. Mais là nous rencontrons une difficulté' (*Peau noire*: 125–6).[8] The phobic object as one that *naturally* arouses fear and disgust? There, Fanon insists, we meet with a difficulty, one that is going to determine his hesitation between a psychoanalysis of the lived experience of the black and a psychoanalytic interpretation of the 'Negro myth' (*Peau noire*: 123; *Black Skin*: 151). The concept of Negrophobia becomes the bridge between the two, the support of Fanon's contention that white culture lies at the origins of every black neurosis: part of the lived experience of the black is living with, and through, the madness of the black imago (*Peau noire*: 123; *Black Skin*: 151). Reflecting on the collision and collusion between the two, Fanon thinks racism – both concept and affect – as a symptom of European culture, its attempt to bind anxiety by institutionalising black men, women and children as its objects.

Anxiety, as Freud puts it in his analysis of 'Little Hans', is 'without an object' (Freud 1909: 24). 'Patients cannot say what it is they are afraid of,' he observes to an audience gathered at the University of Vienna in 1917, 'and, by the help of an unmistakable secondary revision, link it to the first phobias that come to hand' (Freud 1917: 403). As something to be scared of, then, the phobic object belongs to the world of the dream. ('Phobias', declares Charles Odier in *Anxiety and Magic Thinking*, first published in 1947 and one of the key sources for Fanon's thinking on phobia, 'are nightmares of the awakened state' (Odier 1956: 65).) The phobic object belongs to the process of secondary revision that, as Freud describes it in 1900, 'fills up the gaps in the dream-structure with shreds and patches' (Freud 1900: 490). Like the dreamer – or, more accurately, the dreamer on whom the pressure of the censor is being brought to bear – the phobic is unable to bear the 'gap' in the world that threatens him, or her, with senselessness: anxiety without an object, anxiety as the loss of the object that makes sense of the world.

It is another *other scene*, entangling *Peau noire* in the knot that characterises the psychoanalysis of anxiety from its beginnings in Freud's studies of phobia in the 1890s. 'The anxiety belonging to this emotional state,' Freud writes in one of his first forays into 'Obsessions and phobias' in 1895, 'which underlies all phobias, is not derived from any memory; we may well wonder what the source of this powerful condition of the nervous system can be' (Freud 1895: 81). Freud will continue to wonder, and worry, not only about the obscure origin of anxiety but about the mechanism for identifying the phobic object itself – be it 'common' or 'contingent', as he puts it in the same essay (Freud 1895: 80). Some ideas appear to be 'adapted to become the subject of a phobia', Freud continues in a telling phrase which, in one form or another, runs through psychoanalytic approaches to the topic (Freud 1895: 81). In particular, the suggestion that certain fears are 'common' ('night, solitude, death, illnesses, dangers in general, snakes, etc.' are Freud's examples in 1895) brings anxiety and phobia into contact with the idea of the typical – and, by extension, the stereotypical – in psychoanalysis.

It is an odd and complex topic, one that runs through psychoanalytic attempts to talk about the world beyond the consulting room: typical fears, typical symptoms, typical dreams. In his analysis of Negrophobia, Fanon will engage with all three, using psychoanalysis to give some account of the violent articulation between anxiety and object; more precisely, of the articulation between anxiety and object *as* violence. The pressure of the sexual stereotype (black rapist, sado-masochistic white woman) marks the work of that violence in *Peau noire*, driving Fanon towards an interpretation of phobia that veers between insight and cliché – suspending the concept of Negrophobia between (at least) two different representations of anxiety in psychoanalysis.[9] Writing against the fantasm of the black man as rapist, for example, Fanon pits the truth of unconscious fantasy against the delusory literalism of conscious avowal: 'Au fond, cette *peur* du viol n'appelle-t-elle pas, justement, le viol?' In other words, there is phobia because there is desire, anxiety because there is repression, a formulation that repeats Freud's enduring account of anxiety as the effect of a transformation of longing into fear.[10]

Crucially, however, this is an account of anxiety called into question by Fanon's turn to Charles Odier's *Anxiety and Magic*

Thinking; specifically, its debt to Freud's complex and contradictory essay, 'Inhibitions, symptoms and anxiety', published in 1926. 'The reading and study of this paper', Odier declares towards the beginning of *Anxiety and Magic Thinking*, 'was one of the most inspiring moments of my life as an analyst' – inspiration that is clearly directing the course of his presentation on phobia, its emphasis on the 'earliest and most primitive levels of psychic experience' (Odier 1956: 65). 'Appliquant à la compréhension de la phobie la méthode génétique,' Fanon recalls, in an initial attempt to counter Hesnard, 'Charles Odier écrit: "Toute angoisse provient d'une certaine insécurité subjective liée à l'absence de la mère." Cela se passe, dit l'auteur, aux environs de la deuxième année' (*Peau noire*: 126).[11] In other words, countering the idea of anxiousness as the effect of a transformation of libido, Odier renews Freud's emphasis on the fundamental helplessness of being human, on the fearful child as a privileged figure of anxiety in, and for, psychoanalysis.[12] 'The reason why the infant in arms wants to perceive the presence of his mother,' Freud claims in 1926, 'is only because it already knows by experience that she satisfies all its needs without delay' (Freud 1926: 137). Anxiety is a reaction to tension – 'the *growing tension*,' Freud qualifies, '*due to need*, against which it (the infant) is helpless'. It is the menace presented by sensations of need and longing, including the longing to see the mother (Freud 1926).[13] Freud therefore pits transformation against 'tension', libido against 'danger'.

In 'Inhibitions, symptoms and anxiety' the idea of anxiety as adaptive, a response to a real danger – the loss of the mother as a threat to life, say – drives Freud's thinking, fractures it. At the same time, continuing to write against a notion of realistic apprehension in children, Freud is explicit that 'nothing resembling death can ever have been experienced'; death is the very type of a 'gap in the universe', a fear without content, without image, especially in the unconscious that, Freud is convinced, 'contain(s) nothing that could give any content to our concept of the annihilation of life' (Freud 1926: 130, 129). In this sense, the anxiety generated by the infant's apparent fear for itself, its wish to preserve itself *against*, is doubly unbound: anxiety is 'without an object' while death can be neither experienced nor represented. Or, to put the point differently, the infant's wish to preserve itself is driven by the absence of the mother, by a not-being-there that may be one way for the baby to experience a form of death; when the mother is away, as Winnicott puts it, 'she is dead from the point of view of the child' (Winnicott 1971: 22).

It is an unsettling insight, one that suspends the primal scene of anxiety between sexuality and helplessness, longing and a fear of annihilation of self. This suspension is obscured in 'Le Nègre et la psychopathologie' as Fanon immediately runs Freud–Odier's preoccupation with the fearful child into the problematic of sexual trauma and heterosexual and homosexual rape. 'Le choix de l'objet phobogène est donc *surdéterminé*,' Fanon concludes, before seizing on the questions which will prepare the way for his analysis of negrophobia as symptom of sexual anxiety: 'y a-t-il eu traumatisme désecurisant chez cette jeune femme dont nous parlions tout à l'heure? Chez la plupart des négrophobes masculins, y a-t-il eu tentative de rapt?' (*Peau noire*: 126).[14] It is as if, however scandalous, the drama of inter-racial fear and desire is more able to be thought through *Peau noire* than the idea of separation from, and dependence on, the mother as source of phobic fear.[15] Writing, as Ralph Ellison points out, can be a form of acting out, a means to relive – and perhaps to resist – what cannot be subjected to thought (Ellison 1964: xi). Displacing shame, displacing desire, on to the white woman, Fanon discovers a powerful heuristic strategy that, while challenging one of the most tenacious aspects of the Negro myth, repeats the inversion, '*transitivisme intégral*', which he identifies as a determining element of the rape fantasy itself: 'Au fond, cette *peur* du viol n'appelle-t-elle pas, justement, le viol?'

Unsophisticated, untenable, even confused is David Macey's recent judgement on Fanon's uses of psychoanalysis, one that tests *Peau noire* against a (presumed) psychoanalytic orthodoxy (Macey 2000: 135, 193, 323). But the challenge of *Peau noire* – and, in particular, its attempt to mobilise a psychoanalysis of Negrophobia – may not be readable in terms of how far Fanon conforms, or not, to psychoanalytic doctrine. On the contrary, it is *as writing* that *Peau noire* enacts an interpretation of psychoanalysis, one which is at its most original and provocative when it comes in the form of *mise-en-scène* ('Look, a Negro!'), when 'theory' is suffused by the work of condensation (repression?) which marks those few pages of the book devoted to the discussion of phobia – reopening the question of phobia, its articulation between anxiety and object, on to a scene in which the black man is caught up not, or not only, in the dramas of a wayward libido but in the imaginary experience of death.

Notes

1 My thanks to Alan Sinfield, Nicholas Royle, David Marriott and Vincent Quinn for their comments on this chapter.

2 On the question of first aid training, see *The Stephen Lawrence Inquiry, Volume 1*, ch. 10, para. 10.25. Certainly, once the concept of unconscious racism had been introduced, it was no longer possible for the Metropolitan Police to deny any such association and its part in the actions and omissions of its officers. That, precisely, was the ground of Sir Paul Condon's refusal to accept the possibility of institutional racism: 'My anxiety is with this notion of some collective will, that people – intelligent, well-meaning people – don't actually know what they are doing' (Cathcart 1999: 358). Clearly, such a prospect is remarkably unsettling if, as in the instance of a public inquiry, both individuals and institutions are being called to account.

3 'The Negro is an animal, the Negro is bad, the Negro is nasty, the Negro is ugly; look, a Negro, it's cold, the Negro is trembling, the Negro is trembling because he is cold, the little boy is trembling because he is afraid of the Negro, the Negro is trembling with cold, that cold which gets into your bones, the beautiful little boy is trembling because he believes that the Negro is trembling with rage, the little white boy throws himself into his mother's arms: Mother, the Negro is going to eat me up' (tr. mod.: 113–14).

4 This is an objection made on behalf of politics, history and knowledge – 'I claim an authentic Fanon', Gibson concludes – that may blind itself to the specific contexts out of which the disputed reading of this scene was first made. Certainly, the idea of a visual imaginary, of the activity of looking and being looked at subtending the cultural stereotype, has proved remarkably productive in studies of the book. But, if Homi Bhabha's reinterpretation of Fanon is very much at issue – notably, 'The Other question: the stereotype and colonial discourse', first published in 1983, and the Foreword to a new English edition of *Peau noire* in 1986 – a sense of the political need to think the psychoanalytic dimensions of Fanon's text which sparked that reading has become the blindspot of a new criticism which is content to pit the one against the other: psychoanalysis *or* politics. That is not, I think, the question, or possibility, imposed by *Peau noire*: *not* psychoanalysis or politics; not even psychoanalysis *and* politics – the certainty of that 'and' at odds with the process of questioning that

comes with Freud's concept of the unconscious and, of course, with the closing line of *Peau noire*: 'O mon corps, fais de moi toujours un homme qui interroge!' ('Oh my body, make of me a man who always questions') (*Peau noire*: 188; tr. mod.: 232).

5 It is often commented that Fanon is uneasy with psychoanalysis. 'Although Fanon is often described as a "psychoanalyst",' writes David Macey in a critical response to recent Fanon scholarship, 'he was not and his relationship with psychoanalysis was always fraught' (Macey 2000: 134). It is an apparently uncontentious claim: Fanon did not train as a psycho-analyst and his relation to psychoanalysis is nothing if not complex. But that difficulty, together with the issue of training, of institutional affiliation (who is authorised to speak of, on behalf of, psychoanalysis?), is part of Fanon's challenge as a *thinker* of psychoanalysis, one who breaks new ground by bringing the founding concepts of psychoanalysis to bear on racism – and racism to bear on psychoanalysis. As André puts the point – one that is both obvious and curiously overlooked – Fanon's oscillation between psychology and politics is inseparable from the object in question: race, racism (André 1982: 111).

6 In particular, adapting Deutsch's *Psychology of Women* to the vicissitudes of 'a Negro is raping me', Fanon articulates the defensive mechanisms of that projection with the young girl's entry into – her penetration of, her identification with – a culture bound to take up, and contain, the libidinal aggression overrunning the child's relations to the mother-father. It is worth noting that Fanon is giving full weight to a psychoanalytic concept of the Oedipus complex as a structuring of both sexual and collective life. The function of so-called 'Oedipal law' is to route the child into (or out of) culture as well as sexual difference. In this sense, Fanon is describing one way for the young girl to identify with the norms and ethics of her community – an identification which runs counter to an influential idea of the feminine as that which falls outside the law, has no 'stake' (i.e. no penis, nothing to lose) in society.

7 Consider Deutsch's brief reference to the very public life of 'a negro is raping me' in the racially segregated culture of the Southern states: 'It is precisely rape fantasies that often have such irresistible verisimilitude that even the most experienced judges are misled in trials of innocent men accused of rape by hysterical women. My own experience of accounts by white women of rape by Negroes (who are often subjected to terrible penalties as a result of these accusations) has convinced me that many fantastic stories are produced by the masochistic yearnings of these women' (Deutsch 1944: 256). Deutsch's longstanding interest in the idea of what, in 1921, she describes as the 'daydream communicated as reality' – the psychology of pseudology, of *folie à deux* – is crucial to a deeper understanding of this notorious passage. (For further discussion on the controversy of Deutsch's views, see Brownmiller 1975 and Forrester 1990). Deutsch's parenthesis of the violence implicit to this fantasy is also reminiscent of Joan Riviere's influential 'Womanliness as a masquerade', first published in 1929. Fanon's account of the socialisation of white

femininity is remarkably close to that described by Riviere – but the scene of racial violence is literally bracketed out of her account (and, as Jean Walton points out, of most responses to her work (Walton 1995)). Riviere's patient suffers from acute anxiety after appearing in public – anxiety that Riviere tracks back through a variety of daydreams and fantasies, including the following: 'This phantasy, it then appeared, had been very common in her childhood and youth, which had been spent in the Southern States of America; if a negro came to attack her, she planned to defend herself by making him kiss her and make love to her (ultimately so that she could then deliver him over to justice)' (Riviere 1929: 37–8). Deutsch, you might say, opens Riviere's text on to the scene of violent retribution at once recorded and occluded here.

8 'Naturally that object must have certain aspects. It must arouse, Hesnard says, both fear and revulsion. But here we ecounter a difficulty' (*Black Skin*: 154).

9 It is a pressure that recalls Homi Bhabha's Foreword to the new English edition of *Peau noire* in 1986 – in particular, his brief 'Note' warning that the sexual politics of the book should elicit more than a 'facile charge of "sexism"' (Bhabha 1986: xxvi). Bhabha does not elaborate the point, but he is the first reader of Fanon to make the connection between the stereotypes of sexuality and sexual difference in *Peau noire* and its aversion from a 'fuller' psychoanalytic discussion of culture and aggression: 'In chapter 6 he attempts a somewhat more complex reading of masochism but in making the Negro the "*predestined* depository of this aggression" [Bhabha's emphasis] he again pre-empts a fuller psychoanalytic discussion of the production of psychic aggressivity in identification and its relation to cultural difference, by citing the cultural stereotype as the predestined aim of the sexual drive' (Bhabha 1986: xxvi). This is a tantalising conclusion, not least in its call to find in *Peau noire*, in between its lines, an order of psychoanalytic discussion pre-empted, *interrupted*, by the drama of inter-racial desire trafficked through 'The Negro and psychopathology'.

10 On the vicissitudes of Freud's theory of anxiety, see the Editorial Introduction to 'Inhibitions, symptoms and anxiety' (1926), in *Standard Edition*, Vol. XX (or *Pelican Freud*, Vol. 10); see also Weber (1982).

11 'Applying the genetic method to the understanding of phobia, Charles Odier writes: "All anxiety comes from a certain subjective insecurity linked to the absence of the mother." This happens, according to the author, at some time in the second year of life' (tr. mod.: 154–5). That Fanon is quoting from Odier's text at this point is lost in the current English translation of *Peau noire*. The passage appears as paraphrase.

12 The fearful child, the helpless infant, are central to Freud's various debates with himself and others on the problem of *Angst* – calling into question the distinctions between neurotic and normal, drive and real, longing and danger, supposed to organise a psychoanalytic understanding of anxiety. 'Apprehensiveness in children is something very usual,' Freud observes to an audience gathered at the University of Vienna in 1917, 'and it seems

most difficult to distinguish whether it is neurotic or realistic anxiety' (Freud 1917: 405). 'Difficult', but at this point Freud is keen to pit libido, or *longing*, against any common-sense explanation of children's fears as the realistic measure of their weakness in a basically hostile world.

13 Compare this with the account of childhood phobia put forward in the lecture on 'Anxiety' in 1917. 'At the very beginning,' Freud observes, 'what children are afraid of is strange *people*', people who are strange and frightening – cast as the first phobic objects? – because they disappoint the child's *wish* to see his or her mother. Again, this is an account of phobia which derives the fear of strangers – of strangers, foreigners, 'the image of hatred and of the other', as Julia Kristeva puts it – from the vicissitudes of childhood libido (Kristeva 1991: 1). 'It is his disappointment and longing that are transformed into anxiety,' Freud explains, '– his libido, in fact, which has become unemployable, which cannot at that time be held in suspense and is discharged as anxiety' (Freud 1917: 406–7).

14 'The choice of phobogenic object is therefore *overdetermined*'; 'has there been a trauma detrimental to her sense of security in the young woman we mentioned earlier? Among the majority of negrophobic men, has there been an attempt at rape?' (tr. mod.: 155).

15 As Jacques André points out, Fanon does not pursue the significance of the mother, her relation to the white-black imaginary, though the book could be said to be haunted by her (André 1982: 122).

References

André, J. (1982) 'Fanon, entre le réel et l'inconscient: à propos de la relation raciale', *Mémorial International: Frantz Fanon*, 31 Mar.–3 Apr., Paris: Présence Africaine

Arendt, H. (1973) *The Origins of Totalitarianism* (first pub. 1951), London: André Deutsch

Brownmiller, S. (1975) *Against Our Will: Men, Women and Rape*, London: Secker and Warburg

Cathcart, B. (1999) *The Case of Stephen Lawrence*, London: Viking

Deutsch, H. (1944) *The Psychology of Women*, New York: Grune and Stratton

Doane, M. A. (1991) 'Dark Continents: epistemologies of racial and sexual difference in psychoanalysis and the cinema', in *Femmes Fatales: Feminism, Film Theory, Psychoanalysis*, New York: Routledge

Edelman, L. (1994) *Homographesis: Essays in Gay Literary and Cultural Theory*, London: Routledge

Ellison, R. (1964) *Shadow and Act*, New York: Random House

Fletcher, J. and Stanton, M. (eds) (1992) *Jean Laplanche: Seduction, Translation and the Drives*, London: Institute of Contemporary Arts

Forrester, J. (1990) *The Seductions of Psychoanalysis*, Cambridge: Cambridge University Press

Freud, S. (1954–74) *The Standard Edition of the Complete Psychological Works of Sigmund Freud* (hereafter *SE*), London: The Hogarth Press and the Institute of Psychoanalysis

―― (1895) 'Obsessions and phobias: their psychical mechanism and their aetiology', *SE*, vol. III

―― (1900) 'The interpretation of dreams', *SE*, vols IV–V

―― (1909) 'Analysis of a phobia in a five-year-old boy', *SE*, vol. X

―― (1917) *Introductory Lectures on Psycho-Analysis (1916–1917)*, *SE*, vol. XVI

―― (1926) 'Inhibitions, symptoms and anxiety', *SE*, vol. XX

Fuss, D. (1994) 'Interior colonies: Frantz Fanon and the politics of identification', *diacritics* 24 (2–3): 20–42

Gibson, N. (1999) 'Fanon and the pitfalls of cultural studies', in A. C. Alessandrini (ed.), *Frantz Fanon: Critical Perspectives*, London and New York: Routledge, 99–125

Kristeva, J. (1991) *Strangers to Ourselves* (trans. Leon S. Roudiez), New York: Columbia University Press

Laplanche, J. (1989) *New Foundations for Psychoanalysis* (trans. D. Macey), Oxford: Basil Blackwell

―― (1997) *Le Primat de l'Autre en psychanalyse*, Paris: Flammarion

―― (1999) *Essays on Otherness*, London: Routledge

Macey, D. (2000) *Frantz Fanon: A Life*, London: Granta

Marriott, D. (2000) *On Black Men*, Columbia: Columbia University Press

Odier, C. (1956) *Anxiety and Magic Thinking*, New York: International Universities Press

Riviere, J. (1929) 'Womanliness as a masquerade' in V. Burgin, J. Donald and C. Kaplan (eds) (1986), *Formations of Fantasy*, London: Routledge

Roudinesco, E. (1991–2) 'A propos d'une lettre de A. Hesnard', *Les Carnets de psychanalyse* 2: 159–62

―― (1997) *Jacques Lacan*, Cambridge: Polity Press

Rustin, M. (1991) *The Good Society and the Inner World*, London: Verso

Walton, J. (1995) 'Re-placing race in (white) psychoanalytic discourse: founding narratives of feminism', *Critical Inquiry*, 21: 775–804

Weber, S. (1982) *The Legend of Freud*, Minneapolis: University of Minnesota Press

Winnicott, D. W. (1971) *Playing and Reality*, London: Tavistock

8

En moi: Frantz Fanon and René Maran

DAVID MARRIOTT

> But I have that within which passeth show; / These but the
> trappings and the suits of woe (*Hamlet*, Act 1 Scene 2)
> (Mais j'ai ceci en moi qui surpasse l'apparence; le reste n'est que
> faste et parture de la douleur, *Hamlet*, trans. André Gide, Paris:
> Gallimard, 1946)

> La première caractéristique semble être la peur de se montrer tel
> qu'on est
> (The first characteristic seems to be the dread of showing oneself as
> one actually is) (Germaine Guex, *La névrose d'abandon*, cited in
> *Peau noire*: 62; *Black Skin*: 77)

In 1947 the art critic Harold Rosenberg published a long
meditation on *Hamlet*: 'The stages: a geography of human action'
appeared in the first issue of *Possibilities*. Taking as his starting
point Hamlet's 'I have that within which passeth show', Rosenberg presents *Hamlet* as the tragedy of a man 'who attempted in
vain to seize his life as particular to him' – a man caught between
the two worlds, or stages, of the dead and the living (Rosenberg
1947/8: 65). At stake for Rosenberg are the connections between
being and seeming – the wish 'to denote oneself truly' as against
'playing one's part' (Rosenberg 1947/8: 50). 'Why is the grave-
yard so crowded?' he wonders in 'The stages', reflecting on 'the
longing of the dead' who 'have no place to go' – it is a void, an
abyss, an emptiness – producing 'a new ontological anxiety' (for
those still clinging on to life's 'single visible stage'): 'the anxiety
to get into the act. And to decide whether the part assigned is

really one's own part' (Rosenberg 1947/8: 47, 48). To play a part
or to act, this is Hamlet's anxiety; his situation haunted, according
to Rosenberg, by something 'hiddenly particular to him', something beyond 'the visible platform of action' – 'that within'
(Rosenberg 1947/8: 50).

This image of a gap or hiatus is one that runs throughout
Rosenberg's reading of the play – and one which sustains his
vision of Hamlet as a man driven to act 'historically', dialectically,
by the dead 'from whom no history is free'; the dead who act, in
Marx's words, as '"a nightmare on the brain of the living"'
(Rosenberg 1947/8: 52, 53).[1] Certainly, for Rosenberg, Hamlet
learns his 'situation' from the vision of the dead father, the ghost
to whom that within calls: it is an inner (mournful) history
imagined in the form of something intimate, unwilled – and, once
again, part of what links Hamlet to 'the dark offstage' (Rosenberg
1947/8: 49, 50). History, act, situation: suspended between these
three terms, Hamlet is caught up in the difficulty of their relation,
one complicated still further by his 'tortured conscience' (to
borrow Ernest Jones's phrase), his inability to transcend the
contradiction between being and acting, 'is and seems' (Rosenberg 1947/8: 65; Jones 1976: 57). On the cusp between sanity and
madness, at once driven from without and from within, on
Rosenberg's reading Hamlet's conflict opens up on to another
scene: the tragic relation between 'that within' and the 'utter
irony of human existence' (Rosenberg 1947/8: 65).

That irony, of being trapped in a role one can neither finally
satisfy nor forgo, is central to this essay, its exploration of how
the idea of a gap in being that is both inexpressible and yet
deeply haunting comes to inhabit Frantz Fanon's response to the
fiction of René Maran; more specifically, their shared fascination
with the vicissitudes of mourning and history, race and psyche –
Rosenberg's 'that within'. In their different ways, both Fanon
and Maran struggle with an image of black life as one haunted –
as one, in effect, spellbound by a racist imaginary. In a series of
autobiographical novels begun in the 1920s, for example, Maran
portrays black men caught up in the despair of a double life, men
forced to wear existential disguises, pushed deeper inside
themselves by the racial imagos of white reality. The tragedy for
Maran (and Fanon) is that that reality is already part of their

inner lives; hidden behind the self's disguises, encased in its expectations. Theirs is an image of racial subjugation and complicity that embodies not so much existential anxiety as something like the feeling of being out of joint, 'désorienté' ('completely dislocated') by a fantasm or gap, rising between the ego and its others (*Peau noire*: 91; *Black Skin*: 112). The 'that within' is felt to be both outside the self and inside the self at the same time while serving, simultaneously, as a symbol of racism's spectral life. In other words, one of the major impacts of racism is the sense of coming across an intruding double in whose ghostly, enigmatic and hallucinatory movement the ego undergoes 'un décollement, un arrachement' ('an amputation, an excision') (*Peau noire*: 91; *Black Skin*: 112).

Symbolising that amputee – the miserable, neurotic black man at the heart of *Peau noire* – Maran is, for Fanon, a man driven to excise what he simply 'dare not or cannot avow to himself' (Jones 1976: 57). It is a disavowal and a delay which, in one sense, come to Fanon through *Hamlet*. What Fanon uncovers in Maran – through psychoanalysis, through literature – is a 'that within' arising from the roles Blacks are forced to play by, or in, European culture; a massification of what, in *Peau noire*, he describes as the black man's experience of being the 'victime éternel d'une essence, d'un *apparaître* dont il n'est pas le responsable' ('eternal victim of an essence, of an *appearance* for which he is not responsible') (*Peau noire*: 27; *Black Skin*: 35). Wedded to the neuroses and violence of that appearance-disappearance are racist projections and myths, where the desire to play one's part is all. At stake is the part played by the being of the Black. More precisely, it is the drama as posed by Maran's novel, *Un homme pareil aux autres*, with its powerful restaging of Hamlet's mournful address to his mother – 'I have that within which passeth show; / These but the trappings and the suits of woe' – as an image of black selfhood. Not least, it is an image of the black man upset and overwhelmed by a phantasm projected on to him as if on to an imaginary screen. Fanon writes, 'mon corps me revenait étalé, disjoint, rétamé, tout endeuillé dans ce jour blanc d'hiver' ('my body was given back to me sprawled out, distorted, recolored, clad in mourning in that white winter day'), describing the enigmatic effects of a child's phobic speech

(*Peau noire*: 91; *Black Skin*: 113). As I want to show, the idea and (at times) the act of being *overdetermined* by an imago are central to Fanon's reading of the uncanny, spectral logic of racism, its transformation of self and being through an experience of absolute difference and deepest intimacy. That dramatisation of racism's spectral life can become one of the points of connection, or confusion, between psyche and culture, internal life and outside world, as well as part of the dialogue between psycho-analysis and literature in *Peau noire*. It is a dialogue fascinated and fixated by Maran's vision of interracial love in *Un homme pareil aux autres*. Ultimately, I want to suggest, it is a dialogue that takes place over the black man's desire, or longing, for white women, a scene – both imaginary and real – haunted by the loving-hateful dimensions of culture. That scene is going to put before us an image of black inner life as one usurped and invaded, so to speak, by a blackness mournfully worn within.

Spectral sex

There is, it seems, something uncanny in the way we see ghosts, something seen but also not there. Jacques Derrida, in *Spectres de Marx*, refers to 'une structure d'apparition disparaissante' ('a structure of disappearing apparition') to describe this haunted way of seeing the world (Derrida 1993: 165; Derrida 1994: 101). At the same time, as Fanon's ruminations on desire and love make clear, the strangeness, the uneasiness, marking the uncanny return of the ghost is all the graver because of its white flesh, its dreamlike body:

> De la partie la plus noire de mon âme, à travers la zone hachurée me monte ce désir tout à coup *blanc*. Je ne veux pas être reconnu comme *Noir*, mais comme *Blanc*. Or – et c'est là une reconnaissance que Hegel n'a pas décrite – qui peut le faire, sinon la Blanche? En m'aimant, elle me prouve que je suis digne d'un amour blanc. On m'aime comme un Blanc. Je suis un Blanc. Son amour m'ouvre l'illustre couloir qui mène à la prégnance totale. (*Peau noire*: 51)[2]

Where does the wish, the desire to be white come from? 'De la partie la plus noire de mon âme' ('Out of the blackest part of my soul'), Fanon tells us, a phrase which brings the desire to be recognised, to be loved 'like a white man', into implicit contact with both 'une reconnaissance que Hegel n'a pas décrite' ('a form of recognition that Hegel had not envisaged') – and something driven from *within*: in 'le nègre [...] qui cherche à coucher avec la Blanche' ('the Negro who wants to go to bed with a white woman'), Fanon observes in his 'Introduction', lurks 'un désir d'être Blanc' ('a wish to be white') and '(u)ne soif de vengeance' (a 'lust for revenge') (*Peau noire*: 10–11; *Black Skin*: 16).

What (if any) is the connection between love and whiteness? Between wish and revenge – the lust for being over appearance – and a 'revenantial' love conjured up by black longing? Is not this shadow in the soul also haunted? 'The ghost is the unresolved flesh of the event', writes Rosenberg; it is 'the act that will denote him [Hamlet] truly' (Rosenberg 1947/8: 53). Rosenberg's brief, but tantalising, comments on the ghost anticipate Derrida's musings on the revenant:

> Car la chair et la phénoménalité, voilà ce qui donne à l'esprit son apparition spectacle, mais disparaît aussitôt dans l'apparition, dans la venue même du *revenant* ou le retour du spectre. Il y a du disparu dans l'apparition même comme réapparition du disparu. (Derrida 1993: 25)[3]

Something disappeared, departed? Something that appears as the reapparition of the departed? There is indeed something strange and ghostlike in Fanon's desire, something unseen in his wish to be seen as a *white* man. This is a moment that he names, enigmatically, as love – love is what binds the gap between recognition and realisation, love is what fills the gap between a whiteness felt as missing, absent, and a whiteness that returns like an internal foreign body. In this way, love serves as a double site of witnessing: the witness of a claim to be human and the witness of one who cannot be recognised as such – an incommensurable kind of witnessing to be sure. Certainly, the scenario implies a whiteness already there motivating the black man's wish for love and revenge, and one supporting the fantasy of an internally excluded, and so repressed, whiteness. Very quickly, the desire to be loved becomes part of a wish to make the black body disappear – just as the claim to whiteness comes out of the soul's blackest depths. Does this mean that the Black can only receive love via an act of renunciation? In fact, embedded in this scenario is the image of the black man driven by the effects of an unconscious, if latent, masochism inseparably bound up with the workings of a sadistic fantasy. The root of that fantasy is, above all, *spectral*: it speaks to the reapparition of an anxiety-producing imago inside the self, one in whose fantasised scenes the Black is both masochistic and vengeful. The black man, writes Fanon, has to obtain revenge for 'l'*imago* qui l'avait de tout temps obsédé: le nègre effrayé, tremblant, humilié devant le seigneur blanc' ('the imago that had always obsessed him: the frightened, trembling Negro, abased before the white overlord') (*Peau noire*: 49; *Black Skin*: 61). He knows that, when measured against white men, he has failed to *own* or *possess* the only authentic sign of Hegelian lordship: the pleasure that derives from the absolute ownership of self and others.

Part of Fanon's legacy to the work of a psychoanalysis of black self-hatred (more broadly, to the work of hatred and anxiety in culture), the wishful-vengeful intimacies of that self is going to call into question Fanon's earlier description of 'l'amour vrai' ('true love') as a 'don de soi' ('gift of self') (*Peau noire*: 33; *Black Skin*: 41). The wager of that love is high. It is an 'orientation éthique' ('ethical orientation'), he writes, a 'vouloir pour les autres ce que l'on postule pour soi' ('wishing for others what one postulates for oneself') (*Peau noire*: 33; *Black Skin*: 41). What is it, then, that occludes the Black's longing for true love? In question, once again, is a state of being haunted by lack and anxiety. Adopting what he calls an 'analyse ... régressive', in a psycho-analytic sense, of 'l'*exister* du nègre' (a regressive analysis of 'the *state of being* black') (*Peau noire*: 10; tr. mod.: 15), in 'L'homme de couleur et la Blanche' (his chapter on Maran), Fanon insists that what is common to that state is *neurotic* anxiety, or dread; the loss of the self as object that makes sense of the world.

Anxiety becomes one way of dealing with a hostile world in whose fantasmatic coherence the Black simply disappears from view. Fanon writes, 'de la partie la plus noire de mon âme (...) me monte ce désir d'être tout à coup blanc' ('out of the blackest part of my soul (...) surges this desire to be suddenly *white*') (*Peau noire*: 51; *Black Skin*: 63). It is an anxious desire to be loved, to be sexed, but also a desire to have the white woman's sex not only reunite drive with the demands of culture but turn lust (impulse,

wish, revenge, longing) into recognition: 'J'épouse la culture
blanche, la beauté blanche, la blancheur blanche. Dans ces seins
blancs que mes mains ubiquitaires caressent, c'est la civilisation
et la dignité blanches que je fais miennes.' 'On m'aime comme un
Blanc. Je suis un Blanc' (*Peau noire*: 51; *Black Skin*: 63).[4] By loving
me, in other words, the white woman embraces me with the
whiteness of her love. That whiteness dazzles me with its promise,
the conjuration of the white man buried within. In other words,
by possessing her I possess my wished-for self. She is the answer
to my unconscious wish, the means by which I can rectify the
fault of my race, the means by which I can punish and revenge,
via expiation, this expiation of my inner self. Through her I can
transcend all that is inborn in me by redeeming the whiteness
hidden within. Her love betokens what I was *meant* to be, not
what I *am*. It is a wish in which the black subject, once again,
literally vanishes from view, assaulted from within by a repressed
masochist fantasy. Her love is indeed a very discriminate gift and
one that, in its necessity, I regard as both an initiation and a rite.
What her love signifies to me is my own 'authentic' and vigorous
rebirth, one that reverses feelings of impotence by eroticising
racial hatred and passivity. After having recently spoken with
several Antilleans, Fanon calls it 'ce rite d'initiation à l'"authentique" virilité' ('this ritual of initiation into "authentic" manhood')
(*Peau noire*: 58 ; *Black Skin*: 72).

The white woman is here a figure of desire but also of
punishment and retribution. The ethical nature of what she gives
can never entirely be separated from what properly belongs to
law, violence, or vengeance. Alluring, always appealing, she is,
as Fanon discovers in these stories by black men, invariably a
source of anxiety and object of drive-longing. This is why sexual
relations with her are typically described as vengeful, confounded,
fantasmatic. Throughout *Peau noire*, Fanon shows himself to be
an acute reader of such scenes as he passes from the works of
Chester Himes and Richard Wright to those of Paul Morand and
Boris Vian. What basically emerges is a desolate, *perverse* image
of love in which sex and desire are constrained by myths and
longings in which 'authentic love' recedes. If 'l'amour authentique' ('authentic love') is a love freed from 'des conflits
inconscients' ('unconscious conflicts'), it soon becomes clear that

inauthentic, or perverse, love is one burning with unresolved Oedipal conflicts (*Peau noire*: 33; *Black Skin*: 41).[5] In fact, embedded in Fanon's dialectic of love, recognition and desire is the sexual stereotype of the black man driven by the effects of internal and external prohibitions and decrees, displaced on to the typically '"maddening" blonde'.

These prohibitions and decrees are revealed in the following 'anecdote':

> Il y a une trentaine d'années, un Noir du plus beau teint, en plein coit avec une blonde «incendiaire», au moment de l'orgasme s'écria: 'Vive Schoelcher!' Quand on saura que Schoelcher est celui qui a fait adopter par la IIIe République le décret d'abolition de l'esclavage, on comprendra qu'il faille s'appesantir quelque peu sur les relations possibles entre le Noir et la Blanche. (*Peau noire*: 51)[6]

This is a strange scene. From first to last, is there not something rotten in the way that the black man comes, in the way that he is compelled to come? Similarly, why is his coming bound to a spectral mix of sex, death, law and violence? Or is it all just a question of performance? At first glance, what suddenly looms up, at the moment of orgasm, is not the black penis but the apparition of the white man as, perversely, the father-protector of the black man whom he has freed to love white women. The idea that the white liberator-father is there, and agitating, at the very inside of the black man's desire for recognition conjures up a powerfully perverse fantasy at the heart of this scenario. As fantasy, it also quite clearly exhibits the Oedipal dimension of what is otherwise concealed by repression in the text. Hurrah for Schoelcher? What does this imago, this spectre, have to do with that earlier wish for whiteness and its inverse, the apparently sadistic wish to seduce and punish the white woman? Why does the imago of 'le seigneur blanc' return at this most passionate time? And why, at the moment of orgasm, is the black man *inhabited*, that is, haunted by a spectre of liberation-enslavement? This is, perhaps, a mythic vision of the black–white man relation, but one which sustains the image of the Black as host to the violent unfreedoms of culture, as host to the pleasures, the unconscious pleasures, of masochism. What the black man finds – or conjures up – at the point of orgasm is an unconscious which, it seems, is doubly displaced by the paternal spectre of Victor Schoelcher, a white man forever associated with slavery and, inversely, its lynching-castration scenes of fear, desire, retribution and punishment. In other words, it is his apparition – the law-making violence he represents – that supports the black man's discovery of, and wish for, recognition from a white woman who, it seems, is beside herself. But with what – with pleasure, fear or the fearful pleasures of abandonment? Twice displaced – as object of longing and as source of anxiety – she gives way before the imposing, mythic image of Schoelcher, the father who redeems but also the father who potentially cuts and tears away.

In so doing, the anecdote leaves open the issue of whether, in this little *coup de théâtre*, the black man–white woman can ever desire or love, so to speak, without the all-pervasive and intruding fantasm of the dead white father. His is the law and the violence which condemn them to being actors and spectators in perversely voyeuristic scenes. It is *that* ideological, fetishistic image that looms up in the story's stereotype of the blonde made more than a little mad (put out of joint) by the terrible, violating thrusts of the black penis. Or is she one of those sado-masochistic white women who, Fanon suggests elsewhere in *Peau noire*, in making love to the imago of the 'nègre', is really displacing, inverting and transforming her unconscious conflicts on to the stereoptyes of social fantasy?

While it could be said that the story privileges the black man's fears of castration – fears that bind his unconscious wish for whiteness to the white-man-as-enslaver-liberator – the story also brings together the different representations of the white woman as object of both anxiety and phobia, desire and wish. It is almost implied that his (dis)possession is *her* gift to him. For when 'une Blanche … accepte un Noir', Fanon insists, 'il y a don et non pas viol' ('a white woman accepts a black man … it is a giving, not a seizing') (*Peau noire*: 37, n. 5; *Black Skin*: 46). Here the text confirms an association between being black and being in debt, between being white and giving. Naked and abed, what they give each other is precisely the promise of the other as promise, and one that opens up access to guilt, lust, fear and vengeance, but also love, recognition, freedom and gift. That is, the guilty freedom he feels in fucking her is more than matched by what she symbolises: a just future to come where being black

is no longer acting, where being black is an expenditure without
lack. (At the same time, her fantasmatic role also puts into production the dramatic disturbance between patrilineal law as
sanction and patrilineal law as violence.) This is love as disjunc-
ture, an all-and-nothing love, a love enjoyed precisely because it
is haunted by censure and misunderstanding. Nonetheless, what
rears up in this tableau, lifting its death's head, is not the 'black
sword', but the ghost of the dead white father made all the more
powerful for being dead.[7]

This is a typical, ever-persistent social fantasy that, says
Fanon, has been able to 'se maintenir à travers les âges' ('survive
through the years'), and one which 'agite un conflit explicite ou
latent, mais réel' ('renews a conflict that, active or dormant, is
always real') (*Peau noire*: 51; *Black Skin*: 64). On the one hand, the
coal-black Negro and the maddening blonde become the visual
and verbal symbols of the self's blackest unconscious wish to be
recognised as white. On the other hand, Fanon finds the
'attitude' of the black man towards the white woman indissoci-
able from this 'conflict' – of love and recognition, narcissism and
stereotype – which calls out for, at the same time as it confounds,
the hatred and phobia at the heart of the mirroring between
black men and white women, the aggressions and the paranoias
putting pressure on their demands for love. Certainly it is a scene
that plays itself out in the act of writing *Peau noire*. Dictating the
book to his white wife Josie, Fanon addresses her with his words
– the words that render into writing the perverse eroticism of the
negrophobic couple. Those words – and the vengeful, persecutory
delusions they express – are being heard and transcribed by
Josie, who performs the role of witness and accomplice to
practices that she can only suffer and condemn. We are left with
the impression that the writing of *Peau noire* performs part of
that struggle for recognition, that wish to be loved, driving the
black man. Once again, that scene is marked by a secret 'en moi'
projected on to the white woman through Fanon's words, part of
his restless preoccupation with interracial passion and sex. It is a
strange and ambiguous scene of analysis and interpretation, of
interracial transference. What we as readers cannot see or hear,
what must here be excluded, are the nuances conveyed by tones
of voice, the beloved's (the patient's) look, the curve of her body.

In his various commentaries on the fantasies and dreams of white negrophobic women, Fanon not only repeatedly returns to the role played by masochism and perversion; he also shows how the masochistic fantasy of being raped by a black man leads to Oedipal guilt and eroticism (see in particular Chapter 6, 'Le Nègre et la psychopathologie'). It is therefore no surprise that narrative accounts of interracial sex play such a complex role in *Peau noire*. Whether as alienation and engagement, force for psychic and political change or testimony to the affects of racial hatred and/or desire, those narratives are one of the masks to which Fanon returns in order to question and unveil the political and unconscious life of racism.[8] Neither is it any surprise that he restates that concern in the course of his discussion of Maran's *Un homme pareil aux autres*, a story that interests him for what it reveals about the attitude of the black man towards the white woman, an attitude and story to which I now turn.

Phantom texts

On 1 November 1947, in a letter to René Violaines, Maran describes *Un homme pareil aux autres* as an untimely text:

> Hélas, je crois que j'ai eu le tort de publier *Un homme pareil aux autres* beaucoup trop tard. Peut-être aussi ai-je tort de trop vivre en marge de mon temps. Le problème que j'ai posé en toute impartiale bonne foi est pourtant angoissant au possible. On s'en rendra compte un jour, et que j'ai rempli, en le posant, mon devoir social d'écrivain' (Maran 1965: 33).[9]

Here are two errors of timing: out of time and much too late. The time for reading the novel *Un homme pareil aux autres* has, it seems, come and passed; but in another sense it, like its author, has never arrived, its future is still to come. When people realise their true value, both text and author will come back as if for the first time. They will be recognised as the fulfilment of a social duty, an ethical witness to 'angoissant au possible'. This is a question of repetition, perhaps, but one which begins by coming back.[10] In short, Maran is an author who will return from the margins of his times; like a ghost, or 'revenant', his time is not yet.

Is this why readers, interpreters and scholars have had such difficulty deciding between the history of the novel and the time of its writing, between the act of narration and the historical anachronism – time future – of the author?[11] As we shall see, this is a decision with which Fanon will struggle in his attempt to answer whether Maran is *a man like any other*, or whether his anxieties and fears are inseparable from his identity as a *black* man. It is a struggle which will see Fanon constantly switch between fiction and anecdote, history and personal reminiscence as he tries to find a way to speak to what is particularly unique (hidden within) the neuroses of black men: in other words, why black men appear to themselves such uneasy, anxious, negatively enigmatic objects on the margins of history and of time and why, no doubt for the same reason, they seem to produce such haunted texts.

'La personnalité de l'auteur ne se livre pas aussi facilement qu'on le voudrait' ('The personality of the author does not emerge quite so easily as one might wish'), acknowledges Fanon, opening his account of *Un homme pareil aux autres* in the chapter 'L'homme de couleur et la Blanche' (*Peau noire*: 52; *Black Skin*: 64). That wish, to read and interpret *Un homme pareil aux autres* as autobiography, is one endlessly repeated by Maran's critics. Aside from trying to isolate what properly belongs to Maran and his text – Fanon says he wants to put Maran back 'à sa place, à sa juste place' ('into his place, his proper place'), the place of a disjointed future and past (*Peau noire*: 64; *Black Skin*: 79) – such readings tend to address the literature through the lens of Maran's childhood, or, more precisely, the drama of a self haunted by a childhood past. According to an anonymous 1923 profile published in *Opportunity*, Maran's fictions were haunted by loss and by memories of loss that were never transcended: 'Then his father and an elder brother died and, as a consummation of misfortune, came an unhappy love-affair with a (white) girl who was estranged from him by her family. Maran cannot forget her and he makes her the heroine of many of his books' ('René Maran', *Opportunity* I, 1 January 1923: 31). Hence, what cannot be forgotten is both the loss and the trauma that it represents. Further, it is a scene of mourning, of 'Nachträglichkeit', for whatever gets lost along with the girl: her whiteness, perhaps, but also having to abandon that wished-for part of himself, that

demand for recognition which, Fanon argues, forges the connection between black men and white women. What is more, the lost
girl becomes a sign or symbol for what Maran is lacking. It is as
though in the very heart of his destitution, she returns to him as
the affect of loss, as something loved insofar as she is loss, allowing him repeatedly to mourn the being and idea of a whiteness-
that-is-lacking. Never lost because never once possessed, she is
the presence which supports Maran's solitude and the death that
encloses him.

This is a double loss which may partly explain Maran's
obsessive, fascinated self-loathing, his sense of being on the
margins of his present time. We are left with the impression that
Maran's fictions are, to borrow a phrase from Lacan, works of 'an
inexpiable debt', forever suspended in a time of mourning – an
'en moi' projected on to the child who suffers by the man who
mourns (Lacan 1982: 44). More accurately, the hour of Maran's
drama never arrives, he is always too late, which is why he
refuses to act. He is like Hamlet, a man whose will has atrophied
through abnormal development. In other words, what we
encounter when we read Maran are fictions that result from an
obsession with loss and that call forth mourning, fictions that are
unable to fill up the sense of loss that drives them, hence the need
to restage the same story of loss again and again. Between memory
and loss, fiction emerges, then, as a repeated failure to bind the
shattering impact of loss on narcissism and memory. What we are
left with is an absence, a gap, making it difficult for readers to
assign Maran to his proper place and time. This is a gap, an
absence, that, in the words of Rosenberg, makes Maran's fictions
the spectral effect of a 'that within' binding them to the dead.

Un homme pareil aux autres tells the story of Jean Veneuse, a
black man in love with Andrée Marielle, who is white. It should
be said that Jean Veneuse is in no way the same person as Maran
but, for Fanon, is the echo or symbol or metaphor for those
alienated black men whom we encounter throughout *Peau noire*;
men driven to 'annihilate' themselves because of their 'impression
infernale' ('*agonizing* conviction') that they will never gain the
recognition and respect of whites (*Peau noire*: 48; *Black Skin*: 60);
men who, having 'respiré, ingéré les mythes et préjugés de
l'Europe raciste' ('breathed and eaten the myths and prejudices

of racist Europe'), can only express their 'haine du nègre' ('hatred of the Negro') in their desire to be white (*Peau noire*: 152; *Black Skin*: 188).

'De quoi s'agit-il?' ('What are the terms of this problem?') asks Fanon. Veneuse is black, therefore a 'nègre'; but he is also European. 'Voilà le drame' ('There is the conflict') Fanon tells us (*Peau noire*: 52; *Black Skin*: 64). The drama begins on a November day at the Bordeaux docks. Veneuse, heartbroken, is about to set sail for French Equatorial Africa to a post in colonial administration. To his old friend, Coulanges, he explains why he cannot declare his love for Andrée: 'Jean Veneuse, dans le monde colonial, qu'un "sale nègre". Et un "sale nègre", surtout s'il est fonctionnaire colonial, doit de se marier avec une Européenne, s'il aime vraiment cette Européenne et en est aimé' (Maran 1947: 38).[12] Fanon suggests, 'Mais ne nous y trompons point, Jean Veneuse est l'homme à convaincre' ('But let us not be misled: Jean Veneuse is the man who has to be convinced') (*Peau noire*: 53; *Black Skin*: 66). Having 'devoured' French colonial culture in the hope of being accepted as 'un homme pareil aux autres, un homme comme les autres', Veneuse discovers, instead, a troubling paradox, '"le peuple blanc ne le reconnaissant pas pour le sien, le noir le reniant presque"' ('"the white race would not accept him as one of its own and the black virtually repudiated him"' (cited in *Peau noire*: 54; *Black Skin*: 67). Veneuse is a man, then, who, like Hamlet, is troubled by what he *knows*: unable to be white, no longer black, he finds himself affected by a disjunction, a rupture, an 'en moi' that can be neither avowed nor disavowed. That discovery leads to a type of Adlerian 'ressentiment' and 'agressivité', Fanon decides, enjoined to Veneuse's feelings of ambivalence and inferiority – and, once again, part of that 'constellation délirante' ('constellation of delirium') defining interracial desire and love (*Peau noire*: 48; *Black Skin*: 60).

Certainly, what *Un homme pareil aux autres* passes on to its readers is the forlorn image of a black man driven by anguish *and* loss, an anguish expressed by his desire to speak his love and his guilty refusal to bring it about. Suspended between that refusal and desire, the story inevitably falls prey to lack and absence, which are complicated still further by the many diversions, delays, obstacles and postponements that Maran puts in the way of his lovers' consummation. To emphasise the point, we may say that unfulfilment supports the story's defence against the presence and predictability of loss aroused by the loss of Andrée. In fact, what remains, I believe, most striking about this story of loss and delay is the way in which it turns Veneuse's love for Andrée into the fantasy and desire of an unrecoverable emptiness or void, and one which, through the anguish of separation, refigures her loss as a desire for love sustained by its impossibility. To put this another way – and to anticipate Fanon's argument – *Un homme pareil aux autres* tells the story of a man who longs to be redeemed by a white recognition whose threat cannot be borne, a man in love who finds it impossible to be loved, a man terrorised by the pre-Oedipal loss of a black maternal body, yet a man disgusted by black women. *That* man (the remnant of pre-Oedipal break-down or 'décalage') can only love the white woman insofar as she embodies the lack-that-remains, the lack that keeps at bay that libidinal lack-in-being represented by black selfhood.[13] In loving him, she gives him what he does not have, what he lacks in relation to what is lacking in her. Andrée's whiteness allows Veneuse to memorialise feelings of maternal loss by instituting a form of mastery (over himself, over other Blacks) that seeks its own undoing in the wish for whiteness. She is the force allowing him to propel the drive away from what is black toward the objects and signs that acknowledge him in his whiteness. At the same time, she too plays the role of absent auditor in Maran's text (the scene recalls Fanon and Josie), who, through the exchange of letters, will help to secure a representation of perversity that is, once again, inseparable from the experience of writing, and one that sustains the image of a white woman seduced and fascinated (maddened?) by the dramas and drives inhabiting a black man's words.

In common with his wish to protect Andrée from the inevitable scandal that marriage to the 'sale nègre' brings, Veneuse's letters also reveal a debate with himself concerning the meaning of interracial love. Is his love a lust for revenge or a wish for whiteness? In choosing her, is he really any different from those black men driven '"jusqu'à renier et leur pays et leur mère"' ('"to the extreme of denying both their countries and their mothers"') (cited in *Peau noire*: 56; *Black Skin*: 69)? Struggling with the idea of interracial love as a symptom of a more extreme separation from the mother-'motherland', Veneuse gropes his way towards an understanding of the white woman as active participant in the black man's anxious relation to separation and loss. His desire for her seems to require a kind of splitting as a defence against what cannot be knowingly endured. In this way, by loving her, he is struggling to bind feelings of pre-Oedipal loss and his own masochistic relation to whiteness. He is also trying to escape the guilt unleashed by his wish to revenge himself on the mother for the damage she has done him. There is, it seems, no trace here of Veneuse's sense of Andrée's love as a 'gift' – 'le don que vous me faîtes de vous' ('the gift of yourself you are making to me') (Maran 1947: 141) – nor any doubt that his sadistic wishes for '"la satisfaction de dominer l'Européenne"' ('"the satisfaction of being the master of a European woman"') (cited in *Peau noire*: 56; *Black Skin*: 69) were his alone, part of a failed attempt to bind the anxiety unleashed by the phobic demands of cultural life. In fact, embedded in Veneuse's doubts is the image of the white woman as the privileged source of those demands, as the one driven to revenge herself on the imago of the 'sale nègre' by asking for this extreme separation between desire and cultural life. 'A l'extrême', Fanon observes, '… mais justement il s'agit d'y aller' ('At the extreme … but it is exactly to the extreme that we have to go') (*Peau noire*: 52; *Black Skin*: 65).

This is an image which, confirming Maran's vision of interracial love as 'le seul pacificateur, le seul colonisateur, le seul civilisé', ('the only pacificator, the only coloniser, the only civilising entity'), the 'sole motherland', is central to Fanon's reading of Maran as an 'abandonic' (Maran 1947: 95; Maran 1948: 344).[14] That reading presents Veneuse's relation to loss (the loss of Andrée) as the symptom of a prior maternal desertion and Maran's fiction as a defence against the mother experienced as missing or absent. Yet when that anguish (and anger) over maternal separation first appears in Chapter 3 of *Peau noire*, 'L'homme de couleur et la Blanche' (very precisely defined as the extreme rejection of the actual mother and, as such, a form of renunciation), it seems to merit very little interest from Fanon, who dismisses it with the phrase 'Que d'efforts pour se débarasser d'une urgence subjective' ('What a struggle to free himself of a

purely subjective conflict') (*Peau noire*: 56; *Black Skin*: 70). This
remark – the interruption or repression it suggests – is disguised
by a further distortion: 'Je suis un blanc, je suis né en Europe,
tous mes amis sont blancs' ('I am a white man, I was born in
Europe, all my friends are white') (*Peau noire*: 56; *Black Skin*: 70).
What goes missing here, screened out by Fanon's wishful-
vengeful displacement of Veneuse/Maran, is Maran's occlusion
of the mother by Fanon's own occlusion. It is a double occlusion
that runs parallel to the phobic play and fantasy of the (interracial) couple, a play and fantasy that, in turn, casts its shadow
across Fanon's reading of *Un homme pareil aux autres*.

This is a response that also impinges on and disrupts Fanon's
preceding chapter on Mayotte Capécia's *Je suis martiniquaise*,
where interracial desire is linked to the symptom of *lactification*,
the unconscious and cultural fantasy marked by the wish to have
a whiter child.[15] In substituting himself for Maran (and Capécia),
Fanon appears to be caught up himself in that sequence of
disavowal and rejection defining Maran's novel, a scenario
confounding the wish to put Veneuse/Maran back in his 'proper
place' with a disavowal and barely suppressed hatred of the
black mother. Or, to put this another way, as the object of the
black child's phobia, the black maternal body is made central to
that perverse antagonism between drive and the demands of
cultural life, love and recognition, passing between the black
man and the white woman. Like Maran, Fanon uses the mother to
symbolise those anxieties or gaps introduced by the phobic
fantasy of the 'nègre' and, as such, he also seems driven to
exclude her from his writing (and accuse her). 'Je n'ai jamais
pardonné à ma mère' ('I have never forgiven my mother'), Fanon
insists, giving 'l'expression directe' ('direct expression') once
again to Veneuse's 'besoin de revanche' ('need for revenge') in
his own voice (*Peau noire*: 75; *Black Skin*: 60). Fanon's difficulty
in keeping himself apart from Veneuse also impacts on his reading. That indistinction between self and text, at the level of
'énonciation', is a repeated gesture in Fanon's chapter on Maran.
It partly explains why Veneuse's anxieties and doubts do not
even merit a comparison with that fantasising, sado-masochistic
wish for a whiter child defined in Chapter 2 as intrinsic to
Martinican culture and psychopathology. Instead, Veneuse's

anguish over whether to marry Andrée denotes a purely subjective conflict coming between the self and its neurotic history.
However, that moment of repression and of repetition is immediately complicated by Fanon's conjuration of *Hamlet* – or, more
precisely, Harold Rosenberg's 'The stages' and Germaine Guex's
La Névrose d'abandon – an event which leads him to recast
Veneuse's neuroses as the *syndrome* of a black child *abandoned* by
his mother. 'Jean Veneuse n'est pas un nègre, ne veut pas être un
nègre. Pourtant, à son insu il s'est produit un hiatus. Il y a
quelque chose d'indéfinissable, d'irréversible, véritablement le
that within de Harold Rosenberg' (*Peau noire*: 57).[16] (Fanon then
footnotes René Guyonnet's French translation of 'The stages',
'Du jeu au je, Esquisse d'une géographie de l'action', which first
appeared in *Les Temps modernes* in 1948.)

    This is an allusive passage. On the one hand, what is being
described is a moment of denial that is the unconscious affect of a
hiatus: in the 'nègre' who is *not* there is a disarticulation and
derangement that remains fundamentally opaque. On the other
hand, Fanon finds himself up against something that is both
indefinable and *untranslatable*; the words *'that within'* – words
appearing here in English – also register a gap, or hiatus, in the
capacity of French to name this gulf in black identity. Obscurely,
as if groping in the dark, Fanon turns to René Guyonnet's translation to signal this disadjustment between Rosenberg's *'that
within'* and Gide's *'en moi'* as set down in his 1949 translation of
Hamlet.[17] That disparity or dislocation is, to be sure, also a
haunting: the *'that within'* as a figure of, and for, a kind of
unconscious schism breaking forth into the being of the Black,
and the Black as a kind of spectral repository for the aggressions
and phobias of culture. But phobia, too, as the Black's way of
'replac[ing] the (love-hate) object which is missing, absent';
phobia as part of a defence against the psychotic gaps opened up
in the subject when the mother takes on 'the terrifying form of
not-being-there' (Lebeau 2001: 24). As we will see, Fanon turns
to the work of Guex to consider the Oedipal meaning of that
'absence', the ambivalence it evinces, and the psychic vicissitudes
with which it is composed.

    Briefly, and to anticipate my argument: in 'Les conditions
intellectuelles et affectives de l'œdipe', first published in 1949,

Guex describes the neuroses of abandonment as 'obstacles puissants à l'œdipe' ('powerful obstacles to the Oedipus') (Guex 1949: 265). Insecure, dominated by the need to be assured of love, the abandonic is, she says, 'toujours prête à régresser vers une forme d'aimance plus primitive' ('ever ready to regress to a primitive form of love') in his search for 'de l'unité et de la fusion' (Guex 1949: 266; 267). The abandonic is an 'œdipe fruste' ('frustrated Oedipus') whose ego is unable to establish 'rivalités positives' ('positive rivalry') with the 'semblable' ('other') (Guex 1949: 267; 269). These remarks will lead Fanon – in 'L'homme de couleur et la Blanche' – to see Veneuse's neurotic delay in ways differing from the classic Freud-Jones reading of Hamlet's infamous patient-impatience. Hamlet's torment, observes Freud, in a letter of 1877 to Wilhelm Fleiss, is 'roused in him by the obscure memory that he himself had meditated the same deed against his father because of passion for his mother' (Freud 1954: 224). In contrast, Guex's abandonic does not enter on to the stage of such Oedipal compromises; he can only express himself as a frustrated Oedipus, as an Oedipus that is lacking.[18] To the extent that Veneuse's torments, as an abandonic, are also raced, Fanon's reading introduces yet further differences, nuances that return us to Rosenberg. Hamlet acts, so *is*: Veneuse's desire for recognition must be measured differently. The Black cannot be recognised as being unless he succeeds in *seeming* white; yet seeming itself will be weak and ineffectual unless he succeeds in *being* white, which he is destined never to be. Veneuse's decision, then, is not 'to be or not to be', but whether to submit to an endless regress between seeming to be and the being that seems – a regress through whose straits blackness *is* absence, pretence, falsehood, mimicry, proof of the absence of agency.

Seem to Being. Let us go back to that moment in 'L'homme de couleur et la Blanche' when '*that within*' makes its first appearance. In 'The stages', '*that within*' is an exemplary figure of the effect of being haunted. Hamlet comes to know that he is compelled to uncover that which must be most anxiously concealed in others, in himself. His is an 'anguish of possibility' exposed by an 'invisible event' (Rosenberg 1970: 71). Hamlet is compelled to act because of the repressed trace of a secret, a crypt made all the more powerful and mysterious by the disappearing reapparition of his father's ghost (cf. Abraham 1994). The appearance of the ghost is thereby defined in a very particular way: Hamlet's vision of the ghost is not just delusion, which could be perceived as such and understood as deception. Rather, it unfolds an invisible event within that remains unconscious, forcing him to exceed the role of actor via an *act* that goes beyond acting. In 'L'homme de couleur et la Blanche', '*that within*' also marks the *appearance* in the being of the Black, but via a kind of unwilled, ghostly incorporation. It is a mobilisation of affect in which Jean Veneuse is forced to *abandon* himself. Already a stranger within himself, divided in his need to show and hide that division, Veneuse is forced by his role into the neurotic life of racism. This is a scene, then, in which – through Shakespeare's *Hamlet,* through Rosenberg's quasi-existential reading – Fanon not only gives Veneuse the appearance of both being and not-being Hamlet, but, in uncanny fashion, unfolds a series of ghostly effects between *Un homme pareil aux autres* and 'The stages', between a phenomenology of racism and a psychoanalysis of culture.[19]

More accurately, it is through Guyonnet's 'Du jeu au je', with its associations of play, selfhood and being, and its constant italicisation of '*that within*' (an emphasis absent both from Rosenberg's original and Gide's translation), that Fanon uncovers those phantasmal affects of interracial desire in Maran's text: affects which show the black man haunted by the hatreds and anxieties of culture which he in turn projects on to the fantasy of an absent mother. That is, when Fanon tries to discover the content and context of Veneuse's 'hiatus', he finds not only a gap or fault in black identity – that traumatic fissure between being and existence – but also a trace of that division in an 'en moi' derived from maternal separation *and* the spectral histories of race. In *Peau noire*, what remains constant is an idea of the black child as a being threatened by racism, from within and without, a threat that is lived out in relation to the mother both as the repository or source for that child's 'oblativité chargée' ('sacrificial dedication') to white racist culture and as that child's wished-for defence (*Peau noire*: 121; *Black Skin*: 147). Or, what Fanon discovers, finally, is the affect of her separation: hers is a loss unable to be borne, a loss that, in turn, shadows the gaps or faults that threaten the being of the Black, source of those anxieties posed by white, loving demands that he act his part. The lesson she passes on, in other words, is that the unseen is always returned and that its form is a 'that within' irreconcilable to the self. What brings the 'that within' into focus, what makes it visible as a remnant, is the black child's wish to be loved.

The spectral mother[20]

Toute angoisse provient d'une certaine insécurité subjective liée à l'absence de la mère' (All anxiety derives from a certain subjective insecurity linked to the absence of the mother) Charles Odier (cited in *Peau noire*: 126; *Black Skin*: 154).

Arguably, this discovery is also the stage where Fanon develops his reading of Veneuse as a man marked by the shadow of the lost object. It is a reading – of maternal loss and separation – that supports Fanon's decision to tell the story of Jean Veneuse through Germaine Guex's retelling of the pre-Oedipal origins of neuroses and Rosenberg's retelling of *Hamlet*. In these two narratives, Fanon discovers a mother who returns as the ghost reviving the pre-Oedipal insecurities of her child.

It is a familiar enough gesture in Fanon's writing: psychoanalysis emerges as a key insight into the *failed* narcissism of Blacks, part of a wider clinical wish to go beyond the 'consciences aliénées' ('alienated psyches') of the colonised (*Peau noire*: 66; *Black Skin*: 81). As a typical figure of that alienation, Jean Veneuse emerges at the crux of Fanon's discussion of the black man who is symbolically castrated, the Black whose neurosis reveals a sado-masochistic wish for white love. But what is it, precisely, that he is lacking, or missing? A failed 'object relation' to the mother, Fanon maintains. He argues that Veneuse's angry, mournful separation from Andrée is the acting out of earlier childhood scenarios, and these repetitions (the fantasies and impulses they express) echo Veneuse's melancholy attempts to find some kind of restitution for his mother's desertion. On this reading, then, Veneuse's desire for Andrée's love and recognition is closely bound to childhood fantasies of the mother's refusal and abandonment: her spectre, observes Guex, haunts '"toute la symptomatologie de cette névrose"' ('"the whole symptomatology of this neurosis"') (cited in *Peau noire*: 59; *Black Skin*: 73). Guex argues that that traumatic separation '"paralyse l'élan vers la vie"' ('"paralyzes [the abandonic's] enthusiasm for living"') and opens up a gap or 'zone secrète qu'il cultive et défend contre toute intrusion' ('secret zone, which he cultivates and defends against every intrusion') (cited in *Peau noire*: 59; *Black Skin*: 73). Fanon restates that view in the course of his discussion of Veneuse's compromise fantasy: 'je ne veux pas être aimé et je fuis l'objet' ('I do not wish to be loved and I will flee from love-objects'), which he regards as an attempt to ward off the suffering that accompanies the mother's desertion (*Peau noire*: 61; *Black Skin*: 75).

In fact, the figure of an abandoning mother reappears throughout *Peau noire*: 'A la maison', he writes, 'ma mère me chante, en français, des romances françaises où il n'est jamais question de nègres. Quand je désobéis, quand je fais trop de bruit, on me dit de ne pas "faire le nègre"' (*Peau noire*: 155).[21] Hence, as a black child who has been threatened with the loss of love, a threat lived out in relation to the mother's projection of an imaginary white child, Fanon knows why a wish for whiteness may also be a disguised lust for revenge. What remains constant is a wish to be avenged against the unloving black mother, the mother whose Negrophobia is experienced as a point of loss and longing by the black child. That mother, Fanon suggests, is the supreme referent of the conscious-unconscious demand that he act 'white', that he become the white child of her fantasies and desires, that he expel from himself the unwanted imago of the 'nègre'. Or, as Maran writes, imagining Veneuse's imaginary address to a white child: 'j'aimais en toi l'enfant que j'aurais voulu avoir'; 'Je me suis arraché à la douceur d'une vie que je ne dois pas connaître, parce que mon vilain visage noir tout noir me l'interdit, et parce qu'il est à blâmer celui qui, le sachant, se prépare l'inutile amertume des futurs regrets' (Maran 1947: 84–5).[22] This is a perilous and humiliating wish, a wish both to be and to have a white child, and one that finds the mother to be the source and memory of a failure to transcend the persecutory blackness that forbids it.

Once again, Fanon's emphasis is on how the sexualised anxiety of Negrophobia acts out the fantasy of wanting to punish the mother. As Vicky Lebeau (in Chapter 7 in this volume) and Françoise Vergès (1997) point out, in Fanon's analysis of a white girl's fantasy that 'un nègre me viole' ('a Negro is raping me'), it is the Negro who ends up performing this violent retribution against the (white) maternal body; it is he who literally symbolises the 'rod' that beats her (*Peau noire*: 144; *Black Skin*: 178).[23] Such a 'projection of thought, of painful thought, on to the white [mother]', writes Lebeau in her account of Fanon's rebuke to a white mother and her phobic child (p. 135), is experienced as 'liberating' by him. In other words, aggression is a reaction to that 'en moi' which the deserting mother opens up within. And yet Fanon says little about why his response to the black mother's devotion to whiteness is projected on to white women. Nothing is said about Veneuse's love for Andrée being a disguised wish to hurt the mother due to the impact of *her* Negrophobia. Instead, he writes: 'Et nous disons que Jean Veneuse ne représente pas une expérience des rapports noir–blanc, mais une certaine façon pour un nevrosé, accidentellement noir, de se comporter' (*Peau noire*: 64). 'A quoi tend cette analyse?', asks Fanon. 'A rien de moins qu'à démontrer à Jean Veneuse qu'effectivement il n'est pas pareil aux autres' (*Peau noire*: 63), that he is, in short, (not) like me.[24] We are left with the impression that Veneuse's morbid state of mind remains a symptom of a pre-Oedipal crisis provoked by Andreé, who is an echo, of someone or something, which dies away through the pages of *Un homme pareil aux autres* to become the problem, or puzzle, of the book.

Is *Un homme pareil aux autres* the echo of maternal loss and abandonment, an echo that Fanon summons through the image of his own abandoning, an echo that will lead him to see Veneuse's wish not to be seen as a 'nègre' as a restaging of his own pre-Oedipal loss? As Fanon writes, everything in the abandonic is overstepped in favour of an amour and an affect in which the self negates itself, leaving behind it the images (Fanon talks of solitude, anguish, revenge and so on) through which it has stimulated its own passionate desire and through which every possibility of such an intensity of refusal was brought about in the first place. And yet, when he writes on Veneuse, Fanon inevitably calls up his counterpart: the unloving, refusing black mother. Her spectre remains the latent content of Veneuse's sadistic fantasies, the ambivalent source of his persecutory love.

Let us note the drama of this moment in Maran's narrative. It may be said that the entire narrative of *Un homme pareil aux autres*, like that of *Hamlet*, comes in response to a question to the mother, to the memory of her loss. Maran invokes the exemplary figure of a damaged child, a damaged black child:

> Ah! ces larmes d'enfant qui n'a personne pour le consoler ... Il n'oubliera jamais qu'on l'a mis de bonne heure à l'apprentissage de la solitude ... Existence cloîtrée, existence repliée et recluse où j'ai appris trop tôt à méditer et à réfléchir [...] [A] cause de (la vie solitaire) sensible en dedans, incapable d'extérioriser ma joie ou ma douleur, je repousse tout ce que j'aime et me détourne malgré moi de tout ce qui m'attire. (cited in *Peau noire*: 60)[25]

Again, Maran states in relation to Veneuse's unhappy adolescence, '"Mon caractère lui doit cette mélancolie intime et cette crainte de la vie de société qui réprime aujourd'hui jusqu'à mes moindres élans"' (*Peau noire*: 60).[26] Moreover, what is secreted deep within the self emerges most powerfully through a discourse of mourning: 'mais j'ai ceci en moi qui surpasse l'apparence; le reste n'est que faste et parture de la douleur'. Veneuse's feeling of being a man apart from others takes us back to those mournful feelings of liminality. Addressing himself to what he calls, following Guex, Veneuse's '[a]ffective self-rejection', Fanon is sensitive to this image of a self in mourning and the condensed-displaced figure of the child to be found there. But if, as he suggests here, racism is a 'coincidence' to Veneuse's neuroses, why does the novel insist that race and loss are closely bound to the way in which he – Veneuse, the child – associates the mother with the insecure being of the Black? Assuming, along with Fanon, that what is hidden in Maran's text is how the question of the mother *as* memory and fantasy comes to trouble Veneuse's claims to a self, we still need to understand how the experience of racism in the novel itself seems to be uncomfortably like the experience of watching a distraught and anxious child, haunted by isolation and the loss of love. In a key move towards the end of his discussion of Veneuse's '*externalizing* neurosis', Fanon suggests that *Un homme pareil aux autres* is an unhealthy falsehood, a 'sham', in its representation of black–white sexual relations. According to Fanon, part of the problem for Veneuse is what drives the Black to act out the fantasies that, on one psychoanalytic reading, are derived from infantile conflicts.

Rather than a black man seeking recognition, Veneuse, Fanon concludes, is 'un névrosé qui a besoin d'être délivré de ses fantasmes infantiles' ('a neurotic who needs to be emancipated from his infantile fantasies'), revising the original aims of his discussion (*Peau noire*: 64; *Black Skin*: 79).

But after his reconciliation with Andreé at the novel's close, Veneuse says, 'Vous saurez dorénavant que les nègres sont des hommes comme les autres, et qu'ils souffrent peut-être plus que les autres, parce que, lorsqu'ils ont l'affligeant bonheur d'aimer une Européenne, ils sentent peser sur eux une telle réprobation, qu'ils ont vraiment honte d'avouer ou de laisser deviner leur souffrance' (Maran 1947: 248).[27] Painful good fortune? By contrast, when it comes to loving a black woman, Maran can only show incomprehension: 'Je suis un délicat, un rêveur, un sentimental,' he confesses. 'Je ne pourrai donc jamais comprendre ni jamais aimer la femme indigène, inert et simple réceptacle de spasmes désenchantés' (Maran 1965: 125).[28] How does one tell the difference between white and black women? The former offers dream, sentiment and love as opposed to a receptacle cast as void because it can be repeatedly possessed, again and again. 'On n'a qu'à demander,' Maran suggests, 'il n'y a jamais de refus' ('You only have to ask. There is never a refusal') (Maran 1965: 139; trans. Ojo-Ade 1984: 108). The image conjured up is one of hostile and idealised dependence, a splitting that, predictably, takes us back to the black phobic mother. In Maran's view, there can be no question of loving the black woman because, being simple and inert, she signifies the absence of passion as well as its satiated excess. Her sole purpose is to satisfy lust. In her lack of inhibitions and restrictions the debt Veneuse owes to castration cannot be requited. She is life without sentiment, need without desire. In her there is none of that difference driving desire to desire itself in the other. Hers is a presence that will always remain blind to his secretly perverse wish to be his mother's white child. This is why, for Maran, the white woman is a symbol of desire and the black woman a symbol of sex, body, stench and dirt, and why both, ultimately, will never be enough for the Black who wants to have the phallus (rather than just be it). Hence, Veneuse's desire for the white woman is not really a desire for whiteness but rather for the presence of that object (white phallus) whose absence both she and he designate and want. 'On m'aime comme un Blanc. Je suis un Blanc' ('I am loved like a white man. I am a white man'), Fanon writes, giving the lie to his (feigned) distinction between a neurotic who happens to be black and black neurosis (*Peau noire*: 51; *Black Skin*: 63). My final question is this: this wish both to have and to be the phallus, to be revenged, can one call it love?

Afterword: the two scenes

One makes love to a shadow. (Fanon cited in Juminer 1962: 127)

One cannot strike the phallus, because the phallus, even the real phallus, is a *ghost*. (Lacan 1982: 50, original emphasis)

To put all this another way, there is, I think, another figure, aside from Hamlet, haunting Fanon's discussion of white femininity and Negrophobia in *Peau noire*, a figure irreversibly bound to the dream of pre-Oedipal bliss, but someone driven to turn away from the abyssal depths, 'le grand trou noir' ('the vast black abyss') of the pre-Oedipal black-white mother (*Peau noire*: 11; *Black Skin*: 14). That figure is the pining, hate-filled black child whose guilt and anxiety, however disguised, can only restore what he has lost through a confounding repetition. In other words, in refinding the loved object lost he ends up losing himself: he refinds himself as a subject in mourning. In *Peau noire*, the name of that child is, broadly speaking, Orpheus. The following two scenes illustrate, I think, why he remains such a key figure in Fanon's writing on the unconscious vicissitudes of 'se blanchir ou disparaitre' ('*turn white or disappear*') in the black abandonic and his mournful relationship to *that within* (*Peau noire*: 80; *Black Skin*: 100).

Scene 1

In 'Orphée noir', Sartre writes: 'Puisque cette Eurydice se dissipera en fumée si l'Orphée noir se retourne sur elle, il descendra le chemin royal de son âme le dos tourné au fond de la grotte, il descendra au-dessous des mots et des significations ... le dos tourné, les yeux clos pour toucher enfin de ses pieds nus l'eau noire des songes et du désir et s'y laisser noyer' (Sartre 1949: 254–5).[29] A translator's note suggests: 'Sartre seems to have confused his images here, since Orpheus was instructed not to look back while he was ascending from Hades, after he had retrieved Eurydice from Plato [*sic*]' (Sartre 2001: 140). I do not think this is a confused image despite its metaphor of black creativity as some kind of wished-for burial. For Sartre, the meaning of the myth does not lie in ascent followed by loss but in descent followed by gain. As Orpheus drowns, engulfed by surges of dreams and desire, he assumes a new form and humanity, his 'nouveaux soleils' ('new suns') in consort with a 'perpétuel dépassement' ('perpetual surpassing') (Sartre 1949: 257; Sartre 2001: 127). From burial and exile the fiery vision of his 'négritude-objet' appears on the horizon of a new dawn (Sartre 1949: 260). As we look back at Sartre's vision of a black 'chemin royal', whose ending involves a kind of transfiguring union, we see that, in a sense, Eurydice is not as important for this fusion with the loved object as the journey itself. It is not Eurydice that Black Orpheus wants to look on but the black water of dreams and desire in which he drowns and is reborn.

For Sartre the myth reveals an Orpheus bound to the compensations of narcissism, transfigured by a 'torrid obsession' rather than by failure or sacrifice – the endless abyss of black negation in which consciousness ebbs away, consumed by dreams and desires, intimately smothered. Here, once again, the Black appears as the remnant of a search for lost unity and, in his search for that lost unity, all sustained efforts to restore the loss, to be loved, to return to the mother as source, take him back to those deep, pre-Oedipal attachments of the abandonic. Black Orpheus's outward journey therefore charts a descent whose essence is a return; it is a journey in which he surrenders his fears of 'insécurité et ... ses terreurs' as he draws closer to the source (Guex 1949: 276). Fanon accedes to Sartre's vision of black expiation and rebirth – the black man 'de mourir à la culture blanche pour renaître à l'âme noire' ('must die to white culture in order to be reborn with a black soul') – but his approaches to this expiation and rebirth are profoundly different (Sartre 1949: 252; Sartre 2001: 125).

Scene 2

For Fanon, Black Orpheus is the one who descends into the depths of himself to look for a white Eurydice. The illusion and promise of her daylight is what compels him. He will not discover that her promise is illusionary, dream-filled, until after he has lost her. But in losing her he also loses himself, that is, the promise of himself that was, the becoming intimacy with whiteness that he craves, that allows him to forget himself as black, that makes the essential night of his essence disappear. Without that promise, which he pursues for his own sake, he must then confront the law of the vicious circle – neither white nor black but something in between, inessential. In other words, where Sartre sees the revolutionary rediscovery of black desire and dream, Fanon sees an Orpheus blinded by Eurydice, dazzled by her white-black reflection: her absence completes the inner absence of himself. As Orpheus looks back on this absence he cannot repossess it in the way Sartre suggests Negritude's 'absolute' poetry repossesses the word. Instead, it must be endlessly suffered and endured and tarried with. This is not a search for unity and fusion but a search for renunciation. This is why Fanon writes, 'Mais quand on se met en tête de vouloir exprimer l'existence, on risque de ne rencontrer que l'inexistant' ('But, when one has taken it into one's head to try to express existence, one runs the risk of finding only the nonexistent') (*Peau noire*: 111; *Black Skin*: 137). This is also why he states: 'Je me définis comme tension absolue d'ouverture' ('I defined myself as an absolute tension of opening') (*Peau noire*: 112; tr. mod.: 138).

This tension cannot be sublated or surpassed, for its creative force is the achievement of negation, an absolute opening to the future *and* the past that is neither white nor black but beyond the Manichaean. Hence, Black Orpheus must resist the dazzling lure of whiteness if he is to rediscover that tension of opening within himself. This is, I think, to move beyond what Fanon means by 'regressive' analysis, the ability to retrace one's steps, to look back, to reclaim or revendicate what was lost only because never had. Only by returning to himself can he be finally free of himself, free of the self enclosed by the gaze and authority of whiteness. Only by venturing forth into the paths of differentiation can Black Orpheus overcome the insecurities of the abandonic. In short, in Fanon's retelling, it is not Eurydice who disappears after having been set free by the gaze, but Orpheus. But who, then, is abandoning whom? To make Orpheus expose his inner emptiness, to make him open up completely to his nothingness, realise his own unreality by plunging ever deeper into his empty depths – this is one of the tasks undertaken by Fanon in *Peau noire*. It is through his powerful unveiling of the power of the negative, both within and outside himself, that Fanon is able to resist the entrapments and lures of Eurydice in defiance of 'Orphée noir' and, ultimately, in defiance of *that within* his innermost self.

Notes

1 Rosenberg very quickly casts the play as a reflection on the task of bearing witness to those literally buried under the ground. In several essays – 'The stages: a geography of human action', 'The riddles of Oedipus', 'Guilt to the vanishing point', 'The diminished act' – Rosenberg uses *Hamlet* to bring into focus the difference of his thinking about man and actor, politics and history. These are the concepts through which he begins to elaborate *Hamlet* as a play about moral and personal responsibility, a view echoed by Hannah Arendt (see Rosenberg 1970). In 'Personal responsibility under dictatorship', first published in 1964, Arendt writes: 'Whoever takes upon himself political responsibility will always come to the point where he says with Hamlet: "The time is out of joint: O cursed spite / That I was ever born to set it right!"' (Arendt 2003: 27–8).

2 'Out of the blackest part of my soul, across the zebra striping of my mind, surges this desire to be suddenly *white*. I wish to be acknowledged not as *black* but as *white*. Now – and this is a form of recognition that Hegel had not envisaged – who but a white woman can do this for me? By loving me she proves that I am worthy of white love. I am loved like a white man. I am a white man. Her love takes me onto the royal road that leads to total realization' (*Black Skin*: 63). The evocation of the 'royal road' and 'black soul' opens on to two further scenes derived from Sartre's 'Orphée noir' which I discuss in an afterword.

3 'For it is flesh and phenomenality that give to the spirit its spectral apparition, but which disappear right away in the apparition, in the very coming of the *revenant* or the return of the specter. There is something disappeared, departed in the apparition itself as reapparition of the departed' (Derrida 1994: 6).

4 'I marry white culture, white beauty, white whiteness. When my restless hands caress those white breasts, they grasp white civilization and dignity and make them mine.' 'I am loved like a white man. I am a white man' (*Black Skin*: 63).

5 'il demeure que l'amour vrai, réel, – vouloir pour les autres ce que l'on postule pour soi, quand cette postulation intègre les valeurs permanentes de la réalité humaine, – requiert la mobilisation d'instances psychiques

fondamentalement libérées des conflits inconscients [...] Aujourd'hui nous croyons en la possibilité de l'amour, c'est pourquoi nous nous efforcons d'en détecter les imperfections, les perversions [...] [L]'amour authentique demeurera impossible tant que ne seront pas expulsés ce sentiment d'infériorité ou cette exaltation adlériénne, cette surcompensation, qui semblent être l'indicatif de la Weltanschauung noire' ('the fact remains that true, authentic love – wishing for others what one postulates for oneself, when that postulation unites the permanent values of human reality – entails the mobilization of psychic drives basically freed of unconscious conflicts [...] Today I believe in the possibility of love; that is why I endeavor to trace its imperfections, its perversions [...] [A]uthentic love will remain unattainable before one has purged onself of that feeling of inferiority or that Adlerian exaltation, that overcompensation, which seem to be the indices of the black *Weltanschauung*') (*Peau noire*: 33–4; *Black Skin*: 41–2).

6 'Some thirty years ago, a coal-black Negro, in a Paris bed with a "maddening" blonde, shouted at the moment of orgasm, "Hurrah for Schoelcher!" When one recalls that it was Victor Schoelcher who persuaded the Third Republic to adopt the decree abolishing slavery, one understands why it is necessary to elaborate somewhat on the possible aspects of relations between black men and white women' (*Black Skin*: 63).

7 '"L'épée du Noir est une épee. Quand il a passé ta femme à son fil, elle a senti quelque chose"' ('"The black man's sword is a sword. When he has thrust it into your wife, she has really felt something."' (Michel Cournot, cited in *Peau noire*: 137; *Black Skin*: 169).

8 'La littérature officielle ou anecdotique a créé trop d'histoires de nègres pour qu'on les taise. Mais à les réunir, on n'avance pas dans la véritable tâche qui est d'en montrer le mécanisme. L'essentiel pour nous n'est pas d'accumuler des faits, des comportements, mais de dégager leur sens' ('Both authorized and anecdotal literature have created too many stories about Negroes to be suppressed. But putting them all together does not help us in our real task, which is to disclose their mechanics. What matters for us is not to collect facts and behavior, but to find their meaning') (*Peau noire*: 136; *Black Skin*: 168).

9 'Unfortunately, I think I have committed an error in publishing *Un homme pareil aux autres* much too late. Perhaps I have also committed an error in living on the edge of my time ['en marge de mon temps']. The problem that I have raised in all impartial good faith is nonetheless one that is extremely harrowing. People will realise one day that by raising it I have fulfilled my social duty as a writer' (my trans.).

10 'Répétition *et* première fois,' notes Jacques Derrida, 'voilà peut-être la question de l'événement comme question du fantôme' ('Repetition *and* first time: this is perhaps the question of the event as question of the ghost') (Derrida 1993: 31; Derrida 1994: 10).

11 We know, for example, that a version of *Un homme pareil aux autres* first appeared in 1927, as 'Journal sans date', in *Les Œuvres libres* 72 (pp. 105–

236) and that it forms part of an autobiographical sequence beginning with
Le Coeur serré, first published in 1931 but begun in 1928 (Paris: A. Michel).

12 'In the colonial world Jean Veneuse is a "dirty nigger", and a "dirty
nigger", especially if he is in the colonial service, must avoid like the
plague marrying a European, if he really loves that European and is loved
by her' (Maran, trans. Ojo-Ade 1984: 92).

13 The Swiss analyst Germaine Guex uses the word 'décalage' – gap or
rupture – to describe the affects of abandonment. She refers to 'le décalage
entre leur *apparence* dans la vie présente' ('the gap between their
[abandonics] *appearance* and their present life'), and 'le décalage entre le
stade œdipien et le stade adulte' ('the gap between the oedipal stage and
the adult stage') in their 'infantilisme profond' ('profound infantilism')
(Guex 1949: 273, 274; my emphases). As we will see, her clinical
observations on 'le spectre' of isolation and object loss will also have a role
to play in Fanon's reading of Maran (see Guex 1949: 273).

14 In 'Manière de Blanc', an article published in 1948, Maran writes: 'Il n'est
ni de frontière, ni de race, ni de naissance pour les cœurs courageux.
Préventions et préjugés ne peuvent rien contre eux. La passion qui les
anime les rapproche et les unit. Elle est leur seule *patrie*. Tout se plie
devant son pouvoir. Ils lui sacrifient tout, à jamais, et d'abord eux-mêmes'
('There are no barriers, no race, no birth, for courageous hearts. Bias and
prejudice can do nothing against them. The passion that animates them
brings them closer and unites them. It is their *sole motherland*. Everything
gives way before its power. They sacrifice everything for their passion,
forever, and, first of all, they sacrifice themselves' (Maran 1948: 344; my
emphases).

15 'Blanchir la race, sauver la race' ('Whiten the race, save the race'):
'lactification', according to Fanon, is the black woman's fear of 'la
négraille' ('niggerhood'), a fear which drives her to 'choisir le moins noir'
('select the least black of the men') (*Peau noire*: 38; *Black Skin*: 47). But why
restrict this symptom and fear to her alone? If men and women are both
'"feminized"' by 'the pathology of desire and recognition in the colonial
context' – a positioning which continues to identify the feminine with
submission – why does Fanon insist on keeping black men and women
apart as negrophobic subjects of desire (Sekyi-Otu 1996: 214)? Why, if
both are driven by the compensations and impoverishments of narcissism,
is the desire to lactify in the woman invariably a metonym for cultural
betrayal while in the man it remains a metaphor for *self*-alienation? And
why, no doubt for the same reason, is the desire to lactify – to be
recognised and loved – presented as the black woman's degraded *gift*? Is
not the desire to be recognised as a white *man* also encased in an economy
of gift and debt, and one which freely appropriates the *white* man as the
object to be envied, hated, but also loved? Fanon here opens, and closes
very quickly, the door that might lead to such a possibility.

16 'Jean Veneuse is not a Negro and does not wish to be a Negro. And yet,
without his knowledge, a gulf has been created. There is something

indefinable, irreversible, there is indeed the *that within* of Harold
Rosenberg' (*Black Skin*: 71).

17 It is not until Rosenberg rewrites 'The stages' for his 1970 book, *Act and
the Actor*, that he encloses the phrase by italics. This raises an intriguing
issue of precedence, suspense and haunting. The first appearance of the
phrase 'that within', for example, in Guyonnet's translation is left in
English and italicised, a move which exceeds the stage or scene of translation because it does not occur in either of the originals that ostensibly
produces it (that is, Rosenberg's essay and Gide's rendering of an 'en moi'
in his 1949 translation of *Hamlet*).

18 Fanon's reading of Guex may also cast a new light on the enigmatic
sentence 'le complexe d'Œdipe n'est pas près de voir le jour chez les
nègres' ('the Oedipus complex is far from coming into being among
Negroes' [in Martinique]) (*Peau noire*: 123; *Black Skin*: 151–2). I cannot
pursue this complex matter here but there is evidence to suggest that
Fanon linked racist affects to pre-Oedipal forms of attachment and rivalry.
Prior to his famous footnote on Lacan's mirror stage, for example, Fanon
describes a 'déstructuration' of the ego produced by 'l'irruption d'un
autre corps' ('appearance of the body of the [racial] other') (*Peau noire*: 131;
130; *Black Skin*: 161; 160).

19 There is a drama being played out here – a play on the boundaries between
original and translation, fiction and event, but also between hatred and
love. Guyonnet's translation, with its emphasis on the phantom as actor,
not only connects Fanon to Rosenberg, *Hamlet* to *Peau noire*, but also
becomes the subject of several intriguing conjurations: by Rosenberg *and*
Fanon. Indeed, Rosenberg will later credit the French version in the title of
his review of Sartre's *Les Mots*, 'From playacting to self', a text in which
Sartre emerges as a figure hidden 'behind a series of (impostures and)
masquerades', displaced by the 'spectral struggle' of his ego with 'gaps' in
being (Rosenberg 1970: 205). Rosenberg will also claim, again in 1970, that
Guyonnet's existential (read Sartrean) reading was already anticipated by
a 1932 essay of his called 'Character change and the drama', first collected
in *Tradition of the New* in 1959 (Rosenberg 1970: 206). Haunted by the 'en
moi', such echoings allow us a glimpse into writing itself as a kind of
spectral archive. Here what returns – as memory and/or history – is also
what begins as genealogy and/or filiation. Or, more accurately perhaps,
the structure of the 'en moi' is already one of repetition and first time, and
one that is embedded in the relations between writing and the eventuality
of the ghost. In 1952 this 'en moi' reappears in Fanon's reading of *Un
homme pareil aux autres*. But unlike his precursors, Fanon links the 'en
moi' to a form of masquerade, or dissembling, that envelops the racial self
through traumatic seduction.

20 The title of this section is borrowed from Madelon Sprengnether's *The
Spectral Mother: Freud, Feminism, and Psychoanalysis* (Ithaca, NY: Cornell
University Press, 1990). However, what follows is not based on a reading
of her work.

21 'When I am at home my mother sings me French love songs in which there is never a word about Negroes. When I disobey, when I make too much noise, I am told to "stop acting like a nigger"' (*Black Skin*: 191).

22 'I love in you the child that I would have wished to have'; 'I snatched myself from the gentleness of life that I should not know, because I was forbidden by my ugly black face, completely black, and because he who knowingly prepares for himself the useless bitterness of future regrets, is to blame' (Maran, trans. Ojo-Ade 1984: 89–90).

23 Although Vergès's reading leads her to overstate Fanon's investments in an 'Antillean family romance', she is right to point out that 'Fanon resents the Antillean mother for her desire for whiteness yet avoids confronting that desire fully' (Vergès 1997: 584).

24 'I contend that Jean Veneuse represents not an example of black–white relations, but a certain mode of behavior in a neurotic who by coincidence is black.' 'Where does this analysis lead us? To nothing short of proving to Jean Veneuse that in fact he is not like the rest' (*Black Skin*: 79 and 78).

25 '"Oh, those tears of a child who had no one to wipe them ... He will never forget that he was apprenticed so young to loneliness ... A cloistered existence, a withdrawn, secluded existence in which I learned too soon to meditate and to reflect [...] [I]t has made me hypersensitive within myself, incapable of externalizing my joys or my sorrows, so that I reject everything that I love and I turn back in spite of myself on everything that attracts me"' (cited in *Black Skin*: 75).

26 '"It is to this schooling that my character owes its inner melancholy and that fear of social contact that today inhibits even my slightest impulses"' (cited in *Black Skin*: 74).

27 'From now on you will know that Negroes are men like any others and that perhaps they suffer more than others, because, when they have the painful good fortune to love a European woman, they can feel bearing down upon them such reprobation that they really are ashamed to confess or show their suffering' (Maran, trans. Ojo-Ade 1984: 94).

28 'I am a delicate person, a dreamer, a sentimentalist. I can therefore never understand nor love the indigenous woman, an inert and simple receptacle of disenchanted passion' (Maran, trans. Ojo-Ade 1984: 108).

29 'Since this Eurydice will disappear in smoke if Black Orpheus turns around to look back on her, he will descend the royal road of his soul with his back turned on the bottom of the grotto; he will descend below words and meanings ... with his back turned and his eyes closed, in order finally to touch with his feet the black water of dreams and desire and to let himself drown in it' (Sartre 2001: 126).

References

Abraham, N. (1994) 'The phantom of Hamlet', in N. Abraham and M. Torok, *The Shell and the Kernel*, I, ed. and trans. and with an intro. by N. T. Rand, Chicago and London: Chicago University Press, 1994, 191–205

Arendt, H. (2003) *Responsibility and Judgement*, ed. J. Kohn, New York: Schocken Books

Derrida, J. (1993) *Spectres de Marx: l'état de la dette, le travail du deuil et la nouvelle internationale*, Paris: Galileé (*Specters of Marx: The State of the Debt, the Work of Mourning, and the New International*, trans. P. Kamuf, New York and London: Routledge, 1994)

Freud, S. (1954) *The Origins of Psychoanalysis*, ed. M. Bonaparte, A. Freud and E. Kris, New York: Basic Books

Guex, G. (1949) 'Les conditions intellectuelles et affectives de l'œdipe', *Revue française de psychanalyse*, année 13: 257–76

—— (1950) *La Névrose d'abandon*, Paris: Presses Universitaires de France

Guyonnet, R. (1948) 'Du jeu au je. Esquisse d'une géographie de l'action', *Les Temps modernes*, vol. 29, Mar., 1729–53

Jones, E. (1976) *Hamlet and Oedipus*, New York: W. W. Norton

Juminer, B. (1962) 'Hommages à Frantz Fanon', *Présence Africaine*, 40: 126

Lacan, J. (1982) 'Desire and the interpretation of desire in *Hamlet*' (trans. J. Hulbert) in S. Felman (ed.), *Literature and Psychoanalysis: The Question of Reading Otherwise*, Baltimore and London: Johns Hopkins University Press, 11–53

Lebeau, V. (2001) 'Another child of violence', *New Formations*, 42, 19–30

Maran, R. (1947) *Un homme pareil aux autres*, Paris: Arc-en-Ciel

—— (1948) 'Manière de Blanc', *Présence Africaine*, no. 2, 342–5

—— (1965) *Hommage à René Maran*, Paris: Présence Africaine

Ojo-Ade, F. (1984) *René Maran: The Black Frenchman*, Washington: Three Continents Press

Rosenberg, H. (1947/8) 'The stages: a geography of human action', *Possibilities*, vol. 1, Winter, 47–65

—— (1970) *Act and the Actor: Making the Self*, New York: World Publishing Company

Sartre, J.-P. (1949) 'Orphée noir', *Situations III: Lendemains de Guerre*, Paris: Gallimard

—— (2001) 'Black Orpheus', trans. J. MacCombie, in R. Bernasconi (ed.), *Race*, Oxford: Blackwell, 115–42

Sekyi-Otu, A. (1996) *Fanon's Dialectic of Experience*, Cambridge, MA and London: Harvard University Press

Vergès, F. (1997) 'Creole skin, black mask: Fanon and disavowal', *Critical Inquiry*, 23, Spring, 578–95

Notes on contributors

ROBERT BERNASCONI is Moss Professor of Philosophy at the University of Memphis. He is the author of two books on Heidegger and numerous articles on various aspects of continental philosophy, social and political philosophy, and race theory. He has edited *Race* (Blackwell, 2001) and, with Sybol Cook, *Race and Racism in Continental Philosophy* (Indiana University Press, 2003).

BRYAN CHEYETTE is Professor of Twentieth Century Literature at the University of Southampton. He is the author of *Constructions of 'the Jew' in English Literature and Society* (Cambridge University Press, 1993) and *Muriel Spark* (Northcote House, 2000) and the editor of five books. He is currently completing a book called *Diasporas of the Mind* for Yale University Press which will contain a chapter on Fanon.

JIM HOUSE is Lecturer in French Studies at the University of Leeds. He has published articles and chapters on the history of anti-racism and racism in France, the social memories of the Algerian War of Independence, and French colonial governance. With Neil MacMaster, he is currently completing a book for Oxford University Press entitled *Paris 1961: State Terror, Algerians and Post-Colonial Memories in France*.

VICKY LEBEAU is Senior Lecturer in English at the University of Sussex. She is the author of *Lost Angels: Psychoanalysis and Cinema* (Routledge, 1995) and *Psychoanalysis and Cinema: The Play of Shadows* (Wallflower Press, 2001), and has published widely on the topics of psychoanalysis and culture.

DAVID MACEY is a translator and the author of *Lacan in Contexts* (Verso, 1988), *The Lives of Michel Foucault* (Pantheon Books, 1993), *The Penguin Dictionary of Critical Theory* (Penguin, 2002), *Frantz Fanon: A Life* (Granta, 2000) and *Michel Foucault: An Aesthetics of Existence* (2004).

DAVID MARRIOTT teaches at the University of California, Santa Cruz. He is the author of *On Black Men* (Columbia Press, 2000) and *Letters to Langston* (Rutgers University Press, forthcoming). He is currently working on a book of poems called *Incognegro*.

MAX SILVERMAN is Professor of Modern French Studies at the University of Leeds. He is the author of *Deconstructing the Nation: Immigration, Racism and Citizenship in Modern France* (Routledge, 1992) and *Facing Postmodernity: Contemporary French Thought on Culture and Society* (Routledge, 1999), has edited a collection of essays entitled *Race, Discourse and Power in France* (Avebury, 1991) and has published widely on culture and society in contemporary France.

FRANÇOISE VERGÈS is Reader in Political Philosophy and Postcolonial Theory at the Centre for Cultural Studies, Goldsmiths College, University of London. She has written extensively on slavery and the politics of reparation, processes and practices of creolisation in the Indian Ocean, south-south diasporic cultural and political formations, the cartographies of contact zones in the Indian Ocean, and postcolonial slavery. She is currently working on a project in Paris and on Réunion Island on new cultural creolised formations.

Index